A HISTORY OF THE BUREAU OF INDIAN AFFAIRS AND ITS ACTIVITIES AMONG INDIANS

CURTIS E. JACKSON AND MARCIA J. GALLI

San Francisco, California
1977

Published by

R & E RESEARCH ASSOCIATES, INC.
4843 Mission Street
San Francisco, California 94112

Publishers
Robert D. Reed and Adam S. Eterovich

Library of Congress Card Catalog Number

76-55958

I.S.B.N.

0-88247-440-5

The BIA is not an entirely unheard-of unit of the federal government. In fact, it would be rare to find an Indian or a non-Indian who has not read or heard something about what the BIA has done--or, more generally, what it has failed to do--among Indians. But what has been read and talked about popularly is what has been produced for popular consumption--land steals, water right disputes, fights over hunting rights, Alcatraz Island occupation, Wounded Knee 20th Century, the takeover of the BIA by Indians and other emotionally-charged episodes. Sadly, these reports are little more than a snatch here and a piece there about all the goings-on of the BIA among Indians. Actually, it hardly scratches the surface of the multitude of events that really make up the history and activities of the BIA. For this reason, both Indians and non-Indians know, in fact, very little about what the BIA has done and what its programs and work among Indians are all about. Included among these are far too many BIA and other government employees whose work is somewhere in the field of federal activities among Indians.

A book that goes into the history of the BIA and the development of its activities has been needed for a long time. This book is to fulfill that need. Its purpose is to provide Indians and non-Indians with deeper and broader insights about the vast expanse of happenings among Indians and, particularly, about the dealings of the federal government with Indian tribes and their members.

These dealings and the resulting BIA activities are spread across the whole life of the Nation and had their beginnings in the 3 centuries preceding the founding of the Republic.

The so-called conquistadores and the early explorers saw Indian tribes as independent nations and sought to engulf them in the power and protection of the royal sovereignties. Later, the colonists who formed local governments recognized Indian tribes as independent governmental units and treated with them accordingly. The political status of Indian tribes was thus well established by the time of the American Revolution.

Guided by the past, the federal government regarded the tribes as political entities and in its early dealings with them became obligated through treaties and agreements to perform various and many activities among them. The wide spectrum of these activities became known as Indian affairs and was the basis upon which tribes and their members were to seek a cultural, political, social and an economic rehabilitation.

Time and circumstances changed the political relationship of the federal government with Indian tribes. In the changed relationship, the U.S. government nurtured an attitude of moral responsibility for the protection and development of tribes and their members. From the exercise of the responsibility, Indian affairs expanded as the years passed.

Today the scope of Indian affairs is virtually as broad as the ever-widening span of human activities. And there is discernible in the many current programs among Indians the deeper concern of the federal government for the well-being of Indians as American citizens.

In order to administer Indian affairs, a federal agency was created, and with the increasing commitments of the federal government to Indians, the agency grew and expanded. Known first as the Indian Department, the agency has since become titled the U.S. Bureau of Indian Affairs.

This book is a narrative of Indian affairs. It traces the origin and growth of Indian affairs and the federal agency that has administered them. It details the philosophical outlook of the federal government toward Indians as it developed throughout the years, the initiation and development of federal activities among Indians and the effects of the activities in terms of their objectives as related to tribes and their members.

The Indian Department and Bureau of Indian Affairs developed inseparably with the growth of the federal government activities among Indians. For greater clarity, however, the development of Indian affairs and of the federal agency are treated somewhat separately in this book.

The great amount of minutia that represents day-to-day Indian affairs could not possibly be embraced in a single volume. But it is not necessary to include every happening. Details which adequately represent and suggest the daily events are sufficient to portray the larger movements. That is the extent that details are presented in this book.

TABLE OF CONTENTS

LIST OF TABLES

LIST OF FIGURES

CHAPTER 1

THE INDIAN DEPARTMENT

The deep niche carved by American Indians during the making of the West seems ever unfailingly to yield epochs of wild adventure. And each story sparks a tingle that streaks all the way down to the toenails. For who can even so much as think about Sitting Bull, Crazy Horse, Joseph, Black Kettle, Geronimo, Cochise, and dozens others and not be fired with deep-down enthusiasm and admiration for Indian leaders. They were brave, daring, adventurous and excitingly resourceful as they built their war machines and led their warriors in vain attempts to stop the inevitable invasion of their lands.

Tales depicting the boldness and valor of American Indian leaders in the early West probably never will cease to be stirring and enchanting. And, they never should! Those stories are important granules in the abundant garner of American heritage, and they should forever continue to be captivating and exciting.

But, the luster of untamed romanticism radiating from the generations of Indians who dared resist the spread of the American Frontier dims, almost to invisibility, the courage and determination of the generations that came before and after. These Indians were no less glorious than the braves of the battlefields because, in their way, they, too, helped to shape the destiny that is the nonvanishing Americans. These generations are characterized by a multitude of passing events known collectively as Indian affairs.

The term Indian affairs means generally those matters relating to North American Indians that fall within the jurisdiction of the federal government.

Indian affairs are, then, the dealings of the United States government with Indian tribes and their members. These dealings are marked by the development of federal government activities among Indians and of the federal agency established to give effect to the activities. They began in the early days of the Republic and have continued through the years to the present time.

This chapter is about the colonial organizations that handled Indian affairs.

INDIAN DEPARTMENT OF THE CONTINENTAL CONGRESS

Following the French and Indian War, the northern and southern colonies organized into separate quasi-governmental units. Each of the established a superintendency of Indian affairs to resolve the problems arising from colonial settlement. Later on, the Second Continental Congress was organized. Among other things, it assumed the powers of the yet-unborn national government and created 3 departments of Indian affairs to replace the 2 superintendencies in the colonies.

The 3 departments of Indian affairs were known as the Northern Department, the Middle Department and the Southern Department. The jurisdictions of each department extended approximately over the areas of the corresponding colonies.[1]

Each of the departments was headed by a body whose members were called commissioners, and each body was responsible to the Congress. The principal functions of the departments were to preserve peace and friendship with the Indians and to prevent the tribes from taking part against the colonies in the battles for independence.

INDIAN DEPARTMENT OF THE CONFEDERATE CONGRESS

The 3 departments of Indian affairs created by the Continental Congress existed until 1786. On August 7, of that year, the Congress of the Confederation ordained that the "Indian Department" be divided into a southern and a northern district. The southern district was defined to include all the Indian nations south of the Ohio River. The northern district extended over the Indian nations west of the Hudson River.[2]

The Congress of the Confederation, by the language of the Ordinance, acknowledged the existence of an "Indian Department." The term Indian Department had been employed unofficially for a number of years and, by 1786, was common to statesmen whenever they referred to the organization that handled the government's business with Indians.

The 2 specific districts defined to constitute the geographical boundaries of the Indian Department became known as the Northern Department and the Southern Department.

SUPERINTENDENTS OF INDIAN AFFAIRS

The bodies of commissioners established by the Continental Congress to administer Indian affairs were abolished by the Congress of the Confederation. Responsibility for the administration of Indian matters under the Confederation was fixed upon a single head for each of the 2 districts. The Ordinance of August 7, 1786, provided for a superintendent to be appointed for each of the districts. Appointment was for 2 years unless sooner terminated by Congress. Each appointee was required by the Ordinance to reside within, or as near the district as convenient for the management of Indian affairs.[3]

Derived from the language of the Ordinance, the official title for the appointed head of each district was Superintendent of Indian Affairs. The Congress, itself, took over the job of appointing persons to be superintendents of Indian affairs. The Ordinance provided that the same persons could be reappointed for successive 2-year periods.

James White was the first person to be appointed Superintendent of Indian Affairs for the southern district.[4] Duties of the superintendent for the northern district were performed by the governors of the Western Territory. The first of these governors was Arthur St. Clair.[5]

DUTIES OF SUPERINTENDENTS

Broad duties of the superintendents were incorporated in the Ordinance of 1786, as follows:

... The said superintendents shall attend to the execution of such regulations as Congress shall from time to time establish, respecting Indian affairs ....[6]

For the most part, Congress issued directives requiring superintendents to perform specific jobs. The nature and details of these directives are discussed later in this chapter. For now, it is important to note that the Ordinance of 1786 recognized certain commitments of the government to Indian tribes. By issuing directives to the superintendents of Indian affairs, the Congress was attempting to live up to the commitments.

The commitments were formalized in the Northwest Ordinance of 1787. They are basic in Indian affairs and as far reaching as the present and the future. So they should be considered in some detail at this point.

During many years following the landing of the Pilgrims, numerous conflicts arose between Indians and non-Indians. The source of the troubles was chiefly the unscrupulous practices among non-Indians of forcibly dispossessing the Indians of their lands. There were other causes for disagreements, but pushing Indians out of their homes and off their hunting grounds was a major one. By the time of the American Revolution, the frontier rumbled and quaked with Indian wars. Committing its armies to the fight for independence, the promised New Nation could ill afford afford the luxury of sending its troops out to quiet frontier disturbances. Partly, therefore, as a military expediency and partly as an attempt to attach the interests of the Indians to those of the United States, the Congress of the Confederation conceived a plan to introduce some fairness into the squabbles with Indians for lands. The plan was built from fibers of a positive attitude toward Indians and was incorporated in the Northwest Ordinance, as follows:

> ... The utmost faith shall always be observed toward Indians; their lands and property shall never be taken from them without their consent; and in their property, rights, and liberty, they shall never be invaded or disturbed, unless in just and lawful wars authorized by Congress; but laws founded in justice and humanity shall from time to time be made, for preventing wrongs done to them, and for preserving peace and friendship with them ....[7]

This portion of the Northwest Ordinance suggests that the Congress was well aware of the incapabilities of Indians in land transactions. Moreover, it reflects the determination of the Congress to see that the Indians were treated more fairly. As a matter of fact, the Northwest Ordinance indicates several areas in which the rising New Government hoped to establish better practices in dealings with Indians.

The pledged faith, the promises of protection and the covenants to enact just and humane laws represent the early formal commitments of the federal government to Indian tribes and their members. These commitments have endured the passage of time and brought forth a great number of federal programs among Indians.

The work of the government in honoring these commitments is indicated throughout this book. For the present, it is appropriate to consider the part of the Northwest Ordinance relating to Indian lands to illustrate that the directives issued by the Congress to the superintendents of Indian affairs were aimed at fulfillment of the commitments.

By the language of the Northwest Ordinance, the government repudiated the notion of forcibly dispossessing the Indians of lands. To acquire the lands, therefore, the government instituted the policy of negotiating with Indian tribes, as nations, to extinguish their claims. The consent of tribes to give up their lands was to be incorporated in treaties. Gathering the tribes and their members together and making treaties with them became some of the principal duties of the superintendents of Indian affairs.

The directives of Congress and the work of the superintendents are evidenced in a letter written by Arthur St. Clair at New York. The letter, dated June 14, 1789, is pertinent enough to be quoted. It reads, in part:

> ... by the resolution of Congress, of the 29th of August, 1788, I was directed to repair to the Mississippi, in order to hold a treaty with the Indians, who inhabit the land upon that river, for extinguishing their claims to lands, within certain limits, if any such claims existed, and to lay out certain donations of lands to the ancient inhabitants. From thence, I was to proceed to Post St. Vincennes, upon the Wabash, and lay out like donations for the inhabitants there ....[8]

Similarly, James White travelled among the tribes of the southern district in arranging for and negotiating treaties.[9]

GENERAL MANAGEMENT OF INDIAN AFFAIRS

General management of Indian affairs was included among the duties of the Secretary of War. Superintendents of Indian affairs were placed under the administrative direction of the Secretary of War and required by the Ordinance of 1786 to carry out all instructions issued by him.[10]

The Congress of the Confederation wanted to be kept fully informed about Indian affairs, so it issued a directive to the Secretary of War requiring him to provide to it, whenever necessary, pertinent information about what was going on among Indians. The Secretary of War was directed to keep abreast of Indian matters by communicating with the superintendents of Indian affairs. He was also directed to submit periodic reports to the Congress on the work and progress of the Indian Department.[11]

IMPORTANCE OF THE ORDINANCE

The Ordinance of August 7, 1786, established a governmental agency known as the Indian Department in the Department of War and recognized it as the official organization to carry out the national laws dealing with Indians. It also provided the method by which the Congress was to be kept up to date on the happenings among Indians.

The Ordinance was developed primarily to provide an agency to deal with Indian matters existing at that time. It became, however, much more than an instrument for its day. Swept up in the quicksand surge to early national growth, the Ordinance became the sturdy framework for the complex organization that is today the U.S. Bureau of Indian Affairs.

Building up to the BIA necessitated much structuring and restructuring of the ambryonic organization established by the Congress of the Confederation. These additions and refinements were made across a wide expanse of time. They have not yet ended. They were commenced, however, by the Constitutional government in the light of events which gave Indian affairs depth and scope at that time. One of the more significant of the additions and refinements can be considered now.

EXECUTIVE CONTROL OF INDIAN AFFAIRS

In one of its first laws, the Congress of the New Nation established the War Department in the Executive Branch and defined the duties of the Secretary of War to be, among others:

... such duties as shall from time to time be enjoined on, or entrusted to him by the President of the United States, agreeably to the Constitution, relative to ... Indian affairs: ...[12]

This wording of the act placed the administration of matters involving Indians among the functions of the Chief Executive. It fixed responsibility upon the Secretary of War to perform the specific duties relative to Indian affairs that were assigned to him by the President.

The Congress did not abolish the existing northern and southern districts of Indian affairs. Nor did it change the relationship between the Secretary of War and the superintendents of the districts.

In effect, the first Congress simply enacted into law the provisions of the Ordinance of August 7, 1786. This gave legal status to the Indian Department as a suborganizational unit in the Department of War under the U.S. government.

Importantly, however, it gave the President power over Indian affairs. In that way, it aligned the general management of Indian affairs with the concept of Executive administration embraced in the Constitution.

4

1. Laurence F. Schmeckebier, The Office of Indian Affairs: Its History, Activites and Organization (Baltimore: The Johns Hopkins Press, 1927), p. 12. Schmeckebier in his analysis of the organization established by the Continental Congress states "The Northern department extended as far south as to include the Six Nations. The Southern department extended north far enough to include the Cherokees, and the Middle department included all between the others."

2. Walter Lowrie and Mathew St. Clair Clark (eds.), American State Papers, Vol. V, Class II, Indian Affairs, Vol. I (Washington, Gales and Seaton, 1832), p. 14.

3. Ibid.

4. Ibid., p. 15. Dr. White was succeeded by Richard Winn in 1788, and in 1790, William Blount was appointed Superintendent of Indian Affairs for the southern district.

5. Ibid., p. 231.

6. Ibid., p. 15.

7. The Northwest Ordinance of 1787.

8. Lowrie and Clark, op. cit., p. 15. Arthur St. Clair, as governor of the Western Territory, established an office in the summer of 1788 at Marietta on the Ohio River. Later, he moved his capitol to Cincinnati.

9. Ibid., p. 24.

10. Ibid., p. 15.

11. Ibid.

12. U.S. Congress, "An act to establish an Executive Department, to be denominated the Department of War," August 7, 1789, 1 Stat. 49.

Chapter 2

TRADE AND COMMERCE WITH INDIANS

The raw new land pledged to liberate from religious persecution the peoples who formed the one or two settlements that were the beginnings of America. But it promised also a freedom from economic oppression to those who dared search for its material abundance.

So the New World lured numbers of wealth seekers and enterprisers. They had royal charters that granted them parcels of land and the right to exploit it. Their aim was to find and take all the riches the land could produce.

Tobacco, corn, potatoes and other strange products growing in the land were immediate sources of gain to the enterprising businessmen. But they soon saw far greater riches in furs that the braves of the wilderness could supply.

Sedulously the enterprisers nurtured an economic alliance with the Indians and, together with them, built a system of trade and commerce. For the wide and deep stream of furs the Indians caused to flow into the trading posts, there was a backwash of pots and pans, blankets and rum, rifles and powder, feathers, beads, trinkets and many other articles to the villages of the natives.

The system of trade and commerce between the Indians and the European enterprisers proved to be a solid foundation for the buildup of settlements in the New World. It attracted people who were tough enough to withstand rugged hardships and who had capital to risk in colonies and trade. The system was to have its enduring days, too, in the development of the nation's organization for the administration of Indian affairs.

This chapter reviews the early development of commerce between the United States and Indian tribes and suggests how it contributed to the buildup of the Indian Department.

REGULATING TRADE AND COMMERCE

The framers of the Constitution were by no means unmindful of the important part trade and commerce with Indians had played in colonial development. They were not unaware, either, of its significance to the well-being of the nation they had conceived. As a matter of fact, they identified trade and commerce with Indians to be a national concern, and they wrote Section 8 of Article I in the Constitution to confer upon Congress the power to "regulate Commerce with Foreign nations and among the several states, and with the Indian tribes."

Members of the first Congress also recognized that trade and commerce with Indian could help in development of the New Nation. They knew, too, that a number of unscrupulous practices had developed among traders during the many years of keen competition. Continuation of unfair practices, they reasoned, would split the Indians from the government, and the resulting conflicts would seriously hamper the start of the United States.

Seeking to gain the support and confidence of Indian tribes and to correct some of the abuses in trade and commerce with Indians, the Congress passed the act of July 22, 1790, entitled "An act to regulate trade and intercourse with the Indian tribes." The act was a first in a series of similar temporary measures designed, among other things, to achieve a harmony between the trader-businessmen and the Indians. Containing the bases upon which the federal government would eventually develop its more lasting programs of trade and commercial relationships with Indians, the act was renewed every 2 years until a permanent act was passed in a later year.[1]

The act of July 22, 1790, prohibited any person from carrying on any trade or commerce with Indian tribes without a license issued by the "superintendent of the Department," or any other person appointed by the President for that purpose.

Superintendents were required by the act to issue a license to trade with Indians to any person who put up a $1,000 bond. The license was good until revoked. It was revokable if the trader failed to comply with the trading rules and regulations. Full authority was conferred upon the President to issue regulations governing trade and commerce with Indian tribes. Superintendents, as well as traders, were required to conduct the trade according to the rules prescribed by the President.[2]

The President gave the superintendents for the northern and southern districts the job of carrying out the intent of the act locally among the Indian tribes.

The act of July 22, 1790, had no immediate effect upon the organization of the Indian Department. It conferred broad powers upon the President and placed additional duties upon the superintendents of Indian affairs, but it did not initiate changes in the established organization of the Indian Department. In the years following 1790, however, the government became more involved in trade and commerce with Indians, and from this greater involvement, the Indian Department began to expand.

WASHINGTON SUGGESTS TRADING HOUSES

The objective of establishing better order and practices in trade and commerce with Indians was not achieved to the degree anticipated by the act of July 22, 1790. In his fourth Annual Address, delivered to the Congress on November 6, 1792, Washington spoke quite strongly about the lingering frontier difficulties and urged Congress to take swift and effective action in the matter. His message had far-reaching importance and is worthy to be quoted somewhat at length. His words were:

> ... I cannot dismiss the subject of Indian affairs without again recommending to your consideration the expediency of more adequate provision for giving energy to the laws throughout our interior frontier and for restraining the commission of outrages upon the Indians, without which all pacific plans must prove nugatory. To enable, by competent rewards, the employment of qualified and trusty persons to reside among them as agents would also contribute to the preservation of peace and good neighborhood. If in addition to these expedients an eligible plan could be devised for promoting civilization among the friendly tribes and for carrying on trade with them upon a scale equal to their wants and under regulations calculated to protect them from imposition and extortion, its influence in cementing their interests with ours could not but be considerable ....[3]

The ideas of resident agents and promoting civilization among Indians were not new. For many years, agents had been appointed to live among the Indians, and much work had been done toward civilizing the tribes and their members. But the government hadn't done too much about carrying on a liberal trade with Indians. This had been left to the frontier businessmen.

Washington was not content with simply urging Congress to take proper action. To him the nation's welfare required speedy steps toward the settlement of frontier discord. Unlicensed traders were not about to reform, and licensed traders were virtually compelled by competition to follow corrupt practices. Washington wanted to be sure the Indians would not accuse the government of wrong doings in trade. So he and his advisors conceived the idea of providing supplies to Indians through government personnel and scrupulously supervised so that Indians would be dealt with fairly.

Washington submitted the plan of government trading houses to the Congress for its enactment into law. Contrary to his expectations, the plan was rejected by the lawmakers. Washington persisted, suffering more defeats by Congress until, at last, his hopes were realized in the act of April 18, 1796. The act was temporary, but it was reenacted with appropriate modifications, each succeeding 2 years until 1822.

TRADING HOUSES AUTHORIZED

The act of April 18, 1796, empowered the President to establish trading houses at such posts and places on the western and southern frontiers, or in the Indian country, as he judged most convenient for carrying on a liberal trade with the several Indian nations within the limits of the U.S.[4]

The act appropriated $150,000 for the venture and stipulated that the trading houses were to be operated as nonprofit businesses. Prices of the goods supplied to the Indians were to be reasonable yet high enough to assure that the original investment would not be diminished.[5] In other words, commodities were to be sold to Indians at cost plus transportation and administrative expenses.

The trading house system was conceived as a supplement to, but not in intentional replacement of, the system of trade and commerce authorized by the act of July 22, 1790. Thus the system of trade developed over the years between the private businessmen and the Indians was to coexist with the government trading houses.

The importance of the act of April 18, 1796, was its effect upon the growth of the Indian Department. The growth is suggested by the trading house operations, their activities and where they were located. Establishing and operating trading houses were two of the most important administrative functions of the federal government in the field of Indian affairs.[6]

OBJECTIVES OF TRADING HOUSES

The principal object of the federal government in passing the act of April 18, 1796, was to settle frontier difficulties. But other benefits to the government and the Indians were anticipated. Some of the mutual gains expected were reviewed by Ninian Edwards, Governor of Illinois Territory, in 1815. Using the term factories, which was synonymous to trading houses, Governor Edwards wrote:

> ... The Government of the United States thought that, by establishing a system of factories, they would supply all the tribes of Indians, to their satisfaction, with all kinds of goods necessary for their consumption, at such prices that by these means they would get all the furs and pelts of the Indians, and at the same time would also get their confidence, esteem and fidelity ....[7]

The government hoped to become eventually the exclusive middleman in trade and commerce with Indians. This would secure the frontiers and put an end to the disturbances created by the private traders. It would also weld the interests of the Indians to those of the government.

The value to the government of a political and military, as well as an economic, alliance with the Indians was well known to the leaders of the country at that time. The U.S. in 1796 was little more than a daring upstart hemmed within a specific geographical area by European powers. Each of the foreign sovereignties vied for the manpower of Indian tribes to augment their own scanty military resources which were committed to preventing the expansion of the New Nation. To keep the tribal members from joining the forces of the European powers was a compelling reason the government entered into direct trade and commerce with Indians.

But there was another important reason for it. Some of the tribes on the far frontiers had taken to the warpath in their own right. They resented the encroachment of settlers upon the lands that gave them sustenance. They were determined to drive the invaders back to the eastern seaboard and, once again, be masters of their country and destinies.

The federal government, on the other hand, wanted permanent settlements in the land and further expansion of the frontiers. It recognized, however, the effect of its desires upon the well-being of the natives. An attempt by the government to supply the Indians with necessities difficult for them to obtain in their shrinking hunting grounds was another reason for the establishment of trading houses.

OPERATION OF TRADING HOUSES

The government trading houses were operated to suit the convenience of the government more than to accommodate the Indians. They were situated at considerable distances from Indian villages, some of them becoming the first of the frontier settlements.

Usually, detachments of troops were quartered at the sites of trading houses, so they were essentially military outposts. Troops were stationed there principally to protect the U.S. territory and prevent its takeover by European powers. Hunting down and overpowering Indians became a glory to the U.S. Army in later years. But it was not at that time a military objective.

Government trading houses never sold on credit, although the Indians in their trading with private traders and the British companies were accustomed to buying before and paying after hunts. The cash-and-carry policy of the federal government created serious difficulties in the trading system. Generally, Indians had to go up to 300 miles or more from their villages to hunt, and hunting expeditions would take more than 6 months. If the Indians didn't have sufficient furs to buy enough goods to carry them through hunts, they simply couldn't go hunting. It was too hard for them to return to the trading houses during hunts, particularly when snow and ice clogged the trails. Indian hunters stayed at home, too, because they dreaded leaving their camps during hunts to return to trading houses for supplies. Their absence would expose their families to war parties of other tribes and to other inconveniences or hardships. In addition, hunters knew they were vulnerable when they travelled alone or in the company of 1 or 2 other hunters on the way to trading houses and back. They didn't want to be in that kind of a situation, so they just didn't go on hunts when they couldn't obtain supplies on credit.[8]

These difficulties are suggestive of many untold obstacles encountered by the government in its system of direct trade and commerce with Indians. Nevertheless, the government was persistent in its efforts to make the trading house system a successful venture. It took whatever steps it felt were necessary to achieve success.

EXPANSION OF TRADING SYSTEM

Indian country and the frontiers were explored to determine proper and convenient places for trading houses, and the original appropriation of $150,000 was increased gradually as more goods and supplies were required by the Indians. The urgency of expanding the government trading system was revealed clearly by A. J. Dallas, an official in the Department of War, in a letter dated June 9, 1815, to peace commissioners William H. Harrison, Duncan McArthur and John Graham. Dallas referred to the trading houses as factories, the term usually employed by government personnel. The letter sheds much light on the plans, so it is quoted, as follows:

> ... The policy of introducing ... factories generally into the Indian country becomes every day more and more apparent, as well for the sake of the Indians as for our own sake. An opportunity should be taken, therefore, to apprize the Indians that ... the President contemplates ordering a chain of establishments to be gradually extended from Chicago, along the Illinois, to St. Louis ....[9]

Congress appropriated separate and specific funds to be used to explore the frontier for trading house sites. The act of March 3, 1805, for example, appropriated $5,000 to explore "the Indian country and ascertain proper and convenient places for establishing trading houses with the different tribes within the territory of the United States."[10]

To increase the operating funds of the trading houses, Congress took other appropriate action, and the original appropriation of $150,000 was eventually almost doubled.[11]

Local difficulties were met with a determination measurable by the number of trading houses and the results of their operations. By the year 1811, ten trading houses were strung along the southern and western frontiers of the U.S. The results of their operations, although seemingly small compared to the astronomical budgets of today's federal entities, were substantial for their day. The gains and losses for each of the government's trading houses are shown by the following statement covering the period March 31, 1811 to April 1, 1815:

STATEMENT OF GAINS AND LOSSES[a]

Government Trading Houses

Trading Houses	Gains and (-) Losses
Chickasaw Bluffs	$10,241.58
Fort Stephen's (Choctaw)	-82.55
Des Moines	12,739.88
Osage	14,282.90
Natchitoches	12,003.37
Chicago	-11,503.31
Michilimachinac	-11,486.27
Sandusky	-8,053.44
Fort Hawkins	-380.88
Fort Wayne	-5,333.45

[a]Source: Walter Lowrie and Mathew St. Clair Clark (eds.), American State Papers, Vol. V, Class II, Indian Affairs, Vol. 1, p. 68.

The importance of the above tabulation is that it shows the locations of the government trading houses. It is interesting to observe, though, that some trading houses operated at a profit and others at a loss. The net results of all the trading houses was a gain of $12,427.83.

During the period covered by the above statement, the trading houses at Michilimachinac, Chicago, Sandusky and Fort Wayne "were broken up and destroyed by the enemy."[12] The statement reflects losses by the destruction. Two trading houses were constructed during 1816 to replace those destroyed. One of these was at Chicago, and the other at Green Bay.

DISCONTINUANCE OF TRADING HOUSES

The system of direct trade and commerce between the government and the Indians was not too popular with the private traders and the fur companies. They were not denied licenses to trade with Indians, but, almost every day, they saw a bit more of the Indian trade slip over to the government trading houses. So they began agitating for repeal of the act of April 18, 1796.

The government began appraisals of the trading-house system shortly after it established the first trading outpost. Early reports were more or less routine. But when the system fell under the more determined attacks of the private traders and fur companies, superintendents of Indian affairs and other administrators devoted considerable attention to reports on the values and accomplishments of the trading houses.

Their reports reviewed carefully the original objectives of the system and the extent the objectives were realized. They indicated how the system was plagued with numerous difficulties and what was done to overcome them. They warned of more troubles in the future but urged that the system be continued for the benefit of both the federal government and the Indians.

The private traders and fur companies persisted in their efforts to drive the government out of Indian trade. By 1816, their agitation had become so effective that Congress called upon the Secretary of War to recommend whether or not the government should continue the activity.

At that time, James Mason, Superintendent of Indian Trade, wrote a letter to the Secretary of War. Mason summarized the collective views of the administrators of Indian affairs in stating that he doubted the licensed traders were able to supply the Indians with goods in the quantities needed. Elimination of the government trading houses, he reasoned, would force the Indians to trade with the British or suffer greatly from the lack of goods and supplies. "Besides the inhumanity of such a result," Mason wrote, "no circumstance could tend more to alienate them from this government."[13]

The Secretary of War agreed with the administrators of Indian affairs and recommended to Congress that the government stay in the business of trade with Indians.

Temporarily, Congress deferred to the wisdom of the administrators of Indian affairs. But opposition to the government trading houses increased and intensified in the following years. In time, Congress determined the system had lived its days. On May 6, 1822, Congress passed an act which required the President to close down the trading houses and settle the accounts of the government personnel employed in the system.[14]

So the trading-house venture of the government came to an end.

Out of the system had come, however, the rule which endured across the many years to the present time that traders must obtain licenses from the government to trade with Indians.

Out of it came also a position destined to a continuing life as the titular head of the Indian Department.

SUPERINTENDENT OF INDIAN TRADE

The act of April 18, 1796, authorized the President to appoint agents to manage the trading houses. It specified that the agents were to receive goods supplied by the government and to dispose of the goods by trading with Indians for furs and other Indian products. The agents were required by the act to reside at the sites of trading houses.[15]

Trading with Indians involved much work and many details. Some of it was performed by government agencies other than the Indian Department. For example, all goods and supplies for the Indian trading houses were purchased by the Purveyor of Public Supplies, an agency created by the act of February 23, 1795, to purchase supplies for all government agencies. The commodities for Indian trade were hauled in wagons by Army personnel to the scattered frontier trading houses. Accounts of trading houses were examined by the Comptroller of the Treasury as required by the act of September 2, 1789.

These 3 agencies, along with the Indian Department, were the principal government entities involved in Indian trade. Each of them operated with a certain degree of independence. The result was a split of authority and a division of responsibility that added greatly to the many other difficulties arising from the trading-house operations.

Attempting to overcome the disadvantages of divided authority and responsibility, Congress enacted legislation to centralize the management of the trading house system on a single head. The act was passed on April 21, 1806, and is important enough in Indian affairs to be quoted. The act provided that:

... the President of the United States shall be authorized to appoint a superintendent of Indian trade, whose duty it shall be to purchase and take charge of all goods intended for trade with the Indian nations aforesaid, and to transmit the same to such places as he shall be directed by the President ....[16]

As the foregoing portion of the act suggests, the official title for the head of the trading-house system became Superintendent of Indian Trade. The act empowered the Superintendent of Indian Trade to purchase supplies and transport them to the trading houses. Further, it required him to sell at public auction all furs and peltry received from the Indians.

To fix responsibility upon a single head, the act placed the agents at trading houses under the general administrative supervision of the Superintendent of Indian Trade.[17]

The actual result of the act was the formation of a suborganization in the Indian Department. The suborganization was called the Indian Trade Department.

ORGANIZATION OF INDIAN TRADE DEPARTMENT

Trading-house operations increased in scope and volume as the frontier pushed farther and farther inland, and the growth of the Indian Trade Department was as rapid as the building of the network of trading houses.

In 1822, the year Congress passed the act to close the trading houses, the trade department consisted in the office of Superintendent of Indian Trade, located at Georgetown, D.C., and various trading houses situated strategically along the borders of the United States. The organization of the trade department, the general nature of its activities and its size at that time are indicated by the following listing:

INDIAN TRADE DEPARTMENT--1822[a]

Name	Title	Place Employed
Thomas L. McKenney	Superintendent of Indian Trade	Georgetown, D.C.
Jer. W. Bronaugh	Principal clerk	Georgetown, D.C.
Samuel Blount	Clerk	Georgetown, D.C.
M. Fitzhugh	Clerk	Georgetown, D.C.
John W. Bronaugh	Transport agent	Georgetown, D.C.
William Miles	Messenger	Georgetown, D.C.
James Kennerly	Transport agent	St. Louis
John W. Johnson	Factor	Prairie du Chien
F. Barnard	Clerk	Prairie du Chien
John P. Gates	Interpreter	Prairie du Chien
Robert B. Belt	Factor	Fort Edwards
J. Connelly	Assistant factor	Fort Edwards
George C. Sibley	Factor	Fort Clark, Missouri
L. W. Boggs	Assistant factor	Fort Clark, Missouri
Joseph Renoe	Interpreter	Fort Clark, Missouri
Paul Ballio	Factor	Osage Branch Factory
Mathew Lyon	Factor	Arkansas River
Barak Owens	Clerk	Arkansas River
A colored woman	Interpreter	Arkansas River
Mathew Irwin	Factor	Green Bay
Jacob B. Varnum	Factor	Chicago
Wm. McClellan	Factor	Red River
O'Riley Colton	Interpreter	Red River
John Hersey	Factor	Choctaw, T.H.
B. Everitt	Assistant factor	Choctaw, T.H.
J. C. Pitchlyn	Interpreter	Choctaw, T.H.

[a]Source: U.S. Congress, House Document No. 110, 17th Congress, 1st Session, 1821-22, April 12, 1822, p. 11.

The listing is interesting and pertinent in the history of Indian affairs because it discloses the titles of persons employed and the locations of the trading houses. Agents in charge of trading houses were called factors.

Particularly important is Thomas L. McKenney who was Superintendent of Indian Trade for many years. After the trading houses closed, McKenney turned his attention to the task of developing an organizational subdivision in the Department of War to take over Indian matters handled by the Secretary of War. In doing this, he became responsible to a large extent for the creation of the Bureau of Indian Affairs.

1. The bases upon which the Government developed its Indian programs were, among others, the various provisions of treaties under which the Government obtained lands from the tribes. Indian treaties is the subject of a subsequent chapter. The act of July 22, 1790, affirmed the exclusive right of the Federal Government to purchase Indian lands. It was a temporary act in a legislative sense because it contained a clause providing for its expiration. The first permanent trade and intercourse act was the act of March 30, 1802.

2. U.S. Congress, "An act to regulate trade and intercourse with the Indian tribes," July 22, 1790; 1 Stat. 137.

3. James D. Richardson (ed.), Messages and Papers of the Presidents: 1789-1897. (Published by Authority of Congress, 1900, n.p.), p. 127. Other messages dealing with Indian affairs that were delivered by Washington to the Congress are included in the volume.

4. U.S. Congress, "An act for establishing trading houses with Indian tribes," April 18, 1796; 1 Stat. 452.

5. Ibid.

6. Felix S. Cohen, Handbook of Federal Indian Law (Washington: Government Printing Office, 1945), p. 9.

7. Lowrie and Clark, op. cit., p. 66.

8. Ibid.

9. Ibid., p. 47.

10. U.S. Congress, "An act making appropriations for carrying into effect certain Indian treaties, and for other purposes of Indian trade and commerce," March 3, 1805; 2 Stat. 338.

11. U.S. Congress, "An act for establishing trading houses with the Indian tribes," April 21, 1806; 2 Stat. 402.

12. Ibid., p. 67. The destruction occurred during the War of 1812.

13. Ibid., p. 70.

14. U.S. Congress, "An act to abolish the United States' trading establishment with the Indian tribes," May 6, 1822; 3 Stat. 679.

15. U.S. Congress, op. cit., Act of April 18, 1796.

16. Ibid.

17. U.S. Congress, "An act for establishing trading houses with the Indian tribes," April 21, 1806; 2 Stat. 402.

CHAPTER 3

SUPERINTENDENTS OF INDIAN AFFAIRS

The Congress of the Confederation divided the U.S. into 2 districts for the administration of Indian affairs. These districts made up the Indian Department and were designated the Northern Department and the Southern Department. The Northern Department corresponded geographically to the Northwest Territory or, as it was also called, the Western Territory. The Southern Department covered the area known as the Territory South of the Ohio River. By the act of August 7, 1789, the first Congress of the U.S. gave legal status to the Indian Department.

Frontier territories of the U.S. were claimed at one time by the various states, and many dealings with Indians were handled by representatives of the states. However, when the states united to become the original union, the Congress of the Confederation determined that certain Indian matters were the exclusive business of the government. This principle was affirmed by the U.S. government in the Constitution and in some of the laws of the first Congress.

Two of the more important Indian matters at that time were the negotiation of treaties with Indian tribes and the purchase of Indian lands. For these dealings with Indians, specific representatives of the government were appointed by the Congress of the Confederation and, later, by the President. Among them were the superintendents of Indian affairs.

In its early days, a main object of the federal government was to extend its commitments in the Northwest Ordinance to the Indians in the Southern Department. But when the government attempted to do this, it encountered the tough resistance of the states and their citizens.

The task of this chapter is to review the nature of the difficulties in the Southern Department, to show how the government overcame the opposition, and to indicate the significance of these dimensions of Indian affairs in the growth and development of the Indian Department.

SOUTHERN DEPARTMENT

When the union was formed, it was customary for the states to surrender their frontier territories to the U.S. But most of the states that claimed the territory south of the Ohio River hesitated to do that. They were not any more willing, either, to accept the principle of general government supremacy in the management of Indian affairs. These states continued to negotiate treaties with Indian tribes after the adoption of the Articles of Confederation, and many more years passed before all of the land was surrendered to the U.S. In these circumstances, the general government felt obliged to establish its power.[1]

The federal government virtually nullified treaties entered into by the states and the Indian tribes. It sent its own appointees to negotiate new treaties. Likewise, it substantially invalidated all the purchases of Indian lands made by the states, purchased the lands in its own right and, in some cases, restored to the Indians certain lands the states claimed to have purchased from tribes.

These actions by the federal government were the sources of no little unrest in the Southern Department. Undoubtedly, the general sentiments were expressed by a group of "citizens of Davidson county," Tennessee, who wrote to the President. The letter so clearly illustrates the situation that it is worthy to be quoted somewhat at length. It states, in part:

... The people of this State know that their political and individual prosperity is much retarded, and they also believe that their rights are obstructed by two causes, connected with the relations of the United States with the Indian tribes: ... Previous to the formation of the constitution of the United States, and when the State of North Carolina possessed the absolute sovereignty of soil in what is now the State of Tennessee ... the legislature of that State, ... offered for sale her western lands

15

to her own citizens, ... and a fee-simple title was vested in the purchasers to a large portion of the lands in what is now the State of Tennessee. This took place in the years 1783 and 1784 .... Since that period the United States have, by treaties or compacts with the Cherokee and Chickasaw Indians, acknowledged a possessory right in those tribes to a large portion of the lands within this State; and that acknowledgment of title continues to exist, to the exclusion of citizens who have paid a fair price to North Carolina for those lands, more than thirty years since. Nay, the treaties purport to vest an absolute right to those lands in the Indians ...[2]

Protests such as this by settlers in the Territory South of the Ohio River kept the federal government ever mindful of the restlessness created by its course of actions. But the government was firm. It sent its superintendents of Indian affairs into the territory and charged them with the duty of carrying out federal Indian laws and of restoring peace and order. Soon, too, it applied the principles of administration developed in the Northern Department to the Southern Department, establishing its power even more firmly in Indian matters of national importance.

NORTHERN DEPARTMENT

The political problems encountered by the federal government in the Territory South of the Ohio River did not exist in the Northwest Territory. In 1785, the northern states ceded to the general government all the land embraced in the Northern Department of Indian affairs. Two years later, the country was organized as a territorial government headed by a governor.

Management of Indian affairs was an important duty exercised by the governors of the Northwest Territory. The first governor, Arthur St. Clair, assumed that function when the Congress of the Confederation failed to appoint a superintendent of Indian affairs as contemplated by the Ordinance of 1786. In taking over administration of Indian affairs, St. Clair set a precedence in managing Indian affairs that became a federal policy and was followed for approximately 100 years.

INITIATION OF POLICY

The first Congress of the U.S. adopted, with appropriate modifications, the Northwest Ordinance of 1787.[3] Early in its days, the first Congress recognized that the gubernatorial duties in the territory included the broad management of Indian affairs. The act of September 11, 1789, which established salaries for the executive officers of the federal government, evidences this. It reads, in part, as follows:

... there shall be allowed to the officers hereafter mentioned the following annual salaries, payable quarterly at the Treasury of the United States ...; to the governor of the Western territory, for his salary as such, and for discharging the duties of superintendent of Indian affairs in the Northern Department, two thousand dollars ...[4]

This act initiated the practice of conferring upon territorial governors the authority and the responsibility for the broad administration of Indian affairs.[5]

EXPANSION OF POLICY

The policy of putting territorial governors in charge of Indian affairs was broadened to include the Southern Department when the country was set up as a territorial government in 1790. The act creating the territory was quite definite in placing upon the governor the duties of superintendent of Indian affairs. It reads, in part, that:

... the salaries of the officers ... shall be the same as those, by law established, of similar officers in the government northwest of the river Ohio. And the powers, duties and emoluments of a superintendent of Indian affairs for the southern department shall be united with those of the governor ....[6]

With the creation of territorial governments and the unification of the duties of superintendent of Indian affairs and territorial governors, the Northern Department and the Southern Department of Indian affairs passed into the pages of history.

The language to unite the administration of Indian affairs and the gubernatorial duties was included in the acts of Congress that created the Mississippi Territory in 1798, organized the Indiana Territory in 1800, provided temporary governments for the Michigan Territory in 1805 and the Illinois Territory in 1809.

The act of March 30, 1822, established a territorial government in Florida, and the words that place upon the governor the duties of the superintendent of Indian affairs are "He shall ... be ex-officio superintendent of Indian affairs;". This language became common in later acts creating the various territories.

When the frontier in later years hopped across the Mississippi and new territorial governments were hewed out of the wildernesses in the farther west, the uniting of the powers, duties and emoluments of the superintendent of Indian affairs with those of the territorial governors was a standard procedure.

In 1857, Brigham Young was the governor of Utah Territory. As ex-officio superintendent of Indian affairs, he was having some difficulty collecting his salary. He wrote to the Indian department about it and received a reply from J. W. Denver, the head of the Department. A portion of the letter by Denver reveals that the policy was still in effect at that time. It reads:

> ... you became superintendent of Indian affairs by virtue of your appointment as governor of the Territory; and although these offices have since been separated, yet you had not, at the date of your communication, been relieved from the duties appertaining to them ....[7]

Denver's letter suggests that sometime earlier than 1857 the federal government began to break away from the practice of requiring territorial governors to serve as superintendents of Indian affairs. Separation of the offices was, however, a gradual process. As late as 1867, the governors of the territories of Colorado, Dakota, Idaho and Montana were administering Indian affairs for the federal government.

GENERAL SUPERINTENDENTS

Territorial governments ceased to exist when the states carved from the territories gained admission into the Union. These reshapings of the country did away also with territorial governors as superintendents of Indian affairs. But they didn't eliminate the need for representatives of the government among Indians.

So the government redefined geographical areas for the administration of Indian affairs. These redefined areas soon came to be known as general superintendencies. Some of them corresponded roughly to the original areas of territories, while others comprised the area within a new state, or within 2 or more contiguous states. Each general superintendency was put under the supervision of a government appointee whose title, coming down from the past, was Superintendent of Indian Affairs.

The first general superintendency was established at St. Louis, Missouri, in 1822, by an act of Congress. Missouri was admitted into the Union in 1821, and a year later Congress authorized the President to appoint a superintendent of Indian affairs to reside at St. Louis and attend to the affairs of "all Indians frequenting that place."

A number of states were admitted into the Union earlier than 1821. In some of them, Indian affairs ceased to exist because the Indians relocated, voluntarily or otherwise, in the deeper frontiers.

As statehood continued to be acquired in the passing years, the need for federal government representatives among Indians increased, and many general superintendencies came into existence. By 1867, they encompassed practically all the U.S. west of the Mississippi. General superintendencies and their geographical jurisdictions are specified in the following list which shows the applicable states and territories in existence at that time.[10]

Superintendency	Jurisdiction
Arizona	Territory of Arizona
California	State of California
Central	State of Kansas and Indian Territory
Colorado	Territory of Colorado
Dakota	Territory of Dakota
Idaho	Territory of Idaho
Montana	Territory of Montana
Nevada	State of Nevada
New Mexico	Territory of New Mexico
Northern	States of Iowa and Nebraska
Oregon	State of Oregon
Utah	Territory of Utah
Washington	Territory of Washington

General superintendencies, as such, reached a peak in the 1870's. Gradually, in subsequent years, the positions of superintendents of Indian affairs were superceded by similar hierarchies of different titles.

1. The political status of the southern states in the Revolutionary period and in the early years of the Republic is discussed so commonly in standard history books that no documentation appears necessary here.

2. Lowrie and Clark, op. cit., pp. 89-90.

3. U.S. Congress, "An act to provide for the government of the territory northwest of the river Ohio," August 7, 1789; 1 Stat. 50.

4. U.S. Congress, "An act for establishing the salaries of the executive officers of Government, with their assitants and clerks," September 11, 1789; 1 Stat. 67.

5. Felix S. Cohen, op. cit., p. 9.

6. U.S. Congress, "An act for the government of the territory of the United States, south of the river Ohio," May 26, 1790; 1 Stat. 123. William Blount was the first governor of the territory.

7. Annual Report of the Commissioner of Indian Affairs for the Year 1857 (Washington: Wm. A. Harris, Printer, n.d.), pp. 312-14. Hereafter in this book, a citation to an annual report of the Commissioner of Indian Affairs will be briefed as follows: Rept. Com. Ind. Aff. (year).

8. Laurence F. Schmeckebier, op. cit., p. 52.

9. U.S. Congress, "An act to amend an act, entitled 'An act to regulate trade and intercourse with the Indian tribes, and to preserve peace on the frontiers,' approved thirtieth March, 1802," May 6, 1822; 3 Stat. 682.

10. Rept. Com. Ind. Aff., 1867, Table of Contents.

CHAPTER 4

INDIAN AGENTS AND SUBAGENTS

Superintendents of Indian affairs were not the sole representatives of the federal government among Indians. The laws of Congress and the national Indian policies covered matters that, in many cases, touched upon the personal lives of Indians. To carry out these kinds of policies and laws, the Indian Department was expanded, and personnel was employed and headquartered close to the habitats and dwellings of the Indians.

People whose posts of duty were at the sites of Indian communities were called Indian agents and subagents. They formed a level of organization to give local implementation to federal Indian laws and policies. Their headquarters were designated as Indian agencies, and their jurisdictions were confined generally to the geographical areas comprising Indian reservations.

Indian agents of the earliest periods were responsible directly to the President. However, as administrative matters dealing with Indians increased and the Indian Department expanded, they were put under the supervision of superintendents of Indian affairs.

Positions of Indian agents and subagents came into being by various means. Treaties between the government and the Indian tribes contained clauses stipulating that agents reside among Indians to represent the government in Indian affairs. Similarly, some of the early congressional laws specifically provided for the appointment of persons to reside among Indians. Later acts assumed that such personnel existed or that the Indian Department had general authority to employ agents.

This chapter highlights the development of the local administrative level characterized by Indian agents and subagents.

HENRY KNOX SUGGESTS PLAN

The concept of local management of Indian affairs originated principally from the need to reduce friction between the early settlers and the Indians. Washington's Fourth Annual Message included the phrase that "To enable, by competent rewards, the employment of qualified and trusty persons to reside among them as agents would also contribute to the preservation of peace and good neighborhood."

When Washington made this recommendation to Congress in 1792, he reflected the years of sober thought he shared with his advisors on Indian affairs. Henry Knox, Secretary of War, was one of his advisors. In a letter written 3 years earlier, Knox urged the President to consider setting up a program to familiarize Indians with the American way of living. He believed this would be a step in the direction toward peaceful relationships with them. The letter he wrote was dated July 7, 1789. It embodies ideas that shaped the government's attitude, programs and policies among Indians for years to come. It deserves to be quoted in some detail. The letter states, in part:

... Missionaries, of excellent moral character, should be appointed to reside in their nation, who should be well supplied with all the implements of husbandry, and the necessary stock for a farm.

These men should be made the instruments to work on the Indians; presents should commonly pass through their hands, or by their recommendations. They should, in no degree, be concerned with trade, or the purchase of lands, to rouse the jealousy of the Indians. They should be their friends and fathers.

Such a plan, although it might not fully effect the civilization of the Indians, would most probably be attended with the salutory effect of attaching them to the interests of the United States ....[1]

20

From the earliest times after the discovery of America, missionaries of various denominations travelled among Indians trying to spread their particular concepts of Christianity. Knox knew this and felt that Indians were more likely to listen to and follow missionaries then schoolteachers, statesmen and others. So he recommended that missionaries be appointed as agents of the government to show the Indians how to raise crops and livestock and to instruct them in other refinements of the American civilization.

KNOX PLAN IMPLEMENTED

Washington had contributed, no doubt, to the formulation of the Knox plan for local administration of Indian affairs. Since he was committed to the objective of establishing peaceful relationships between the promised New Nation and the venerable nations of Indians, he desired that every possible means be employed to put the plan into operation.

One way was to recommend necessary legislation authorizing and establishing positions of agents among Indians. This method was used quite extensively to implement the plan of resident agents among Indians.

Another way was to get the consent of tribes to send government agents to reside among Indians. This method was the more expeditious one in the early days of the Republic. It was accomplished by inserting clauses in treaties for agents to manage Indian affairs. Some of the details of this method are worthy of a few comments now.

The Constitution conferred power upon the President to make treaties "by and with the advice and consent of the Senate ... provided two-thirds of the Senators present concur." There was no question at the beginning of the U.S. that the various tribes of Indians were nations with which peace could be established through treaties. Neither was there any doubt that developing articles for treaties and seeking concurrence in them by the tribes were prerogatives of the President.[2]

Previous to the ratification of the Constitution, the general government entered into certain treaties with Indian tribes. The first of these was with the Six Nations on August 25, 1775. Ten other treaties were made with as many different tribes prior to the framing of the Constitution.[3] Some of them contained provisions for government agents to reside among Indians. For example, the treaty of September 17, 1778, with the Delaware Indians provided for:

> ... a well-regulated trade, under the conduct of an intelligent, candid agent, with an adequate sallery, one more influenced by the love of his country, and a constant attention to the duties of his department by promoting the common interest, than the sinister purposes of converting and binding all the duties of his office to his private emolument ....[4]

This treaty, as well as other early treaties, and the influence of agents upon the Indians were well known to Washington and his advisors. So it was clear to them that they could include articles in treaties providing for agents and defining their duties.

The way treaties were negotiated with Indian tribes is an item proper for consideration at this point.

INDIAN PEACE COMMISSIONS

In the treaty-making process, the U.S. was represented by committees of persons called peace commissioners. These committees were formed as the need for them arose throughout the infancy and growth of the Nation. They were more generally referred to as Indian Peace Commissions. Each of the commissions was required to perform its functions in accordance with instructions issued by the President.

The act of August 20, 1789, for example, provided funds for the purpose of defraying expenses incurred in connection with negotiations of treaties with Indian tribes. Additionally, the act empowered the President to appoint commissioners to represent the U.S. in the treaties. The appointees became known as Indian peace commissioners, and they composed groups called Indian peace commissions.

An important function of the superintendents of Indian affairs under the Confederation was negotiating treaties with Indian tribes. By the act of August 20, 1789, the constitutional government transferred this responsibility to Indian peace commissioners. The superintendents of Indian affairs were not eliminated entirely from the treaty-making process. Their work was to inform the applicable tribes that the federal government was sending its commissioners to negotiate treaties and to assemble the tribes at designated places for that purpose.

Essentially, the act of August 20, 1789, authorized the formation of organizations apart from the Indian Department to deal with Indian tribes in the making of treaties. The act became a legislative precedence in prescribing the manner that treaties were to be made between the government and Indian tribes. Similar acts were passed as the need arose during the following 100 years.

The numerous acts authorizing Indian peace commissions need not be listed for illustration at this point. However, evidence that the concept expressed in the act of August 20, 1789, did endure for almost an entire century is relevant.

A man whose name was Felix S. Cohen was the Solicitor for the Department of the Interior during the Roosevelt administration. He wrote a treatise on Indian law and, in it, he presents a brief history of Indian treaties. He starts with the treaty of September 17, 1778, which was said by Chief Justice Marshall to be the first treaty made with the Indians, and ends with the treaty of August 13, 1868. Cohen's work contains the following paragraph:

> ... In the summer of 1868, many Sioux, together with a scattering of Cheyenne and Arapaho warriors, renewed hostilities, which were terminated by the treaty of April 29, 1868. A month later the Crows and the Northern Arapaho and Cheyenne put an end to hostilities in two agreements concluded May 7, 1868, and May 10, 1868. By summer, the Navajo, the eastern band of Shoshones and the Bannock, and the Nez Perce had also become signatories to treaties of peace. These were the last treaties made by the United States with Indian tribes ....[5]

The federal government was represented in these last treaties by an Indian peace commission composed of Nathaniel G. Taylor, William T. Sherman, William S. Harney, John B. Sanborn, S. F. Tappan, C. C. Augur and Alfred H. Terry. The commissioners were appointed by the President pursuant to the act of July 20, 1867, to conclude treaties with such "bands or tribes of Indians as are now waging war against the United States or committing depredations upon the people thereof."

AGENT BY TREATY

One of the earliest peace commissions formed under the New Nation was composed of Benjamin Lincoln, Cyrus Griffin and David Humphreys. This trio of peace commissioners was organized to treat with the southern Indians. In their instructions from Washington, they were required to direct a fair amount of careful attention to the concept of resident agents whose principal functions would be to secure an ultimate peace with the Indians and introduce and promote the American civilization among them. Washington's directives to the peace commissioners are dated August 29, 1789. They illustrate so clearly the concern of the government about agents and their work that they deserve to be quoted. In part, they are:

> ... You will, also, endeavor to obtain a stipulation for certain missionaries, to reside in the nation, provided the General Government should think proper to adopt the measure. These men to be precluded from trade, or attempting to purchase any lands, but to have a certain reasonable quantity, per head, allowed for the purpose of cultivation. The

object of this establishment would be the happiness of the Indians, teaching them the great duties of religion and morality, and to inculcate a friendship and attachment to the United States ....[6]

Peace commissioners Lincoln, Griffin and Humphreys negotiated separate treaties with various tribes of southern Indians. One of these was the treaty of August 7, 1790, with the Creek Indians. Article 12 of that treaty provides for agents, defines their duties and specifies the restrictions placed upon them. The article is quoted at length because of the significance to the point at issue. The applicable part of it reads:

... that the Creek Indians may be led to a greater degree of civilization, and to become herdsmen and cultivators, instead of remaining in a state of hunters, the United States will, from time to time, furnish gratuitously the said nation with useful domestic animals, and implements of husbandry. And further, to assist the said nation in so desirable a pursuit, and at the same time to establish a mode of communication, the United States will send such, and so many persons, to reside in said nation, as they may judge proper, and not exceeding four in number, who shall qualify themselves to act as interpreters. These persons shall have lands assigned to them by the Creeks for cultivation, for themselves and their successors in office; but they shall be precluded exercising any kind of traffic ....[7]

Although the treaty article provided for as many as four persons, qualified as interpreters, to act as agents and reside among the Creeks, the government appointed only one person at a time as agent. The first of these was Alex McGillivray.[8]

Similar articles were included in many of the subsequent early treaties. For example, the treaty of July 2, 1791, with the Cherokee Indians, the treaty of November 11, 1794, with "the tribes of Indians called the Six Nations" and the treaty of December 9, 1795, with the "Wyandots, Delawares, Shawanese, Ottawas, Chippewas, Pattawatamies, Miamies, Eeel Rivers, Weas, Kickapoos, Piankeshaws and Kaskaskias," stipulated that the government furnish animals and implements of husbandry and send an appropriate number of agents to reside among the Indians.[9] A number of later treaties with the tribes west of the Mississippi contained the provision for agents to reside among the Indians.

This section has shown that the inclusion of appropriate stipulations in treaties was one of the important ways the federal government arranged to send its agents to reside among Indians.

Another way, equally important in the buildup of the local level of administration, was legislation. This method can be examined now.

AGENTS BY LEGISLATION

The recommendation Washington made in 1792 that Congress enact laws authorizing the employment of agents to reside among Indians came alive a year later in the act of March 1, 1793. The act reads, in part, that:

... in order to promote civilization among the friendly Indian tribes, and to secure a continuance of their friendship, it shall be lawful for the President of the United States ... to appoint such persons, from time to time, as temporary agents, to reside among the Indians, as he shall think proper ....[10]

It is difficult to ascertain the name of the first agent appointed under this legislation. The general government in earlier years employed agents for specific purposes. Some of them might have been recruited to implement the act of March 1, 1793. Previous to the passage of the act, too, the general government appointed deputy temporary agents to reside among Indians and to handle Indian affairs. Israel Chapin, Leonard Shaw and James Robertson, to mention 3 of them, were appointed in the early months of 1792 as deputy temporary agents to the Five Nations, the Cherokees and the Chickasaws, respectively. These men continued in the same capacity after the act passed.[11]

The act of March 1, 1793, was one of the temporary trade and intercourse acts. It specifically stated, nevertheless, that the agents were "temporary."

The legislators hoped or expected the objects of the law would be accomplished in a year or two and agents among Indians would no longer be necessary. Soon, though, they began to realize that perpetuating the friendship of Indians and promoting the American civilization among them was a big job, complicated by the turbulent times and requiring a mutual confidence built across many years. So every 2 years for about the next decade, the lawmakers renewed the authority of the President to appoint Indian agents. They omitted the authority, however, in the permanent trade and intercourse act passed in 1802. For approximately 30 years thereafter, no legal basis existed, except as provided in treaties, for many of the positions of agents.

Meanwhile other relationships developed between the various Indian tribes and the federal government. These relationships evolved in large part from treaties, and it is appropriate now to explore this matter in some detail. The following chapter is devoted to it.

1. Lowrie and Clark, op. cit., pp. 53-54.

2. Felix S. Cohen, op. cit., pp. 33-46. The political status of Indian tribes was, in later years, particularly 1872, the subject of legal deliberations, and the question of the extent of Executive powers in treaty-making has been brought before courts several times since the founding of the nation.

3. U.S. Congress, Senate Executive Documents, Ex. Doc. No. 95, 48th Congress, 2nd Session, Indian Education and Civilization, March 4, 1885, p. 132.

4. Treaty of September 17, 1778; 7 Stat. 13.

5. Felix S. Cohen, op. cit., pp. 65-66. Chief Justice Marshall refers to the first treaty with the general government. This particular treaty was superceded by the treaty of January 9, 1789, which was the first treaty entered into by the constitutional government and Indian tribes.

6. Lowrie and Clark, op. cit., pp. 65-69.

7. Ibid., p. 100. The treaty of August 7, 1790, was superceded, in later years, by other treaties, notably the treaty of August 7, 1814.

8. Ibid., p. 127.

9. Ibid., p. 125, p. 545, p. 562.

10. U.S. Congress, "An act to regulate trade and intercourse with Indian tribes," March 1, 1793; 1 Stat. 329.

11. U.S. Congress, House Report No. 474, Vol. IV, 23rd Congress, 1st. Session, Regulating the Indian Department, May 20, 1834, p. 42.

CHAPTER 5

INDIAN TREATIES

Nearly everyone knows something about the countless were generated by the rugged insistence of the Indians that none spoil their virgin lands and the dogged determination of the federal government that the country be populated and exploited to yield its greater abundance. The fact that many of the conflicts ended with treaties is also generally known. Less familiar are some of the treaty articles and the numerous activities of the federal government that sprang from them. Activities resulting from stipulations in treaties made the system of resident agents among Indians permanent and enlarged the Indian Department. This chapter goes into how treaties were made and some of the treaty articles.

In making treaties with Indians, the government encountered a unique situation. This situation and how it was handled are interesting and significant highlight in Indian affairs. A review of this uniqueness is an apt beginning for this chapter.

UNIQUENESS IN TREATY MAKING

The period of time during which treaties were made spanned nearly a century. In those many years, 645 separate treaties were made with the various Indian tribes.[1]

Peace commissioners sometimes were able to meet with the many different tribes inhabiting a large area the U.S. wished to acquire. At this kind of a conference, it was customary to negotiate one treaty with all the tribes convened. At other times, the peace commissioners met with only the tribe they thought possessed the lands to be acquired and negotiated a treaty with that tribe.

The particular type of meeting held was up to the peace commissioners. In 1862, a treaty was contemplated with the Shoshones and other Indians of Utah. Duane Doty, Luther Mann and Henry Martin were appointed as peace commissioners. Instructions issued to them state that, if practicable and possible, they should assemble and negotiate with all Indians in the area. But if that were not feasible, they should make treaties with one tribe or band at a time. Specifically, the instructions were:

... Should you find it impracticable to make one treaty which will secure the goodwill and friendship of all the tribes or bands of Shoshones Indians, you will then negotiate only with that tribe or band which is most dangerous to emigrants and settlers upon the route of travel to the Pacific ....[2]

At treaty meetings, it was usual for the commissioners to incorporate in the treaties whatever land descriptions were supplied by tribal leaders or those who represented themselves to be authorized to act for the tribes. Areas claimed by the Indians were described by physical landmarks, such as rivers and mountains.

Formulation of treaties in these ways commenced with the earliest of the treaties and continued throughout the years during which the country was settled.

Many of the treaties gave rise in the immediately following years to disputes between the federal government and the Indians. In some cases, the disagreement was about what land had actually been relinquished. In other cases, the power of the Indian signatories was challenged by tribal members, leaders and other tribes.

These kinds of quarrels might have led to more Indian wars. However, early in its dealings with Indians, the federal government adopted an easy solution and avoided further troubles. The government simply renegotiated treaties with whichever tribe or tribes denied having relinquished the land, or with the tribal members or leaders who challenged the power of the Indian signatories to treaties.

NATURE OF INDIAN TREATIES

Some of the early Indian treaties were purely declarations of peace. The fundamental nature of these kinds of treaties was indicated by peace commissioners William Clark, Ninian Edwards and August Chauteau in their report made in 1815 about the treaties they made with 21 different tribes of the Mississippi valleys. Their report reads, in part:

... According to our instructions, we confined those treaties to the sole object of peace; but the Indians were in several instances extremely solicitous that they should also have embraced other subjects; and some further negotiation with some of them seems to be recommended by every dictate of policy ....[3]

Both the Indians and the government were aware that treaties restricted solely to the "objects of peace" failed in many other points of significance to both parties. Furthermore, the declared peace was, at best, temporary. Subsequent wars ended with superceding treaties that included items of importance to the parties, won a more-enduring peace and set a pattern for original treaties with some of the newly-contacted tribes.

Treaties which went beyond simply declaring the existence of peace were, basically, instruments for the sale and corresponding purchase of land. They were documents by which Indian tribes relinquished huge blocks of their claimed territory to the U.S. for agreed-upon consideration. These kinds of treaties honored the commitments of the government recited in the Northwest Ordinance. The agreed-upon consideration was a variety of stipulations from which many of the government's activities among Indians originated.

To list and describe every stipulation in the many treaties would not be practicable. But some common to the greater number can be explored.

PEACE DECLARED

Since peace and friendship were objects of the parties, treaties usually included an article similar to the following Article I from the treaty of September 14, 1816, negotiated by peace commissioners Andrew Jackson, David Meriwether and Jesse Franklin and the Cherokee tribe:

... Peace and friendship are hereby firmly established between the United States and the Cherokee nation or tribe of Indians ....[4]

Treaties made about 50 years later with the tribes of the west included an article declaring peace and friendship between the parties. In 1863, for example, a number of treaties were made with Indians of the west. Among them were those between the various Shoshones tribes and the government. One of these tribes was designated the Eastern bands of Shoshones Indians. Article I of the first treaty made with them at Fort Bridger, Utah Territory, on July 2, 1863, states:

... Friendly and amicable relations are hereby reestablished between the bands of the Shoshones nation, parties hereto, and the United States; and it is declared that a firm and perpetual peace shall be henceforth maintained between the Shoshones nation and the United States ....[5]

Declarations of peace were followed generally by articles requiring the parties to bring to justice "bad men" of the nations who jeopardized the peace and friendship.

TERRITORIES DESCRIBED

Treaties contained descriptions of the land purchased by the federal government. The territory was described by physical landmarks. Article II of the treaty of September 14, 1816, with the Cherokee tribe illustrates the language. The article reads:

... The Cherokee nation acknowledge the following as their western boundary south of the Tennessee river: commencing at Camp Coffee, on the south side of the Tennessee river, which is opposite the Chicksaw Island, running from thence, a due south course, to the top of the dividing ridge between the waters of the Tennessee and Tombigee rivers; thence easterly, along said ridge, leaving the headwaters of the Black Warrior to the right hand, until opposed by the west branch of Will's creek; down the east bank of said creek, to the Coosa river and down said river ....[6]

This description of land lacks engineering precision. But it was considerably more detailed than descriptions in later treaties. In the treaty of July 30 , 1863, with the Northwestern bands of Shoshonee Indians, Article IV states:

... The country claimed by Pokatello, for himself and his people, is bounded on the west by Raft River and on the east by the Porteneuf Mountains ....[7]

Pokatello was the recognized chief of the Northwestern bands at that time. The city of Pocatello, Idaho, was named after him.

LANDS RELINQUISHED

One of the principal objects of the government in making Indian treaties was to extinguish the aboriginal title to the lands. Treaties , therefore, included language to the effect that all title, claims or rights of the Indians to the lands described were relinquished to the U.S.

The treaty of September 14, 1816, with the Cherokee nation is illustrative. It provided by Article III:

... the Cherokee nation relinquish to the United States all claim, and cede all title, to lands lying south and west of the line as described in the second article ....[8]

By these kinds of treaty articles, the federal government obtained from Indians virtually all the lands, other than the original colonies, which today comprise the continental U.S.[9]

LANDS RESERVED

Many treaties contained descriptions of lands reserved to the tribes for the use of their members. This is particularly the case in a good many treaties made with Indian tribes west of the Mississippi river. The areas of lands reserved to the tribes were not relinquished to the government. The second treaty between the U.S. and the Eastern Bands of Shoshonee Indians is a good example of this. The treaty was concluded on July 3, 1868. The applicable portion of Article II reads:

... the United States further agrees that the following district ... shall be and the same is set apart for the absolute and undisturbed use and occupation of the Shoshonee Indians herein named ... and henceforth they will and do hereby relinquish all title, claims, or rights in and to any portion of the territory of the United States, except such as is embraced within the limits aforesaid ....[10]

Lands reserved by tribes were some of the original Indian reservations. The reservation created by Article II of the treaty of July 3, 1868, was the original Shoshone Indian reservation in the Wind River country of Wyoming. It is popularly known as the Wind River Indian Reservation.

Territories reserved in treaties were not gifts of lands to Indian tribes by the federal government. Treaties recognized Indians to be the landowners, and the government dealt with the landowners accordingly in acquiring title to the lands.

Treaties were not the sole means by which Indian reservations were established. Some of the treaties failed to reserve lands to the Indians. In such instance, however, it was understood that reservations would be created by legislation or Executive Order. As a matter of fact, a number of Indian reservations were created by these means. The Isabella reservation in Michigan was the first Indian reservation created by Executive Order. It was set aside on May 14, 1855. In the following 30 years, 60 Indian reservations were created by Executive Orders.

In its dealings with Indians, the federal government extended basic benefits to tribes and their members even though the detailed stipulations varied and, in some cases, benefits were left out. The creation of Indian reservations by Executive Order is an example of the federal government providing a benefit not included in some of the treaties.

PAYMENT FOR LANDS

The federal government agreed in treaties to compensate the Indians for the lands relinquished to it. The forms of payment, as well as amounts, varied widely in treaties. Virtually all treaties, however, contained a provision for part of the payment to be annuity payments. This form of payment has been described with particular reference to Indian treaties, as follows:

> ... Periodic payments of either money or goods are called "annuities." According to the terms of the instrument, an annuity may be a specific amount for a specified number of years, or it may be a specified amount for life or while the Indians are at peace ....[11]

The life of an annuity in the case of Indian treaties can be forever.

Some of the treaties provided for money annuities, others for annuities of goods. The treaty of September 29, 1817, with the "Wyandots, Senecas, Delawares, Shawanees, Pattawatamies, Ottowas and Chippewas" illustrates treaties stipulating money annuities. This particular treaty superceded a treaty made in 1795 with these and other tribes who inhabited the Northwest Territory. This treaty, too, was superceded in later years by treaties applicable to the separate tribes. It illustrates, nevertheless, the provision for money annuities. Since Indian annuities have been of more or less general interest, the treaty provision is quoted at length. Article 4 of the treaty states:

> ... In consideration of the cessions and recognitions stipulated in the three preceding articles, the United States agree to pay to the Wyandot tribe, annually, forever, the sum of $4,000, in specie, at Upper Sandusky; to the Seneca tribe, annually, forever, the sum of $500, in specie, at lower Sandusky; to the Shawanee tribe, annually, forever, the sum of $2,000, in specie, at Wapaghkonetta; to the Pattawatomie tribe, annually, for the term of fifteen years, the sum of $1,300, in specie, at Detroit; to the Ottawa tribe, annually, for the term of fifteen years, the sum of $1,000, in specie, at Detroit; to the Chippewa tribe, annually, for the term of fifteen years, the sum of $1,000 in specie, at Detroit; to the Delaware tribe, in the course of the year 1818, the sum of $500, in specie, at Wapaghkonetta, but no annuity; and the United States also agree that all annuities due by any former treaty to the Wyandot, Shawanee, and Delaware tribes, and the annuity due by the Treaty of Greenville to the Ottawa and Chippewa tribes, shall be paid to said tribes, respectively, in specie ....[12]

The Wyandot, the Seneca and the Shawanee tribes were to be paid money annuities forever. This kind of annuities is called permanent annuities. Money annuities for the term of 15 years were provided to the Patawatamie, the Ottawa and the Chippewa tribes. Annuities with a time limit are known as term annuities. The Delaware tribe was to receive full payment in one lump sum.

Some of the Indian treaties provided for annuities in goods rather than money. The first treaty with various tribes of the Northwest Territory, concluded on August 3, 1795, and the treaty of August 9, 1814, with the Creek nation are among the early treaties providing that payment for the relinquished lands be made in the form of goods.

Payment in goods was particularly common in later treaties with tribes of the west. The treaty of October 1, 1863, with the Western bands of the Shoshonee nation illustrates these kinds of treaties. Article VII of that treaty reads:

... The United States, being aware of the inconvenience resulting to the Indians in consequence of the driving away and destruction of game along the routes traveled by white men, and by the formation of agricultural and mining settlements, are willing to fairly compensate them for the same; therefore ... the United States promise and agree to pay to the said bands of the Shoshonee nation, parties hereto, annually for the term of twenty years, the sum of five thousand dollars in such articles, including cattle for herding or other purposes, as the President of the United States shall deem suitable for their wants and condition, either as hunters or herdsmen ....[13]

Another form of payments made to Indians was services, such as health, law and order, education and other services. Some of the treaties provided for these kind of services, but many did not. The federal government, nevertheless, provided these services to practically all the tribes.

Treaties in the nature of land-sales contracts created a relationship of mutual obligations between Indian tribes and the federal government. The obligations of the Indians were to relinquish their vast hunting grounds, settle down upon specifically designated tracts of land, called Indian reservations, and work toward acquiring the desirable characteristics of the non-Indian civilization. The federal government became obligated to pay for the lands in lump sum or installments of money, goods and services. Agents were to reside among Indians to represent the government and to aid the Indians in adopting the culture of the American civilization.

The material in this chapter indicates a broad movement of the federal government to hem Indians within defined geographical boundaries to bring an end to frontier warfare and to Americanize the tribesmen. Two of the larger specific projects in this broad movement were the Indian Removal Act and the creation of Indian Territory.

Both of these projects are touched upon in histories about the growth and development of the U.S. But they are not generally tied together. They were actually glaring examples of the consistent policy of the federal government to push Indians as far from settlements and lines of communication as possible. A brief review of these projects can show clearly what the government was attempting to accomplish.

REMOVAL ACT AND INDIAN TERRITORY

The Indian Removal Act and the creation of Indian Territory were separated by many years.

In the early 1800's no one believed the U.S. would extend its borders beyond the Mississippi. Lands to the west loomed as wildernesses that would forever be uninhabitable by the Americans. On the other hand, frontier troubles between Indians and non-Indians in the east were scarcely lessened by the measures taken by the federal government. More thinking about how to stop the fights led to the idea of removing the Indians to lands west of the Mississippi where they would be no more bother to the settlers.

This idea became known as the removal policy. Its first expression was in a treaty of July 8, 1817, with the Cherokee nation. In that treaty, the Cherokee Indians agreed to cede to the U.S. certain lands they claimed in the Southern Department. In exchange, they were promised as much land west of the Mississippi and a lifestyle undisturbed by settlers and the American civilization.

Andrew Jackson represented the U.S. as peace commissioner in the treaty, and he applied a good deal of pressure in getting the Indians to agree to the treaty provisions. Many leaders of the Cherokee nation bitterly opposed it. Moreover, the Cherokee tribe at that time was split into 2 groups. One of the groups denied it was a party to the treaty. This group felt no obligation to abide by the treaty provisions, so it remained east of the Mississippi in the territory it claimed. The other group relocated west of the Mississippi in the area of the Arkansas and White rivers.[14]

Treaties such as this were negotiated with other tribes, particularly the Five Civilized Tribes. The major object of these treaties was removal of the Indians to the uninhabitable country west of the Mississippi. Partial success of the removal policy was achieved by the treaties, but those Indians who refused to leave their claimed territories persisted in their resentment, hostilities and wars against the non-Indians. Resolution of the continuing frontier disturbances remained a challenge to the federal government.

Andrew Jackson became President of the U.S. in 1829. He was fired with a determination to push the Indians across the Mississippi. In his first message to Congress on December 8, 1829, he urged legislation calling for voluntary removal for the benefit and protection of both the Indians and the settlers. But Congress went further than the President requested. In the following year, it passed the Indian Removal Act, empowering the President to proceed in the matter with increasing vigor.[15] The ultimate effect of the act was the removal, voluntarily or involuntarily, of almost all tribes of the east to lands across the Mississippi.

A few years after the Indian Removal Act, the idea that the western lands were uninhabitable by non-Indians fell apart. Westward expansion proceeded with undreamed rapidity. The facts and incidents in the conquest of the west are a substantial part of history texts and other works. They need no amplification in this book. Indian wars of the west did, however, renew the thought that the way to end hostilities was to confine the warriors and their tribes to a specific area along the fringe of civilization.

In 1866, new treaties were negotiated with a number of tribes. Those treaties contained provisions for the formation of a federated Indian government in an area called Indian Territory and for the removal of the different tribes to the Territory. The plan was pushed for a while, but eventually, it failed. One cause of failure was the refusal of many tribes to relocate in Indian Territory. R more significant reason was "Land-hungry whites overflowed into Indian Territory and reached about a quarter of a million at the beginning of the last decade of the nineteenth century."[16] Under the impact of these forces, Indian Territory became, in time, the State of Oklahoma.

FOOTNOTES--CHAPTER 5

1. U.S. Senate, Ex. Doc. No. 95, op. cit., p. 132.

2. U.S. Court of Claims, No. M-107, The Northwestern Bands of Shoshone Indians v. The United States, March 2, 1942, pp. 9-10.

3. Lowrie and Clark, op. cit., p. 10.

4. Ibid., p. 92.

5. Treaty of July 2, 1863; 18 Stat. 685.

6. Lowrie and Clark, op. cit., p. 92.

7. Treaty of July 30, 1863; 13 Stat. 663.

8. Lowrie and Clark, op. cit., p. 92.

9. Felix S. Cohen, op. cit., Frontispiece.

10. Treaty of July 3, 1868; 15 Stat. 673.

11. Felix S. Cohen, op. cit., p. 199.

12. Lowrie and Clark, op. cit., p. 131.

13. U.S. Court of Claims, No. M-107, op. cit., pp. 21-22.

14. Felix S. Cohen, op. cit., pp. 55-56.

15. U.S. Congress, "An act to provide for an exchange of lands with the Indians residing in any of the states or territories, and for their removal west of the river Mississippi"; 4. Stat. 411.

16. Felix S. Cohen, op. cit., p. 427.

CHAPTER 6

GROWTH AND PROBLEMS OF INDIAN DEPARTMENT

Many tribes of Indians were encountered by the people who burst the seams of the Infant Nation and took the mighty lunge across the continent. Practically every contact with a different tribe, or subgroup of large tribes, brought about treaty relationships, necessitating more agents or subagents to reside among Indians and increasing the activities of the Indian Department. In fact, the job of paying annuities, attempting to preserve peace on the Frontier, trying to promote the American civilization among Indians and other activities was more than agents and subagents could handle alone. So other personnel, particularly interpreters and blacksmiths, were provided to help out. Increasing activities and more personnel gave growth to the Indian Department. But its growth became the source of a number of organizational and other problems.

The task of this chapter is to examine the early growth of the Indian Department and the resulting problems.

GROWTH INDICATED BY APPROPRIATIONS

The early growth of the Indian Department is evident by the increasing amounts of money needed to finance Indian affairs.

The first act of the U.S. Congress to recognize the existence of the Indian Department was the act of December 23, 1791. That act appropriated $39,424.71 for "defraying all expenses incident to the Indian Department" during the fiscal year 1792.[1] In the following 30 years, the Indian Department grew and expanded rather rapidly. The sum of $123,638.00 was appropriated in fiscal year 1822 for the following expenses:[2]

Pay of agents	$22,300
Pay of subagents	11,338
Presents to Indians	15,000
Contingent expenses	75,000

The difference of $84,213.29 is the approximate increase in the cost of operating the Indian Department in fiscal year 1822 compared to 1792. The amount needed for Indian Department expenses tripled in the 30 years.

In those days, the sum of $123,638.00 was a significant portion of the federal budget. But additionally, Congress had to appropriate funds for annuity payments and other treaty obligations.

GROWTH REVEALED BY INCREASES IN PERSONNEL

Increases in personnel also indicate the early growth of the Indian Department.

From January 1, 1820 to April 12, 1822, the Indian Department added on 3 superintendents of Indian affairs, 17 agents and 25 subagents. They were administrative personnel. In addition, 34 interpreters and 21 blacksmiths were put on the payroll.[3]

These statistics suggest the broadening functions of the Indian Department and the widening geographical area over which it extended its jurisdiction in the approximate 2 year and 3 months.

INTERNAL PROBLEMS OF INDIAN DEPARTMENT

The early fast growth of the Indian Department brought about a few problems from the way people were appointed to positions.

Superintendents of Indian affairs and territorial governors, who were ex-officio superintendents of Indian affairs, were appointed by the President. Generally, too, the President appointed Indian agents. The War Department appointed subagents, interpreters, blacksmith and other personnel at the local levels.[4]

In these circumstances, appointees felt responsible to their appointing authorities, and they had little regard for the hierarchy of authority in the Indian Department. Ninnian Edwards, Governor of Illinois Territory, summed up the problems and his dilemma in a letter to Secretary of War, William H. Crawford. The letter was dated November, 1815, and in it, Edwards stated:

... As to the Indian agents, the law is perfectly silent with regard to their powers and duties, or those of the superintendent in relation to them; and really I have been much at a loss to know what orders I could legally give to those who have been directed to report to me, and receive my orders; ...[5]

Agents and subagents assumed a very wide degree of personal judgment in deciding what their duties were and how to perform them. The hierarchy of authority was powerless in giving them directions and defining their duties.

FIRST ATTEMPTS TO SOLVE INTERNAL PROBLEMS

In time, the personnel problems of the Indian Department were brought to the attention of Congress, and Congress passed the act of April 16, 1818. The act revised the appointment system for Indian Department jobs. It required that the superintendent of Indian trade, the agents and assistant agents at Indian trading houses and Indian agents at Indian reservations be nominated by the President and appointed by and with the advice and consent of the Senate. The act made appointees accountable for their judgments and actions and required them to furnish bonds of $10,000 to ensure faithful performance of duties.[6] Lines of authority were redrawn and management functions were overhauled so that appointees were made responsible to higher-ups in the pyramid of authority. This revamping put some temporary order into the personnel structure.

But "growing pains" continued to annoy and agonize. A cluster of problems developed in getting money, paying annuities and accounting for expenditures. As an agency of the government, the Indian Department had to obtain money for its operations and account for its expenditures in the same way as other federal agencies. But as treaty annuities increased and federal activities among Indians expanded, the Indian Department was deluged with more work than it was staffed to do.

The search for solutions to this "bucket of worms" had a lot to do with renaming the Indian Department the Bureau of Indian Affairs and setting up the position of Commissioner of Indian Affairs as its titular head. These incidents are important milestones in Indian affairs. So it is well to go into how money was obtained, how annuity payments were made, what accounting was required and how the headaches developing from these jobs led to those organizational titles.

APPROPRIATION PROCESS

Section 9 of the Constitution places certain restrictions upon public moneys. Paragraph 7 of Section 9 states, in part, that "No money shall be drawn from the Treasury, but in Consequence of Appropriation made by law."

This provision of the Constitution is the source of a method used to draw money from the treasury. The method is known as the appropriation process. At the end of the process, federal agencies are authorized by congressional laws to withdraw funds from the U.S. Treasury to finance their operations. Since the Indian Department was a federal agency, it was subject to the appropriation process.

Over the many years of its use, the appropriation process has been modified and refined several times. In essence, however, it has remained unchanged since the early years of the Republic.

The appropriation process is lengthy, involved and technical. Its development, ramifications and details are beyond the scope of this book. But bare outlines need to be presented to suggest some of the work of the Indian Department, particularly in connection with treaty annuities.

ESTIMATES OF APPROPRIATIONS

During the appropriation process, agencies develop estimates of the funds they need for their operations. For these estimates, operations are called programs and subprograms. Each program is shown separately, and it is broken down by subprograms and their estimated costs.

In the case of the Indian Department, one of the programs was fulfilling Indian treaties. Subprograms were the separate treaties. For each treaty, the costs were estimated for annuities and other obligations. The combined cost was the estimate of funds needed for the program of fulfilling Indian treaties.

Estimates are submitted to Congress by the President, and specific House committees and subcommittees hold one or more hearings to consider the estimates of particular agencies. These conferences are attended by members of the House committee and representatives of the agency whose estimates are under consideration. Feasibility of programs and their purposes are considered at these hearings, along with the reasonableness of estimated costs.

In early periods, representatives of the War Department and the Indian Department met with the House Committee on Indian Affairs to go over the estimates of appropriations for the Indian Department.

House committees and subcommittees may agree fully with the proposals of the agencies and estimates of appropriations, or they may revise the programs and amounts.

Indian treaties generally provided for specific amounts of annuities, so early House committees usually didn't change these estimates. However, they did alter other estimates and programs when they believed costs were too high or too low or proposed programs were not feasible.

APPROPRIATIONS

The outcome of appropriation hearings is proposed bills the House committees recommend for enactment into law. Many details make up this phase of the appropriation process. It is not necessary to go into them here.

Proposed bills eventually become appropriation acts authorizing named agencies to withdraw from the U.S. treasury stated amounts of public funds for the purposes specified in the acts.

Indian treaties that provided for annuities of goods were treated in the appropriation process in the same manner as those for money annuities. The Indian Department needed money to buy the annuity goods, and this money was obtained through the appropriation process.

In the youthful days of the federal government, a number of appropriation acts were passed each year to fund the Indian Department. Usually, each act was for a specific program, or for several subprograms. The act of May 6, 1796, for example, provided money to fulfill the treaty of August 3, 1795. The treaty provided for annuities of goods, and the act appropriated money to the Indian Department to buy the goods. The act reads, in part:

> ... for the purpose of defraying the expenses which may arise in carrying into effect
> the treaty made between the United States and the tribes of Indians ... the moneys
> arising under the revenue laws of the United States, ... not already appropriated to
> any other purpose, ... be, and are hereby pledged and appropriated for the payment of
> the annuity stipulated in the said treaty, to be paid to said Indian tribes; that is
> to say, to the Wyandots, one thousand dollars; to the Delawares, one thousand dollars,
> to the Shawanoes, one thousand dollars, to the Ottawas, one thousand dollars, to the
> Chippewas, one thousand dollars, to the Putawatimes, one thousand dollars, to the
> Miamies, one thousand dollars, to the Eel River, Weea, Kickapoo, Piankashaw and
> Kaskaskia tribes, each five hundred dollars: and to continue so pledged and appro-
> priated, so long as the said treaty shall be in force ....[7]

This act illustrates the way the constitutional requirement is met that money withdrawn from
the treasury must be in "Consequence of Appropriations made by law." It gave the Indian Department authority to withdraw money for the annuity payments.

The act also depicts the type of appropriation known as a permanent appropriation. This
kind of an appropriation is a recurring appropriation. The stipulated amounts were pledged and
appropriated "so long as the said treaty shall be in force." No other acts were necessary for
the money in succeeding years.

The act applied to a treaty with Indians in the Northwest Territory. Treaties in later years
superceded this treaty, but many of them provided for permanent annuities.

Expansion of the nation, contact with more and more tribes and one Indian war after another
brought on increasing numbers of treaties. By 1822, 95 treaties were in force with 50 different
tribes. These treaties contained stipulations for annuities and other services valued in that
year at $468,251.25.[8]

Generally, Indian treaties spelled out where annuities were to be paid and services performed. In the earliest periods, these places were frontier settlements. Later they were the
Indian reservations scattered across the land.

ACCOUNTANT FOR THE WAR DEPARTMENT

Payments of money annuities were no great problems to the Indian Department. Money was withdrawn from the treasury and paid out to the Indians at reservations or other designated places.
Difficulties were overcome by better practices in the handling of money.

But many problems developed with annuities of goods. They came about when Congress passed
some laws to establish and streamline purchasing and accounting procedures of federal agencies.

The need to account adequately for public funds was recognized early by Congress, and the
act of May 18, 1792, was passed to make the War Department responsible for its own accounting.
Previous to the act, the accounting of the War Department was performed by the Treasury Department. The act transferred this function to the War Department. For some unknown reason, however, the transfer of the function was delayed.

Six years later, in 1798, another act was passed, and the function of accounting was then
transferred. The effect of this act upon the accountant of the War Department was indicated by
a report dated December 9, 1816. The report was made to the Senate by a committee of the President's cabinet members consisting of James Monroe, William H. Crawford, George Graham and B. W.
Crowninshield. The report stated:

> ... The business of the Accountant's office was confined to the duties prescribed by
> the act of the 8th May 1792, until the year 1798. On the 16th July of that year,

Congress passed "An Act ...," by which the duties heretofore performed by the accounting officers of the Treasury Department, ..., were annexed to those of the Accountant, making it his duty to settle accounts of every description growing out of the military service of the United States ... and also for the Indian Department, including the Indian annuities ....[10]

In essence, the act of July 16, 1798, placed upon the accountant for the War Department the job of processing all claims arising from activities of the War Department. This included paying the annuities to Indians and settling up with vendors for goods, supplies, equipment and whatever else was purchased by the Indian Department.

PURCHASE OF ANNUITY GOODS

The act of May 18, 1792, provided that all purchases and contracts of federal agencies be made by or under the direction of the Treasury Department.[11] Three years later, by the act of February 23, 1795, Congress authorized the position of Purveyor of Public Supplies and transferred to it the job of purchasing and contracting for federal agencies. The Purveyor of Public Supplies entered into contracts with vendors who agreed to furnish supplies.

When Annuity goods or other supplies were needed, the Indian Department sent purchase orders to the contracting vendors. If the particular goods needed were not under contract, the Purveyor of Public Supplies bought them from noncontracting vendors for the Indian Department.[12] After the goods were furnished, vendors issued bills or invoices to the War Department.

As the number of Indian treaties mushroomed, the volume of transactions for annuity goods and other Indian Department expenses shot up, and the Accountant for the War Department was swamped.

DUTIES OF SECRETARY OF WAR

Frontier discord was not always firmly settled by treaties. In some places, friction continued between the Indians and non-Indians and minor skirmishes broke out. In these conflicts, Indians sometimes came out semi-victorious. But in practically all these uprisings, they damaged or destroyed property in settlements and outlying non-Indian farms and ranches.

Non-Indians didn't go for this too much. They had worked hard to make a go of their settlements, farms and ranches, and they didn't like to see it all lost by Indian outbursts.

The idea finally occurred to them that they ought to be paid for the damages. They took their grievance to Congress, and the lawmakers decided that damages be paid out of annuities. This way of making Indians pay for damages was written into law for the first time in the Act of May 19, 1796. It was included in subsequent temporary trade acts and finally made a part of the permanent trade act in 1802.

Briefly, the act empowered the President to deduct from annuities any proven claim for loss of property resulting from theft or destruction by Indians.[13]

The practical meaning of the legislation and the burden it placed upon the Secretary of War was explained by William H. Crawford, Secretary of War, in a letter to the Senate dated March 13, 1816. A portion of the letter reads:

... From the payment of annuities to the various Indian tribes within the United States, a new species of jurisprudence has sprung up, which operates as a heavy tax upon the time of the Secretary of War ...

All losses of property by American citizens, from the robberies, thefts and depredations of those tribes, are to be remunerated out of the annuities payable to them. The evidence in all these cases is extra-judicial, and requires the examination and approbation of the Secretary before remuneration can be made. The presents which are made to them; the allowances to artificers settled among them by the Government; in fact, every disbursement of money connected with the Indian Department, except in the prosecution of trade with them, has to receive the special sanction of the head of this Department ....[14]

The report went on to state that the act substantially made the Secretary of War the auditor of all the Indian accounts and the courtroom judge of all the claims cases. Claims made by citizens of the U.S. had to be looked into, examined and decided by him. If claims were proved to his satisfaction, he directed payment for the damages to the injured party from annuities, presents, allowances or other money of the offending tribe.[15]

None of the work could be delegated. It had to be done by the Secretary of War personally. Crawford made this plain when he wrote:

... the duties incumbent upon this officer, resulting from control of the Indian Department, are so mulfifarious, so impossible to be reduced within general regulations, that a considerable portion of his time is necessarily devoted to them ....[16]

Indian annuities, claims of citizens, purchasing Indian goods and all the other work of the Indian Department became so voluminous and detailed that the Secretary of War and the accountant for the War Department were unable to get it done.[17] How far behind they were in their work was revealed by the Monroe, Crawford, Graham and Crowninshield committee. Their report stated that the accounts of the Indian Department, without a solitary exception, had remained unsettled from 1798 to the date of their report in 1816.[18]

The way this situation was cleared up and how it fit into the creation of the Bureau of Indian Affairs is the subject content of the following chapter.

FOOTNOTES--CHAPTER 6

1. U.S. Congress, "An act making appropriations for the support of the Government for the year 1792," December 23, 1791; 1 Stat. 226.

2. U.S. Congress, "An act making further appropriations for the military service of the United States for the year 1822, and for other purposes," May 7, 1822; 3 Stat. 686.

3. U.S. Congress, House Document No. 110, Vol. VIII, 17th Congress, 1st. Session, Report on Indian Department, April 11, 1822, pp. 7-10.

4. Ibid., p. 10.

5. Lowrie and Clark (eds.), American State Papers, Vol. VI, Indian Affairs, Vol. II, p. 62.

6. U.S. Congress, "An act directing the manner of appointing Indian agents, and continuing the 'Act for establishing trading houses with the Indian tribes,'" April 16, 1818; 3 Stat. 428.

7. U.S. Congress, "An act making appropriations for defraying the expenses which may arise in carrying into effect a treaty made between the United States and certain Indian tribes, northwest of the river Ohio," May 6, 1796; 1 Stat. 460.

8. U.S. Congress, House Report No. 474, Vol. IV, 23rd. Congress, 1st. Session, Regulating the Indian Department, May 20, 1834, pp. 49-59.

9. U.S. Congress, "An act making alterations in the Treasury and War Departments," May 18, 1792; 1 Stat. 279.

10. Lowrie and Clark, op. cit., p. 64.

11. U.S. Congress, "An act making alterations in the Treasury and War Departments," May 18, 1792; 1 Stat. 279.

12. U.S. Congress, House Report No. 474, op. cit., p. 10.

13. U.S. Congress, "An act to regulate trade and intercourse with the Indian tribes, and to preserve peace on the frontiers," May 19, 1796; 1 Stat. 469.

14. Lowrie and Clark, op. cit., p. 27.

15. Lowrie and Clark (eds.), American State Papers, Vol. XXI, Miscellaneous, Vol. II, p. 397.

16. Lowrie and Clark, op. cit., Indian Affairs, p. 28.

17. Ibid.

18. Lowrie and Clark, op. cit., Miscellaneous, p. 197.

CHAPTER 7

CREATION OF BUREAU OF INDIAN AFFAIRS

Organizations that carry out the laws of Congress are called federal agencies. They are also known as departments, bureaus, independent offices and commissions, authorities and boards. Literally hundreds of federal agencies are in existence. Most of them are in the Executive Branch, since the job of the President is to execute Congressional laws.

Ordinarily, federal agencies come into existence by acts of Congress. These acts establish positions to head the agencies and define broadly what the agencies are set up to do. A separate act is passed customarily to create each agency.

An act of Congress establishing a federal agency is an organic act. Two examples of organic acts are the acts of Congress which created the War and the Treasury Departments. These acts established the positions of Secretary of War and Secretary of the Treasury to head the agencies and broadly specified their functions.

The Indian Department was not created in that way. The colonies set up organizations to handle Indian affairs, and these organizations were recognized and named the Indian Department by the Congress of the Confederation. The first Congress of the U.S. adopted the Ordinance of 1786, giving legal status in the constitutional government to the Indian Department. Employees were added to the Indian Department as its activities and work increased with the spread of the American civilization.

The organization administering Indian affairs today is the Indian Department of the yester-days. Restructured, refined and modified in the passing years, it is still the organization that has administered Indian affairs from the beginning of the Republic. But it is known now as the Bureau of Indian Affairs , or the BIA.

The way the Indian Department was changed to the BIA is an interesting episode and important event in Indian affairs. This chapter tells about it.

SENATE REQUESTS PLAN

The War Department was not the only agency behind in its work in the early days. Every department was just getting started; trying to organize, seeking out what its job really was, looking for ways to do the job and going through other "growing pains." They were all submerged in work.

The U.S. Senate became aware and concerned about slowups and delays of the departments in getting their work done, particularly accounting for the public funds and settling up their accounts. Determined to have the departments do something about the situation, the Senate passed a resolution on April 20, 1816, requiring:

... Secretaries of the Departments to report jointly to the Senate, in the first week of the next session of Congress, a plan to insure the annual settlements of accounts , and a more certain accountability of the public expenditures in their respective Departments ....[1]

The resolution didn't specifically mention the Indian Department. It directed the Secretaries to go into the financial affairs and accounting procedures of all the departments, to get their heads together and come up with a plan whereby agencies could keep up with their accounting work and promptly settle their accounts. The Secretaries were given leeway to decide the scope and depth of investigations needed to find out what the specific hangups were and how to overcome them.

40

Eventually, they made it around to every department and departmental subdivision. They found problems in all of them. But the War Department and the Indian Department were in worse shape and in more of a frustrating predicament than any other department.

DETACHMENT OF INDIAN DEPARTMENT PROPOSED

The Secretaries discovered the trouble was that the Secretary of War and the accountant for the War Department were bogged down with Indian Department work. The volume of this work was so massive that neither of them could do justice to the War or the Indian Department. Going on, the Secretaries came to the conclusion that the Indian Department really had nothing to do with the mission of the War Department, so the Secretary of War should not be required to do its work.

In their report to the Senate, the Secretaries stated:

... It is obvious to the mind of every reflecting man that the duties upon the Secretary of War in relation to the Indian Department have no rational connexion with the administration of the military establishment. From the point of view which has been presented, it is conceived that the public interest requires that the Secretary of War should be relieved from further attention to those duties ....[2]

Having determined that administration of Indian affairs was not a proper function of the War Department, the Secretaries had to decide which department the work could logically fit into. They came to the conclusion that the work was beyond the primary function of every other department and that no other department was able to take it over.[3] In fact, they found that each of the departments was burdened with extraneous work. They believed all the departments should be relieved of their miscellaneous duties.[4]

NEW DEPARTMENT RECOMMENDED

The Secretaries reasoned that the extraneous duties of all the departments, when lumped together, "would furnish employment for the head of another independent Department." So they recommended that:

... another independent Department of the Government be organized, to be denominated the "Home Department." That the Secretary of this Department shall execute the orders of the President in relation to

1. The Territorial Governments

2. The national highways and canals

3. The General Post Office

4. The Patent Office

5. The Indian Department ....[5]

The Senate requested the Secretaries to submit a plan to insure better practices in relation to the public accounts. But it was not prepared to accept the recommendation to propose legislation creating a new department. In fact, many years were to pass before this would be done.

BRANCH STATUS FOR INDIAN DEPARTMENT

The burdens of the Indian Department upon the Secretary of War and the accountant for the War Department became heavier and heavier. By 1822, the Secretary of War concluded that the new department recommended by the Secretaries was a far-too-distant hope or realization. For the immediate need, therefore, he urged Congress to establish a separate branch for Indian affairs in the War Department. This branch would be under the general supervision of the Secretary of

War, but it would take over and be responsible for the work of the Indian Department, freeing him and the accountant of the work.

The Secretary of War made this recommendation to the Chairman of the Committee on Public Expenditures in a letter dated February 12, 1822. Contemplating the closing of the government trading houses and visualizing it would increase the work of the Indian Department, he wrote:

... Should the Government discontinue the trading houses, the whole trade with Indians would be placed in the hand of individuals, which would require on the part of the Government increased vigilance and attention to give that mode of carrying on the trade a salutary direction, and would render it the more necessary that this important branch of our public affairs should be placed under the direction of a distinct subordinate hand. Such an organization of the Indian Department would render it analogous, in its organization, to that of other branches of this Department, and would doubtless be attended with the same desirable results. An officer specially charged with a single department would have leisure to superintend its affairs, and examine its disbursements carefully and minutely ....[6]

Congress was not willing to enact the legislation to give branch status to the Indian Department. Two years more passed and, finally, the Secretary of War decided to take the matter into his own hands.

SECRETARY OF WAR ACTION

The Secretary of War decided he had the power to establish a position and assign to it the conduct of Indian affairs. This decision was connoted in a letter written by Thomas L. McKenney. The letter reads, in part:

... In March 1824, the officer charged with the bounty land office, died. His salary was $1600. It was then determined to transfer that salary to some person, and place in his charge whatever related to Indian affairs ....[7]

McKenney's letter suggests the Secretary of War was urged to his decision by a startling incident of fate.

Something more than that was necessary, however, for the Secretary to get the particular person he wanted for the job. He wanted McKenney to take it.

McKenney was for many years the Superintendent of Indian Trade, and he occupied that position when the Government trading houses were abolished in 1822. He was quite familiar with the weight of Indian Department work and didn't relish the idea of bearing the burden for the salary offered. He stated in his letter:

... I was offered the place, but on understanding the amount of salary which could be made applicable to it, declined its acceptance. I knew from my experience in Indian affairs enough to satisfy me that the compensation was not equivalent for the labors which would be required to be performed ....[8]

The Secretary of War made a second offer to McKenney some time later. Again McKenney declined. But the Secretary persisted. He made a third offer, promising McKenney a salary more in line with the duties. McKenney accepted the position. Writing about the second and third offer, he wrote:

... It was offered a second time, and again declined, for the same reason, when another offer was made, accompanied by the assurance of the estimate taken of the extent of the duties, and of the justice of the corresponding compensation. The pay of an Auditor was spoken of; I intimated my willingness to be satisfied with that ....[9]

It was not, however, the salary alone that attracted McKenney. He shared the thought of the Secretary of War that the Indian Department ought to be a branch with status similar to other branches, and he wanted to work toward getting it elevated to that status.

BUREAU OF INDIAN AFFAIRS CREATED

About the time McKenney decided to take the job, Congress was taking another look at the recommendation that a branch be established in the War Department to handle Indian affairs. McKenney was encouraged by the likelihood that this legislation would be enacted in the next session of Congress. He wrote about it, as follows:

... I was told there could be no doubt of the disposition of the Congress to create a branch similar to those already existing in the Department. I then accepted the place ....[10]

The Secretary of War felt certain the Congress would enact, at last, the legislation which would transfer the burden of Indian affairs from him to the head of the new branch. Anticipating favorable congressional action, he wrote a letter to McKenney. The letter is dated March 11, 1824, and was said to have created the Bureau of Indian Affairs "by the Executive."[11] The letter is important enough to be quoted in full. It reads:

Department of War

March 11th, 1824

Sir: To you are assigned the duties of the Bureau of Indian Affairs in this Department, for the faithful performance of which you will be responsible. Mr. Hamilton and Mr. Miller are assigned to you, the former as chief, and the latter as assistant clerk.

You will take charge of the appropriation for annuities, and of the current expenses, and all warrants on the same will be issued on your requisitions on the Secretary of War, taking special care that no requisition be issued, but in cases where the money previously remitted has been satisfactorily accounted for, and on estimates in detail, approved by you, for the sum required. You will receive and examine the accounts and vouchers for the expenditure thereof, and will pass them over to the proper Auditor's Office for settlement, after examination and approval by you; submitting such items for the sanction of this Department as may require its approval. The administration of the fund for the civilization of the Indians is also committed to your charge, under the regulations established by the Department. You are also charged with the examination of the claims arising out of the laws regulating the intercourse with Indian tribes, and will, after examining and briefing the same, report them to this Department, endorsing a recommendation for their allowance or disallowance.

The ordinary correspondence with the superintendents, the agents, and sub-agents, will pass through your Bureau.

I have the honor to be,

Your obedient servant,

J. C. CALHOUN

Thos. L. M'Kenney, Esq.[12]

This letter officially employs, for the first time, the title Bureau of Indian Affairs.

The letter purports to give bureau status to the Indian Department, renaming it accordingly and broadly defining duties and responsibilities. It purports to transfer all the accounting functions and all the work connected with claims against Indians from the Secretary of War to the head of the Bureau of Indian Affairs.

LEGISLATION DELAYED

In a few short months following his acceptance of the position, McKenney felt a change in the pulse of Congress. He advised the Secretary of War not to request Congress to enact legislation giving bureau or branch status to the Indian Department. McKenney wrote about this, as follows:

> ... The proposition to carry the measure into effect, was not made to the last Congress, and I did not wish it to be made. I was not willing to risk it in the eddy of other matters which was large and rapid enough to whirl down any proposition of twice its size ....[13]

Bureau status for the Indian Department, which McKenney called "the proposition" was not brought before the next session of Congress either. In fact a decade passed before the Congress went back to it. By then, McKenney was long since a victim of the Jackson "spoil" system.

1. Lowrie and Clark, op. cit., Miscellaneous, p. 397.

2. Ibid.

3. Ibid., pp. 397-398.

4. Ibid., p. 398.

5. Ibid.

6. U.S. Congress, House Document No. 146, 19th Congress, 1st. Session, On Establishment of a General Superintendency of Indian Affairs in Department of War, March 21, 1826, p. 12.

7. Ibid., p. 9.

8. Ibid.

9. Ibid.

10. Ibid., p. 8.

11. Ibid., p. 4.

12. Ibid., p. 2.

13. Ibid., p. 10.

CHAPTER 8

ORGANIC ACT OF BUREAU OF INDIAN AFFAIRS

Agencies of the federal government ordinarily are created by acts of Congress called organic acts. The Indian Department, however, didn't originate that way. It grew from a small organization in the Revolutionary period and, in 1824, had its name changed to the Bureau of Indian Affairs. Nevertheless, an act of Congress passed in 1834 is said to be the organic act of the BIA.[1]

The Secretary of War in 1824 named Thomas L. McKenney head of the BIA, but he didn't give McKenney a title. An act of Congress, preceding the organic act by 2 years, provided the title Commissioner of Indian Affairs for the head of the BIA.[2]

Actually, these 2 acts were congressional laws to remove legal doubts about the administration of Indian affairs. Challenges of legality came about during an investigation of the Indian field service when a bundle of questionable management practices by the BIA were uncovered. One of the judgments of the investigators was that the action of the Secretary of War did not in fact set up the Bureau of Indian Affairs as a legal governmental agency nor establish a position to head it. The 2 acts were necessary to do that.

This chapter goes into the dubious management practices that led to the passage of the 2 acts of Congress.

BUREAU HEAD BY CONFIDENCE

Secretary of War Calhoun established the BIA, selected McKenney to head it and defined McKenney's duties in a letter dated March 11, 1824. This move relieved Calhoun of many details, but it was actually no more than an office arrangement to get the work of the Indian Department accomplished more expeditiously. It gave no power or authority to McKenney. So after McKenney attended to the details of claims, disbursements and other such financial work and administrative jobs, he packaged them up and sent them on for Calhoun's review and signature. Calhoun was still the authority in Indian affairs. McKenney explained the fundamental nature of the BIA and his assigned duties, as follows:

> ... with its constitution, no power was conveyed. The business, though it be arranged, has yet, at every step, to be carried up to the head of the Department, without regard to its importance; otherwise the most unimportant correspondence upon matters of mere detail, is not authorized, except by the general confidence of the head of the Department in the Officer in charge of the Indian business ...[3]

McKenney's comments need to be looked at in the light of the way the federal government operates by delegation of authority.

The act of August 7, 1789, which created the Department of War, recognized that Indian affairs were Executive functions. But it authorized the President to assign any of the functions to the Secretary of War. In other words, the act made it possible for the President to delegate his authority in Indian affairs to the Secretary of War. Assignments of fun-tions by the President empowered the Secretary of War to act for the President, and actions taken by the Secretary of War in assigned functions carried the weight of Presidential authority.

No congressional act, however, provided for the delegation of authority from the Secretary of War to a subordinate official. For this reason it was not legally possible for the Secretary of War to transfer to the head of the BIA any authority related to Indian affairs. McKenney could attend to the details in Indian affairs, but he could not act for the Secretary of War. Even routine and unimportant correspondence had to be reviewed personally by the Secretary of War and signed by him.

McKenney's explanation was, in effect, that when Congress places authority in a position, that authority cannot be delegated or transferred to another position unless Congress provides for such delegation. Fundamentally, then, the arrangement Calhoun made with McKenney could not legally exist. Despite Calhoun's seeming creation of the BIA and his assignment of McKenney to head it and perform its functions, the Secretary of War was still legally held accountable for the duties related to Indian affairs. He could not convey power to another to make decisions about Indian affairs or authority to act for him. This limitation was brought out clearly by Secretary of War, James Barbour, in a letter dated March 24, 1826. Barbour succeeded Calhoun, and in his letter addressed to the Chairman of the House Committee on Indian Affairs, he affirms his confidence in McKenney's ability but admits that McKenney had no power or authority in Indian affairs. In part, the letter stated:

> ... I take pleasure in bearing a most unqualified testimony to his ability and industry, and promptness, and to his experience in our Government. But he is responsible to the head of the Department only, and not to Congress ....[4]

Barbour went on to say that no legal authority or responsibility rested upon the head of the BIA. All Barbour could rely upon was his confidence in the person he selected to head the BIA. Even then, much of the work had to be taken up with him for his approval and authorization.[5]

ESTABLISHMENT OF POSITION OF COMMISSIONER OF INDIAN AFFAIRS

Secretary Barbour was no less desirous than his predecessor that the Indian affairs be legally transferred to a responsible position. In his letter to the House Committee on Indian Affairs, he specifically requested that the Indian Department be made a branch with its head subordinate to the Secretary of War but with power and authority to take care of the financial and administrative work of Indian affairs.

His request went unheeded. Six more year passed. Meanwhile the Secretary of War kept on pushing for a branch to handle Indian affairs. Finally, Congress passed the act of July 9, 1832, establishing the position of Commissioner of Indian Affairs to take over all functions of the Indian Department. The act reads, in part:

> ... the President of the United States shall appoint, by and with the advice and consent of the Senate, a commissioner of Indian affairs, who shall under the direction of the Secretary of War, and agreeably to such regulations as the President may, from time to time, prescribe, have the direction and management of all Indian affairs, and of all matters arising out of Indian relations ....[6]

The act particularly empowered the Commissioner of Indian Affairs to examine and approve all claims, accounts, disbursements and other financial transactions. So it was no longer necessary for the Secretary of War to perform these functions. The Commissioner of Indian Affairs was given authority in these and all other financial and administrative affairs of the Indian Department.[7]

Since the passage of the act of July 9, 1832, the position of Commissioner of Indian Affairs has been held by 40 persons. The first of these was Elbert Herring. At the time the act passed, Herring was serving in the same capacity under Secretary of War Cass as McKenney served under Calhoun. The 40th person was appointed by President Nixon in 1974.[8]

HOUSE COMMITTEE STUDY OF BUREAU OF INDIAN AFFAIRS

Soon after passing the law establishing the position of Commissioner of Indian Affairs, Congress took up the proposal of branch status for the Indian Department. By this time, however, branch status was not the sole interest. The lawmakers wanted to know about all the functions, work and organization of the Indian Department. The task of taking this in-depth look fell upon the House Committee on Indian Affairs. Congress requested the Committee to come up with whatever recommendations it found appropriate.

The House Committee studied trading with Indians, expenditure of the Indian Department, education and civilization of Indians and the organization. All these areas are important, but the study and findings about the structure of the BIA is particularly significant to this chapter.

The Committee reported its general observation of the BIA and the administration of Indian affairs in the following words:

... The present organization of the department is of doubtful origin and authority ....[9]

In support of this judgment, the Committee stated it had searched the statutes to determine the legal bases for the appointment of agents and subagents. No such laws were discovered. The Committee found rather that appointments were made on the supposition that it was "the thing to do" whenever a tribe or group of Indians was subdued and relocated on an Indian reservation. In its own words, the Committee stated:

... Your committee has sought, in vain, for any lawful authority for the appointment of a majority of the agents and subagents of Indian affairs now in office. For years, usage, rendered colorably lawful only by reference to indirect and equivocal legislation has been the only sanction for their appointment ....[10]

Many treaties provided for the appointment of agents to reside among Indians. The Committee hadn't overlooked this. It admitted, also, that the act of March 1, 1793, and subsequent trade acts provided for the appointment of temporary agents. But the Committee concluded that Congress had no intention by these acts to make resident agents among Indians a permanent institution.

The system of resident agents was commenced in the early days of nationalism as an appropriate measure of defense and peace with Indians. But this justification for many years back was no longer valid. Nevertheless, the BIA continued to use it as the basis for appointing more agents. Findings of the Committee were:

... Our Indian relations commenced at an early period of the revolutionary war. What was necessary to be done, either for defence or conciliation, was done; and being necessary, no inquiry seems to have been made as to the authority under which it was done. This undefined state of things existed for nearly 20 years ....[12]

The management of Indian affairs was an Executive function, and the Indian Department grew in response to needs identified by the President. Appropriations for Indian affairs were general, the Committee found, and in the appropriation process, "the whole subject of the organization of the Indian Department passed on in silence, and almost in secrecy, until 1818." At that time, there were 15 agencies and 10 subagencies and an oversized body of other personnel whose jobs were obtained through the system of political patronage.[13]

The Committee noted that on April 16, 1818, Congress passed an act setting up guidelines for the appointment of Indian agents. This act was construed by the Indian Department as authority to expand the system of resident agents. According to the Committee, this construction of the law was erroneous. The object of that act, the Committee stated, was to realign the appointment of agents and subagents with the constitutional requirement that all officers of the government be appointed by and with the advice and consent of the Senate. The act did not establish agencies or create the office of Indian agent as the Indian Department held. According to the Committee, it merely directed and restricted the mode of appointment.[14]

The Committee also found that the Indian Department interpreted the act of April 20, 1818, as approval of the system of Indian agents. The Committee disagreed with this interpretation, stating the act merely fixed the compensation of the 15 agents employed at that time. The Committee explained further that both the act of April 16 and April 20, 1818, were passed "with reference to the existing state of things, without inquiring whether these agencies had been previously established by law."[15]

48

The Committee implied that the Congress had been quite negligent in keeping tab on the build-up of the Indian Department and was, therefore, at fault for the illegal way it had grown. In reference to the acts of April 16 and April 20, 1818, the Committee stated:

> ... The committee consider this as indirect, and, therefore, vicious legislation. A recognition of the exercise of power without right is usually followed by the claim of the right; and such seems to have been the consequence in this instance. Indian agencies have been created by the power of appointment; and so long has the power been exercised, that for years, no examination has been made respecting its legality ....[16]

In summary, the Committee found that the Indian Department developed almost entirely under the power of Executive appointment rather than by an organic act and subsequent legislation authorizing its growth and expansion.

RECOMMENDATIONS OF HOUSE COMMITTEE

The House Committee recommended legislation to give legal status to the BIA and to limit the President in appointment of Indian agents. The report of the Committee stated:

> ... it is time that, ... the legislation of Congress should be direct; and that the creation of offices, and the fixing their salaries, should not be left to Executive discretion or to legislative implication ....[17]

At the time of its study, the House Committee found the administrative field service of the BIA to be composed of 4 superintendents of Indian affairs, 18 Indian agents, 27 subagents and 34 interpreters. Many other positions made up the Indian field service, but they were not administrative. The Committee decided the field service had too many administrators. It recommended cuts. The bill proposed by the Committee provided for 2 superintendents of Indian affairs, 8 agents, 12 subagents and 23 interpreters.

Moreover, the House Committee recommended a restructuring of the authority in the field organization so that Indian agents would be legally under the direction and supervision of the superintendents of Indian affairs. The Committee reported on its proposed bill, as follows:

> ... The agents, being subject to no immediate control, have acted under scarcely any other responsibility than that of accountability for moneys received. Although such is expected from the personal character of the agents, yet it is not deemed safe to depend entirely upon it. The superintendents are, therefore, authorized to exercise a general supervision and control over the official conduct of the agents and sub-agents, and to suspend them from office for malconduct, reporting their reasons therefor to the President ....[19]

The House Committee defined subagents "a class of agents whose appointments and salaries are different from those of agents" and recommended that their appointment and setting up subagencies remain at the discretion of the President. Relations with many of the western tribes at that time were quite unsettled, the Committee stated, making it difficult to limit the number of sub-agents and subagencies.

SIGNIFICANCE OF LEGISLATION

Most of the recommendations of the Committee were incorporated in a bill that became the act of June 30, 1834. That act is said to be the organic act for the BIA. It was really more in the nature of an act to restrict the appointment of Indian agents. It had no effect on the established organization at the national level. Felix Cohen analyzed it, as follows:

... It was in effect, a reorganization of the field force of the War Department having charge of Indian affairs, and in no way altered the power of the Secretary of War or the Commissioner, or changed the status of the Bureau of Indian Affairs in the War Department ....[18]

In addition to reorganizing the field force, the act of June 30, 1834, provided lawful existence to the BIA and legal bases for its future growth. The act established particular Indian agencies, authorized Indian agents for them and fixed their salaries. By the language of the act, some of the Indian agents were to be dismissed at specified future times. Others were to be removed when their jobs were determined to be unnecessary or when their work could be performed by the subagents. All Indian agencies other than those authorized by the act were abolished, and the act prohibited the setting up of other Indian agencies without specific ongressional authority.[20]

The act climaxed the long struggle to obtain branch status for the Indian Department. It changed the name of the organization to Bureau of Indian Affairs. It didn't do away entirely with Executive appointments. As territories were created, duties of superindents were joined with those of territorial governors who were Presidential appointees. Establishment of Indian agencies and the appointment of Indian agents were forbidden by the act except when specifically authorized by Congress. But the authority of the President to designate Indian subagencies and appoint subagents remained unchanged.

The act had far-reaching importance in the overall organizational structure of the BIA. In conjunction with the act of July 9, 1832, it established the hierarchy of authority that since has been evident in the BIA.

The Commissioner of Indian Affairs and his staff became the top echelon of authority with headquarters in the nation's capitol. Superintendents of Indian affairs and their staffs formed the regional level of authority. Situated in the field, they were responsible for Indian affairs related to specified geographical areas covering several reservations or Indian tribes. They were the connecting links between the Washington level of authority and the Indian agents and subagents who formed levels of authority at local sites among Indian tribes or groups.

Fundamentally, then, the acts of July 9, 1832, and June 30, 1834, established a tri-level organization with recognizable lines of authority from the Commissioner of Indian Affairs to the superintendents of Indian affairs, and from them, to the various Indian agents and subagents. This type of organization has continued through the many years. Numerous changes in titles of positions have occurred with the passing of time, but the tri-level organization exists today as the basic structure of the BIA.

1. Office of the Federal Register, <u>United States Government Organization Manual</u> (Washington: Government Printing Office, 1965-66), p. 251.

2. Felix S. Cohen, <u>op. cit.</u>, p. 12.

3. U.S. Congress, House Document No. 146, <u>op. cit.</u>, p. 4.

4. <u>Ibid.</u>, p. 1.

5. <u>Ibid.</u>, p. 2.

6. U.S. Congress, "An Act to provide for the appointment of a Commissioner of Indian Affairs, and for other purposes," July 9, 1832; 4 <u>Stat.</u> 564.

7. <u>Ibid.</u>

8. Felix S. Cohen, <u>op. cit.</u>, p. 12. Cohen lists 32 persons who served as Commissioner of Indian Affairs from 1832 to 1945. Eight persons were appointed since then. In the order of their appointment, they were William Brophy, John Nichols, Dillon Myer, Glen Emmons, Philleo Nash, Robert Bennett, Louis Bruce and Morris Thompson. Four of the appointees were of Indian descent. They were Ely Parker, Robert Bennett, Louis Bruce and Morris Thompson, an Alaskan. One of the appointees served at 2 different times, so there have been 41 appointments of 40 persons.

9. U.S. Congress, House Report No. 474, <u>op. cit.</u>, p. 2.

10. <u>Ibid.</u>

11. <u>Ibid.</u>, p. 4.

12. <u>Ibid.</u>, p. 3.

13. <u>Ibid.</u>, p. 6.

14. <u>Ibid.</u>

15. <u>Ibid.</u>, p. 7.

16. <u>Ibid.</u>

17. <u>Ibid.</u>, pp. 7-8.

18. Felix S. Cohen, <u>op. cit.</u>, p. 10.

19. U.S. Congress, House Report No. 474, <u>op. cit.</u>, p. 8.

20. <u>Ibid.</u>

CHAPTER 9

MILITARY AND CIVIL POLICIES TOWARD INDIANS

Increasing relations between the federal government and Indian tribes filled the passing years. More than half a century of wars raged across the continent, and the era boomed with a long series of treaties as one tribe followed another to the crushing fell of the sabre. Reservation after reservation sprang into existence; generally, beyond the brinks of the sprawling American civilization. To these reservations, the Indians were removed--forcibly, if necessary. There they were to remain--forcibly, too, if necessary--to allow for the peaceful settlement of the country.

Responsive to the stir of events, the BIA broadened in personnel and activities. Indian agents and subagents multiplied. Superintendents of Indian affairs increased and the staff of the Commissioner in Washington expanded.

But the BIA was not alone in Indian affairs. Indian wars were the lifeblood of Army troops and the chances for them to build a new kind of glory in the plains and deserts. And after the wars ended, the troops stayed on to keep the Indians penned up on reservations and to prevent them from marauding and terrifying settlements.

Indian wars and their aftermaths revived and revitalized a dichotomy in Indian affairs, and out of it, the military and civil policies of the federal government were conceived and developed.

This chapter is about these policies and the fight between the two government agencies that championed them. It also includes a review of the reckoning that the once-compelling drive to do Indians in must give way to more profound and purposeful activities.

CONTROL OF INDIAN AFFAIRS TRANSFERRED

In the early 1800's, members of the President's cabinet made a study of the Indian Department and other departments of the federal government and recommended, in 1816, that a new cabinet department be created to administer domestic functions, including Indian affairs, that were scattered among the departments.

Creating a cabinet department is an undertaking of great magnitude and requires deliberations spread across many years. At least, that seems to have been the case in the creation of the department recommended by the President's cabinet in 1816. More than 30 years passed before Congress finally incorporated that recommendation in legislation. The act was approved on March 3, 1849. It created the Home Department of the Interior and, among other purposes, provided that:

> ... the Secretary of the Interior shall exercise the supervisory and appellate powers
> now exercised by the Secretary of the War Department, in relation to all the acts of
> the Commissioner of Indian Affairs ....[1]

This law established the position of Secretary of the Interior and transferred administration of Indian affairs from the Secretary of War to it.

TRANSFER OF CONTROL DELAYED

Congress intended by the act of March 3, 1849, for Indian affairs to pass from military to civilian control. But when the act passed, the concept held in 1816 by the President's cabinet members that Indian affairs had no "rational connexion with the administration of the military establishment" was fast becoming a fiction. The actual transfer of Indian affairs was becoming, just as rapidly, an increasingly difficult job.

By 1849, the federal government had acquired from foreign powers virtually all the land in the continental U.S. Settlement beyond the Mississippi, only a few years earlier supposed to be highly improbable, was definitely more than an unfulfillable dream. The trek of the Mormons to the interior of the continent in 1847, the wild bolt of treasure-seekers to California in 1849, the already substantial settlements rooted in southern regions and the matrix of frontier outposts lacing the northern areas were omens and signs of the Great Migration to come.

Tough and rugged Indian wars marked the westward expansion. This gave prominence anew to the military establishment in Indian affairs and delayed for nearly half a century the transfer contemplated by the act of March 3, 1849. Moreover, the importance of the military in the settlement of the west magnified and intensified a dualism in the conduct of Indian affairs.

THE DUALISM

Two opposing nations regarding Indians developed during the many years preceding the founding of the nation. One was positive; the other negative.

The positive viewpoint was that Indians were a people, rich in human potential and deserving of dignity and respect as an inalienable right. This concept was spearheaded, in the main, by missionaries who labored to convert Indians to the Christian faith and to teach them some of the ways of the non-Indians. They had a following in this viewpoint of those whose deeper consciences were sparked by the idea of the brotherhood of man.

The negative viewpoint was manifested in the feeling that Indians were hardly more than brute savages, beyond hope of becoming human and destined to the fate of peoples unable to move in a changing and dynamic world. For the most part, the searchers for material gains shared this negative point of view about Indians, and they found no little support among the many who worked hard to obtain little from the land.

This dualism, born of the past and existing at the nation's beginning, was observed by Henry Knox in a letter he wrote to Washington on July 7, 1789. Knox recapped what happened to Indians under the negative approach and recommended the positive approach to Washington. The applicable portion of his letter is interesting and informative enough to be quoted somewhat at length. It reads:

> ... As population shall increase, and approach the Indian boundaries, game will be diminished, and new purchases may be made for small consideration. This has been, and probably will be, the inevitable consequence of cultivation.
>
> It is, however, painful to consider, that all the Indian tribes, once existing in those states now the best cultivated and most populous, have become extinct. If the same causes continue, the same effects will happen; and, in a short period, the idea of an Indian on this side of the Mississippi will only be found in the pages of the historian.
>
> How different would be the sensation of a philosophic mind to reflect, that, instead of exterminating a part of the human race by our modes of population, we had persevered, through all difficulties, and at last had imparted our knowledge of cultivation and the arts to the aboriginals of the country, by which the source of future life and happiness had been preserved and extended. But it has been conceived to be impracticable to civilize the Indians of North America. This opinion is probably more convenient than just ....[2]

Knox is clear that extermination of Indians was the negative approach and preservation of them was the positive.

These opposing principles came to be policies of the federal government in its dealing with Indians. Separately, they were the military policy and the civil policy. They loomed as profound and resolute causes in the War Department and the Department of the Interior during the settlement of the west.

THE MILITARY POLICY

The military policy was total defeat of the frontier enemy. Under this policy, Army campaigns against Indians were inevitable. Indian retaliation was equally unavoidable.

Theodore Roosevelt, in his book describing westward expansion, penned the thought that it was wholly impossible to avoid conflicts with the Indians because they claimed the land and were not about to sit around and let another people take it away from them without a struggle. Even if the Americans had adopted the "ludicrous policy" of allowing a European power to gain and retain the land, the Indians in their own right, Roosevelt said, would still have made war on the U.S.[3]

Damages wreaked upon Indians by troops of the U.S. Cavalry were parts of the business of war. And ravages by Indians among the settlers and the soldiers were no less accomplished missions of combat. The destructions, waste, carnage and brutalities of Indian wars have come down as depressing blots in U.S. history. But they were nothing other than representations of the firmly unchanging nature of war.

In a discussion of wars, particularly Indian wars, Reverend Joseph Doddridge explained the essence of conflicts between nations. Wars, he said, bring out the most terrifying and revolting features in humans. A vindictive spirit of revenge and a thirst for blood pour into the soldiers and warriors. Indiscriminately, they slaughter enemies of all ranks, ages and sexes by weapons of war, by torture and by any other means imaginable. Doddridge shuddered at the destruction and sometimes senseless butcheries in Indian wars. But destroying and killing, he said, were inherent in those wars as in all wars.[4]

Enemies on the western frontiers of the U.S. asked for and gave no mercy. The decree to whip the Indians was pitted against Indian determination to drive the Americans out. Indians slammed into their enemies with all the tactics and strategies they could devise, and the Army smashed back with every combat plan in the books. Cruelty, barbarity, treachery and intrigue were normal expectations of Indian wars.[5]

Some of the encounters reached the peak of armed purpose. Among these were the well-known San Creek Massacre, where Black Kettle and his band of Cheyennes were wiped out, and the battle of the Little Big Horn that put an end to Custer and his command.

Eventually, the long-awaited secret weapons of the U.S. surfaced from the drawing boards. They were the repeater rifles and Gattling guns. Toted and wheeled to the battle lines, they ripped through and cut down the ranks of the unsuspecting warriors. Then pushed on to the villages, they heaped up piles of sliced-up and dead women, children and old folks.

This was the beginning of the end of Indian wars.

THE CIVIL POLICY

The civil policy was stated conclusively by the Commissioner of Indian Affairs, George W. Manypenny, in a letter dated October 5, 1855. His letter was addressed to Colonel A. Cummings, Superintendent of Indian Affairs at St. Louis. It commented upon a report by Indian Agent, John Montgomery, who described the Indians under his jurisdiction, as follows:

> ... I am constrained to say that the Kansas are a poor degraded, superstitious, thievish, indigent, tribe of Indians; their tendency is downward, and, in my opinion, they must become extinct, and the sooner they arrive at this period, the better it will be for the rest of mankind ....[6]

Commissioner Manypenny was quite disturbed by Agent Montgomery's report. In his letter, he instructed Colonel Cummings to make certain Montgomery understood the nature and extent of government policy towards Indians. Instead of designing the extinction of Indians, Commissioner

Manypenny said, Agent Montgomery should employ the best means within his reach to promote their welfare and improvement. He went on to say that Montgomery's description of the Indians and his opinion about them were inappropriate and inconsistent with an Indian agent's relation and obligations to the Indians and wholly unacceptable to the BIA.[7]

In the civil policy, no place was open for the thought of exterminating Indians. The policy encompassed only the thinking to employ the best means that could be conceived to promote their welfare and improvement.

The civil policy was known, also, as the peace policy.

THEORETICAL APPLICATION OF POLICIES

In theory the military policy was to prevail during hostilities, and the civil policy was to obtain when the Indians surrendered and relocated on Indian reservations. This relationship was explained to Major General Pope by Secretary of the Interior, James Harlan, in a letter dated July 6, 1865. Pope had complained about the failure of Indian agents to act in harmony with the policy of the War Department, and he wanted Secretary Harlan to bring about some reforms among Indian agents. Secretary Harlan wrote:

> ... It is the desire of the Secretary of the Interior to subordinate the actions of the agents of the department to the policy of the Secretary of War, in relation to Indian tribes at war, and to secure the support of the military authorities in carrying out the civil policy of the government in relation to those Indians at peace ....[8]

Grave difficulties were encountered in attempts to restrict the policies to their defined areas. One of these difficulties was psychological. An example is the reaction of Indian Agent Montgomery to the civil policy. A difficulty, equally as baffling, was administrative, arising from differing opinions as to where the military policy ended and the civil policy began. Major General Pope's complaint about the Indian agents is an example of this difficulty.

PRACTICAL APPLICATION OF POLICIES

The greater number of Indians complied with peace treaties, relocating on reservations and seeking rehabilitation. But some of the incorrigible and more-daring braves simply couldn't endure confinement. They sneaked away; sometimes to hunt, but more often as impulsive reversions to their customary ways of life. They kept right on trying to drive settlers out.

A faction of administrators of Indian affairs believed the military policy, modified to the type known today as 'military occupation,' should prevail on Indian reservations to prevent or quell disturbances created by the unsettled and adventurous braves. Commissioner of Indian Affairs, Francis A. Walker, shared this view. He pushed the idea quite strongly. This use of military was a necessity, he felt, not precluded by or contrary to the civil policy. From the nature of Indians and the background of their circumstances, he said, it couldn't be expected the "entire body of wild Indians should submit to be restrained in their Ismaelitish proclivities without a struggle on the part of the more audacious to maintain their traditional freedom."[9] Something had to be done to keep them under control. The presence of troops on reservations, Walker believed, might sufficiently discourage the Indians from reverting to their native inclinations. If it didn't and the Indians broke out, troops were needed to hunt them down and herd them back to the reservations.

Other administrators felt the mission of the Army ended with the defeat of the enemy, and no part of Indian affairs thereafter was a concern or responsibility of the Army. To them, even the matter of treaty negotiation was not a proper function of military personnel. Major General Pope asked for an Army officer to negotiate a treaty with the Sioux Indians. James Harlan, Secretary of the Interior, informed him that according to a law of Congress an Indian treaty had to be negotiated by an officer of the BIA.[10]

Despite differences of opinion, troops under the command of military officers were stationed at practically all Indian agencies. In fact, many Indian agencies were constructed as military forts and, even today, they bear such names as Fort Hall, Fort Duchesne, Fort Sill and Fort Berthold.

In some instances, Army officers were the officials in charge of the Indian agencies. In other cases, commanding officers were subordinate to civilian Indian agents. This division of authority caused all kinds of administrative unrest, especially among Army officers and Indian agents unable to reconcile the military and civil policies.[11] These troubles were compounded by charges and countercharges of corruption, inefficiency and other types of mismanagement. The seriousness of the situation became prominent in 1867 by a report of a Congressional committee directed to look into the conditions of Indian tribes and how they were treated by military and civilian authorities. The committee report stated:

> ... While it is true many agents, teachers, and employees of the government are in-
> efficient, faithless, and even guilty of peculations and fraudulent practices upon
> the government and upon the Indians, it is equally true that military posts among the
> Indians have frequently become centers of demoralization and destruction to the Indian
> tribes, while the blunders and want of discretion of inexperienced officers in command
> have brought on long and expensive wars, ...[12]

The Congressional committee found neither the military nor the civilian personnel guiltless in the failure to implement the policies of the federal government in Indian affairs.

REMEDIES FOR DIFFICULTIES

The search for a way to clear up the troubles in applying the military and civil policies led to a proposal to put Indian affairs back in the War Department. This idea didn't receive the warmest reception in some quarters. In fact, it fomented heated debate spread across many years. The 1867 Congressional committee reported the status of the argument, as follows:

> ... The question of whether the Indian bureau should be placed under the War Department
> or retained in the Department of the Interior is one of considerable importance, and
> both sides have very warm advocates ....[13]

Actually, the squabble over primary jurisdiction of Indian affairs began almost concurrently with the passage of the act of March 3, 1849. The fight was not solely between the War Department of the Interior. Various appointees to the position of Commissioner of Indian Affairs kept the kettle boiling from within.

Commissioner Manypenny (1853-57) opposed the notion of transferring the BIA back to the War Department. He urged full control of both the military and civil policies by civilians, re-questing authority to organize a BIA quasi-military force to replace Army troops. In his 1854 report, he told about a battle near Fort Laramie between a band of Sioux Indians and an Army detachment. The Indians had killed and eaten a head of beef that strayed away from a Mormon emigrant train and wandered into the Sioux village. The troops were ordered to chastise the Indians. The battle ended with the complete annihilation of Lieutenant Gratten and his command of 30 men. Manypenny described the incident to support his idea of a BIA quasi-military organization. He stated:

> ... Occasions frequently arise in our intercourse with the Indians requiring the employ-
> ment of force; although the Whites may be, and often are, the aggressors. The Indian
> bureau would be relieved from embarrassment, and rendered more efficient, if, in such
> cases, the department had the direct control of the means to execute its own orders. A
> force better adapted to the Indian service than any now employed, could, it is believed,
> be readily organized. But careful attention and kind and humane treatment will, generally,
> have more influence upon the savages than bayonets and gunpowder ....[14]

Commissioner Nathaniel G. Taylor (1867-69) opposed the idea of Indian affairs going back to the War Department. His successor, Ely S. Parker, (1869-71) supported the measure to the extent that troops were needed to remove Indians to reservations and keep them there. Commissioner Francis A. Walker (1871-73) favored the use of troops to further the civil policy. Walker's successor, Commissioner Edward P. Smith, (1873-75) despite a clause in the treaty with the Sioux Indians prohibiting the presence of Army troops on the reservations, favored the military in Indian affairs.[15]

In an effort to settle the difficulties and long controversies over jurisdiction of Indian affairs, Congress passed the act of July 15, 1870. The act prohibited the appointment of military officers to civil positions, such as Indian agents and subagents, unless the officers resigned their commissions.[16]

This act adjusted the issue to a certain extent. But, the passing of time that saw the final settlement of the west and a gradual reorientation of the Indians to reservation life eventually brought an end to the military policy.

1. U.S. Congress, "An act to establish the Home Department and to provide for the Treasury Department and Assistant Secretary of the Treasury, and a Commissioner of the Customs," March 3, 1849; 9 Stat. 395.

2. Lowrie and Clark, op. cit., Indian Affairs, Vol. I, p. 53.

3. Theodore Roosevelt, The Winning of the West (New York: 1889-96), Vol. I, p. 333.

4. Wiscomb E. Washburn (Ed.), The Indian and the Whiteman (Garden City, New York, Anchor Books, Doubleday and Co., 1964), p. 270.

5. Ibid., pp. 274-5.

6. Rept. Com. Ind. Aff., 1855, p. 114.

7. Ibid., p. 115.

8. Rept. Com. Ind. Aff., 1865, p. 200.

9. Rept. Com. Ind. Aff., 1872, p. 5.

10. Rept. Com. Ind. Aff., 1865, p. 200.

11. Felix S. Cohen, op. cit., p. 18.

12. U.S. Congress, Senate Report No. 156, 39th Congress, 2nd Session, Report on Condition of Indian Tribes, January 27, 1867, p. 7.

13. Ibid., p. 6.

14. Rept. Com. Ind. Aff., 1854, p. 17.

15. Rept. Com. Ind. Aff., 1873, p. 6.

16. U.S. Congress, "An act making appropriations for sundry civil expenses of the Government for the year ending June 30, 1871, and for other purposes," July 15, 1870; 16 Stat. 291.

CHAPTER 10

EARLY GOVERNMENT ACTIVITIES ON INDIAN RESERVATIONS

The federal government in its early dealings regarded Indian tribes as independent nations and treated with them accordingly. Treaties, for example, were instruments of conciliation and agreement between the U.S., a sovereignty, and Indian tribes recognized to be nations.

In time, however, the idea that Indian tribes were nations was challenged, and the dispute went the rounds of government circles for a number of years. The controversy was settled when the relationship of the government and Indians was defined to be guardian and ward.

This definition spurred the BIA to increasing activities among Indians particularly in the early years following their relocation on reservations.

The term ward has many legal meanings in Indian affairs.[1] Examining them and their implications is beyond the scope of this book. Furthermore, a look at the legal inferences wouldn't aid greatly in understanding what the government did about it. But it is helpful to know some of the major incidents in the development of the definition and the increasing activities on Indian reservations resulting from it. They are important phases in the history of Indian affairs.

The present chapter goes into these topics.

INDIANS BECOME WARDS OF THE GOVERNMENT

The U.S. Supreme Court was among the first to think Indian tribes were wards of the government. Its announcement of this was in a decision for a suit by the Cherokee nation against the state of Georgia in 1831. The Cherokee nation wanted to stop Georgia from taking over lands recognized in treaties as belonging to the Indians. In deciding the case, the Court went into the relationship of the Indians and the federal government. The opinion of the Court was written by Chief Justice John Marshall, and, in it, he stated the relationship was similar to guardian and ward. His own words are important enough historically to be quoted. He wrote:

> ... it may well be doubted whether those tribes which reside within the acknowledged boundaries of the United States can, with strict accuracy, be denominated foreign nations. They may, more correctly, perhaps, be denominated domestic dependent nations. They occupy a territory to which we assert a title independent of their will, which must take effect in point of possession when their right of possession ceases. Meanwhile they are in a state of pupilage. Their relation to the United States resembles that of a ward to his guardian ....[2]

This view of the Supreme Court had little immediate effect on the way the federal government dealt with Indian tribes. Many treaties subsequent to 1831 regarded Indian tribes as nations. As a matter of fact, more than 30 years later, on July 2, 1863, a treaty was made "by and between the United States of America, represented by its Commissioners, and the Shoshone Nation of Indians, represented by its Chiefs and Principal Men and Warriors of the Eastern Bands." This way of recognizing the Shoshone Nation is illustrative of the wording in many other treaties made after the Supreme Court rendered its decision.

Meanwhile, however, the thought that Indian tribes were wards of the government was kept alive in Indian affairs officialdom.

George W. Manypenny was one of the first commissioners to suggest Indian were wards. But he used the term only in passing on to a larger concern before him. He instructed Colonel A. Cummings by letter in 1855 to "apprise Agent Montgomery of the nature and extent of his duties to those untutored wards of the government."

Some years later, in 1862, Caleb B. Smith, Secretary of the Interior, analyzed the relationship of the federal government and Indian tribes. He contended the government adopted a mistaken policy in regarding Indians as quasi-independent nations and making treaties with them. They had none of the elements of nationality, Smith stated, and since they were within the recognized boundaries of the U.S., they were subject to control by the federal government. He went on to say a change needed to be made in the dealings with Indian tribes. Rather than considering them nations, the government should regard them as wards, entitled to its fostering care and protection.[3]

No identifiable change resulted from Smith's suggestion. Seven years later, in 1869, Commissioner Ely S. Parker urged that no more treaties be made with Indians. His ideas of treaty making and Indian nationalism were:

... The Indian tribes of the United States are not sovereign nations, capable of making treaties, as none of them have an organized government of such inherent strength as would secure a faithful obedience of its people in the observance of compacts of this character. They are held to be wards of the government ... But, ... they have become falsely impressed with the notion of national independence. It is time that this idea should be dispelled, and the government cease the cruel farce of thus dealing with its helpless and ignorant wards ....[4]

Commissioner Parker had no doubt Indian tribes were wards of the government. As such, they didn't have the power of treaty making or enforcement. His words did not go unheeded. Two years later, on March 3, 1871, Congress passed an appropriation act which brought an end to the making of treaties with Indians. The applicable portion of the act reads:

... hereafter no Indian nation or tribe within the territory of the United States shall be acknowledged or recognized as an independent nation, tribe, or power with whom the United States may contract by treaty ....[5]

Actually, the last treaties were made in 1868. But this declaration had great influence in molding the point of view that Indian tribes and their members were wards of the government. Any further questions about this were dispelled in 1886 when the Supreme Court ruled Indian tribes were wards, dependent upon the U.S. for their political rights. The Court further explained it was a duty of the federal government to protect tribes and their members, its obligation to do this having come about in dealings, in treaties and in recognition of their weakness and helplessness under the impact of the spreading American government and its people.[6]

It is interesting to note the period of time Indian tribes were regarded as nations extended from 1775 to 1871. In that century of time, nearly 650 treaties were made with them.

Coincidentally, the treaty-making period ended approximately with the close of the American Frontier. Documents called agreements took the place of treaties in the few years from 1871 until the final settlement of the country. Agreements were legal documents, binding the parties to their stipulations. They contained commitments similar to treaties and, together with treaties and legislation, became the sources of further governmental activities on Indian reservations.

PAYMENT OF MONEY ANNUITIES

From among the first treaties to the last, annuities of money or goods were stipulated as part of the compensation to Indians for lands they relinquished. So payment of annuities became a major activity of Indian agents and their staffs on reservations.

Usually at each Indian reservation, a specific day was set aside for the payment of annuities. The day came to be known as payment day for the money annuities and ration day for annuities paid in food, clothing and other goods.

Payment day was an annual, or sometimes semiannual, gala event for the members of the tribe. Practically every Indian on the reservation congregated at the place of payment. Generally, this was the Indian agency. Consisting in an office building, houses for employees, storehouses, school buildings, dormitories, barns, stables and other structures, an agency was something of a small settlement. Often an agency was under protection of the Army, so officer and troop quarters, warehouses and other military buildings and equipment were parts of an agency complex.

The total sum of an annual annuity was generally small; although, for large tribes it became more sizable, approximating $75,000 to $100,000. Populations of tribes varied from less than 100 to thousands. Annuities were not paid to a tribe as a whole, but rather on a per-capita basis to the Indian men, women and children. In those days a part of the work of annuity payments was preparing and keeping up an accurate list of tribal members. The list was called a census roll. The agent needed it to obtain annuities through the appropriation process, to keep track of individuals entitled to payment and to have a record showing where the money went. Each Indian received the same amount of money in gold, silver or specie.

Payment day was not complete without upward to 100 traders. These frontier travelling businessmen constructed temporary stands of poles and canvas where they displayed merchandise they learned was in demand by the Indians. Grains of all kinds, cooking pans, pots and utensils, washtubs and washboards, coffee mills, a wide assortment of household articles, calico, muslin and other fabrics, blankets, clothing, salt, pork, flour and bacon were the usual stocks in trade of the businessmen. Saddles and bridles and a flashy assortment of jewelry, bound to catch the eye of every Indian, complemented the traders wares. Sometimes payment day became a 3 or 4 day celebration or pow-wow. Rum runners and whiskey peddlers were generally close at hand on payment day.

PAYMENT OF ANNUITIES IN GOODS

Ration day was the same general character as payment day. However, since goods rather than money were issued, ration day didn't include traders, and it was not as colorful as payment day. Government personnel issued goods similar to the merchandise offered for sale by traders. Ration day was weekly rather than annually or semiannually, and in time, a coupon system developed. To obtain rations then, an Indian had to have a coupon issued by the Indian agent.

Interesting stories have been told in recent times about annuities of goods. One of these used to circulate a few years ago around the Fort Hall, Idaho, reservation. It touched the funny bones of the Indians whenever they told it or heard it because it was about some of the troubles old-time Indians experienced in trying to fit into the lifestyle of non-Indians.

An object of the government in the ration-day period was to transform Indians into images of the dominant culture. Goods supplied in payment of annuities were often commonplace to non-Indians but quite strange to the Indians. Flour was one of these strange items to Indians on the Fort Hall reservation. They didn't know what it was or how to use it when it first appeared among rations. But they didn't turn it down when it was issued. They had something in mind by taking it. On their way home, a mile or so from the agency, they ripped open the sack and emptied the flour into the bushes and gullies. They kept the empty sack because it had an important value to them. On it was the reproduction in color, a reddish-orange, of a portrait of an Indian in headdress. The women traced the outline on to a buckskin jacket then beaded it into a work of art.

DISCONTINUANCE OF ANNUITY PAYMENTS

Some of the Indian agents felt Indians were quite deficient in the handling of money. These agents were not too sold on the program of money annuities. They observed as time went on that many Indians spent a good deal of their annuity money on liquor, in gambling and in other such pursuits. Feeling these were not the best types of expenditure, these agents sent a stream of letters to the Commissioner of Indian Affairs reporting the goings-on. They eventually succeeded in bringing about the discontinuance of money payments. Annuities were then paid in goods.

Payments of annuities in goods became known generally as rations, and with the continued use of that word, they were soon thought of as gifts, or doles, to the Indians by the government rather than annuity payments for lands given up. In the early 1870's, some of the administrators of Indian affairs began to feel rations encouraged indolence and idleness among tribal members. They urged a stop to rations and the start of policy requiring Indians to work for the food, clothing and other ration items. A part of their ideas was written into the act of March 3, 1875. That act required able-bodied male Indians to earn the supplies and other articles distributed to them by working.[7]

Discontinuance of rations was but a step away from this. In 1877, the Commissioner of Indian Affairs issued a directive that agents insist upon some kind of work by the individual Indians for the food and clothing issued to them.[8] This policy remained in effect for the ensuing years and finally led to the complete discontinuance of rations in the early 1900's.

PROMOTION OF CIVILIZATION

Payment of annuities was a major activity in the early days of Indian relocation on reservations. Another principal work of the Indian agents and their staffs was providing the means and opportunities for Indians to learn the lifestyle of Americans and encouraging them to adopt it. This activity was officially called civilization of Indians.

In the history of Indian affairs, civilization often denotes a program separate and distinct from education. Sometimes, however, the two words are used synonymously or interchangeably. In this book, civilization is distinguished from education to the extent possible. Education is taken generally to mean training in an educational institution, such as a school. This section takes up the meaning and implications of civilization.

Henry Knox was one of the first to come out in favor of civilization of Indians. In a letter to Washington dated July 7, 1789, he told the President "all the Indian tribes once existing in those States now the best cultivated and most populous, have become extinct." He predicted this trend could be stopped in the frontier country and among newly-contacted tribes if the government took on the job of civilizing the Indians. Admitting the task to be difficult, but not impossible, he wrote:

> ... That the civilization of the Indians would be an operation of complicated difficulty ... cannot be doubted. But to deny that, under a course of favorable circumstances, it could not be accomplished, is to suppose the human character under the influence of such stubborn habits as to be incapable of melioration or change--a supposition entirely contradicted by the progress of society, from the barbarous ages to its present degree of perfection ....[9]

This suggestion was the foundation and framework for the civilization program. Stipulations that the government provide the means for civilizing the Indians were built upon this suggestion and included in treaties and laws of the land in the passing years.

TREATY STIPULATIONS FOR CIVILIZATION

Article 12 of the treaty of August 7, 1790, with the Creek Indians was among the first treaties to provide for civilization. It is illustrative of the stipulation in many other treaties, so it is worthy to be quoted in some detail. The treaty stated:

> ... that the Creek Indians may be led to a greater degree of civilization, and to become herdsmen and cultivators, instead of remaining in a state of hunters, the United States will, from time to time, furnish gratuitously the said nation with useful domestic animals, and implements of husbandry. And further, to assist the said nation in so desirable a pursuit, ..., the United States will send such, and so many persons, ..., as they may judge proper ....[10]

The meaning of civilization in that treaty was transformation of Indian hunters into herdsmen and cultivators. The federal government pledged to provide animals, farm implements and personnel to assist the Indians in changing their lifestyle.

Two years later, on May 22, 1792, Secretary Knox issued instructions to Brigadier General Rufus Putman who represented the U.S. at a general council of "hostile" Indians in the Lake Erie region. Knox instructed Putman to inform the Indians the U.S. was "highly desirous of imparting to all the Indian tribes the blessings of civilization as the only means of perpetuating them on the earth." Knox also told Putman to assure the Indians the federal government would provide teachers, supplies, materials and other articles so they could learn "to read and write, to plough, and to sow, in order to raise their own bread and meat, with certainty, as the white people do."[11]

According to these instructions, civilization of Indians meant teaching them to read, write, cultivate the land and raise crops and livestock.

Providing for the civilization of Indians was a huge desire and firm commitment of the government, so a civilization article was written into nearly all the treaties.

LEGISLATION PROVIDING FOR CIVILIZATION

Treaties were not the only documents providing for civilization of Indians. Acts of Congress show the desire and policy of the government to do this.

On March 1, 1793, Congress passed the first trade and intercourse act. Among other things, the act stated:

... in order to promote civilization among the friendly Indian tribes, and to secure the continuance of their friendship, it shall and may be lawful for the President of the United States, to cause them to be furnished with useful domestic animals, and implements of husbandry, and also to furnish them with goods and money, in such proportions, as he shall judge proper ....[12]

This act was the first to provide the means to promote civilization among Indians in general. Farming and stockraising were singled out in the act as the meaning of civilization. The act authorized a sum not to exceed $20,000 a year for the project. Pledges in the act expired in 1795, but they were renewed every 2 years until 1802.

On March 30, 1802, Congress passed the permanent trade act. That act lowered the amount for civilization from $20,000 to $15,000.[13] Civilization programs were continued on authority of the 1802 act for more than a decade and a half. At the end of that time, on March 3, 1819, Congress passed another act, and it was the legal basis thereafter for continuance of the program. This act reduced the amount to $10,000, but made it a permanent annual appropriation. By then, however, the term civilization was beginning to lose its separate meaning and identity to the broad program of education.

EARLY PROBLEMS AND THEIR REMEDIES

Paying annuities and promoting civilization among Indians enlarged the BIA in scope of activities and personnel, and this expansion ushered in its share of problems. Some of the problems were compounded by the charges and countercharges of inefficiency, corruption and mismanagement arising from the military and civil policies of the government.

The congressional committee organized in 1865 to look into the condition of Indians and how they were treated by the military and civil authorities drafted a bill to remedy some of the irregularities they discovered. The bill proposed division of territories and states into 5 districts and a yearly checkup of Indian affairs by an inspection board for each district. Each inspection board was to be nonpolitical and consist in an Assistant Commissioner of Indian Affairs, an officer of the Army and a person selected by the President upon recommendation by religious societies. A statement of the committee in urging enactment of the proposed bill is important enough in the history of Indian affairs to be quoted. It indicates the committee's deep concern about mismanagement of Indian affairs and its desire to bring about adjustments. The report stated:

> ... Such a board not organized upon political grounds at all, and possessing, as they
> will, the important powers conferred in the third section of the bill, will, in the
> judgment of the committee, do more to secure the faithful administration of Indian
> affairs than any other measure which has been suggested ....[15]

The proposed bill was not enacted into law; although, some of the recommendations were incorporated into later legislation. For example, the act of July 15, 1870, prohibiting the appointment of Army officers to civilian posts was based upon the committee's recommendations. But further study and thinking were necessary on the recommendation to cut the country up into 5 districts and set up 5 nonpolitical inspection boards. In the meanwhile, time brought other complications in Indian affairs.

The organic act of the BIA was intended to wipe out some of the abuses in appointment to BIA jobs, and it did bring about a temporary reformation. It didn't prohibit appointments, and it didn't make all appointments subject to Senate approval. Superintendents of Indian affairs, subagents, clerks and other employees continued to be appointed by the President, the Secretary of War, the Secretary of the Interior or some other official down the line. In time, these appointments became quite political. They were attended by more of the evils than virtues in that kind of appointments.

By 1869, lively scandals of dishonesty, inefficiency and other corrupt practices in Indian affairs surfaced again. In fact, the observation was beginning to emerge that a superintendent, agent or subagent could retire wealthy after 5 years of BIA employment although his salary was no more than $2,000 a year. This observation reveals the type of dishonesty in Indian affairs at that time and how great it was.

When Grant moved into the White House, he wanted to correct the abuses. He urged and secured in an appropriation act the authority to establish an organization, apart from the BIA, called the Board of Indian Commissioners. The Board was made up of 10 persons "eminent for intelligence and philanthrophy, to serve without pecuniary compensation" and was authorized to exercise joint control with the Secretary of the Interior over BIA appropriations. The original purpose of the Board was to correct fraudulent and disgraceful practices in the purchasing and handling of Indian supplies. However, as years passed, the Board assumed the function of studying and advising the President on important questions relating to Indian affairs.[17] The Board remained in existence for more than half a century before it was abolished in 1933.

President Grant took another step to correct abuses in Indian affairs. He came up with a system limiting political patronage in BIA jobs. His system was designed to assure appointment of Indian agents and other employees "for other than political reasons."[18] It provided that the Society of Friends select personnel to fill the positions of Indian agents in the Nebraska, Kansas and Indian Territories and that other religious organizations select Indian agents for other specified geographical regions.

Measures taken by President Grant were a partial and temporary solution to the difficulties in administration of Indian affairs. But there were later problems.

LATER PROBLEMS AND REMEDIES

President Grant was desirous of eliminating the system of political patronage from appointments to positions in the BIA. But he was concerned also with the sad effects of political appointments in other governmental agencies. So in taking steps to correct abuses in Indian affairs, he did the spadework for other reforms. One of the more important of these was the act of January 16, 1883. The assassination of President Garfield by a disappointed political aspirant to a federal post hastened the passage of the act.[20]

The act of January 16, 1883, was called the Civil Service Act. Among its outstanding features was the requirement of competence as a basis for eligibility of applicants to fill positions in government agencies. The act was applicable to departments in Washington, certain of the custom houses, post offices across the nation and, in the discretion of the President, to other agencies. The President didn't place the BIA under the act at that time, so a few more undesirable problems were added to the BIA.

In the early 1880's, the system established by President Grant was abandoned. By 1901, a new dimension of renewed political appointments was revealed. Appointments were so rapid and extensive that BIA programs could hardly get off the ground. A report made about the situation is informative and important enough to be quoted. It reads:

> ... During President Cleveland's first administration, in sixty agencies, all the agents were changed but two; during President Harrison's administration, while the number of agencies remained unchanged, there were seventy six appointments, and only eight agents were allowed to serve out their four-year terms; during President Cleveland's second administration, in the same number of agencies, there were eighty-one changes and only four agents were allowed to serve out their terms; and during the first term of President McKinley, in fifty-eight agencies, there were seventy-nine changes, only nine agents were allowed to serve out their terms and only one was reappointed at the expiration thereof ....[21]

About 10 years before this report, in 1891, a reattempt was made to free appointments to BIA jobs from political control. In that year, school superintendents, physicians, matrons and teachers were placed under Civil Service rules. In the following 15 years, other positions went under the Civil Service. Positions of agents and subagents were eventually taken out of the political appointment category and put into the pool of Civil Service jobs.

Today most of the BIA employees are appointed in accordance with the rules and regulations of the Civil Service Commission. The position of Commissioner of Indian Affairs, however, is filled as provided by the act of July 9, 1832, and Indians, under authority of various statutes, may be placed in positions for which they are qualified without regard to the rules and regulations of the Civil Service Commission.[22]

1. Felix S. Cohen, op. cit., pp. 163-173.

2. Cherokee Nation v. Georgia, 5 Pet. 1, 1831, p. 20.

3. Rept. Sec. Interior, 1862, p. 9.

4. Rept. Com. Ind. Aff., 1896, p. 6.

5. U.S. Congress, "An act making appropriations for the current and contingent expenses of the Indian Department, and for fulfilling treaty stipulations with various Indian tribes for the year ending June 30, 1872, and for other purposes," March 3, 1871; 16 Stat. 544.

6. United States v. Kagama, 118 U.S. 375, 1886, pp. 383-384.

7. U.S. Congress, "An act making appropriations for the current and contingent expenses of the Indian Department, and for fulfilling treaty stipulations with various Indian tribes, for the year ending June 30, 1876, and for other purposes," March 3, 1875; 18 Stat. 420.

8. Rept. Com. Ind. Aff., 1877, pp. 1-2.

9. Lowrie and Clark, op. cit., Indian Affairs, Vol. I, pp. 53-54.

10. Ibid., p. 100.

11. Ibid., p. 235.

12. U.S. Congress, op. cit., Act of March 1, 1793; 1 Stat. 329.

13. U.S. Congress, "An act to regulate trade and intercourse with Indian tribes, and to preserve peace on the frontier," March 30, 1802; 2 Stat. 139.

14. U.S. Congress, "An act making provision for the civilization of Indian tribes adjoining the frontier settlements," March 3, 1819; 3 Stat. 515.

15. U.S. Congress, Senate Report No. 156, op. cit., p. 21. The Board recommended by this committee was not established. However the appropriation act for fiscal year 1874 (17 Stat. 437, February 14, 1873) established an Office of Inspectors in the BIA and authorized 5 inspectors.

16. Felix S. Cohen, op. cit., p. 18.

17. Ibid., p. 11.

18. Lawrence F. Schmeckebier, op. cit., pp. 54-55.

19. James D. Richardson, (ed.), Messages and Papers of the Presidents: 1789-1897 (Published by authority of Congress, 1900), pp. 3992-3993.

20. O. Glen Stahl, Public Personnel Administration (New York: Harper and Brothers, 1956), p. 23.

21. National Civil Service Reform League, Abuses in the Appointment of Agents in the Indian Service (No publisher shown, 1901), p. 1.

22. Among the statutes which provide that preference by given to Indians in the filling of BIA positions are the act of June 30, 1834, the act of March 3, 1875, the act of March 1, 1883, the act of February 8, 1887, the act of August 15, 1894 and the act of June 18, 1934.

CHAPTER 11

EARLY EDUCATION OF AMERICAN INDIANS BY RELIGIOUS ORGANIZATIONS

Indian affairs is, in a way, a history of education among Indians. The BIA is not, by law, an agency which exists unto itself. Some of its functions and work derive from its existence as an organization. But its major programs have been helping Indians to acquire the knowledges and competencies needed to attain the economic, social, political and cultural status befitting to the promise in the American society. That is its real purpose and reason for being. And that is the essence of Indian affairs. But it is customary to think of Indian education as a particular program of the BIA or as a specific part of Indian affairs.

Indian education, in its broad meaning, is the various opportunities for institutionalized or formal learning and training. It consists in the programs developed and offered by all the many different types and kinds of educational institutions. This includes public schools, private schools and institutions of special and higher learning, together with adult education, employment assistance, adult vocational training and similar programs to train and school adult Indians.

By definition, then, Indian education is a vast field with many facets and ramifications. In this book, however, it is restricted to the BIA educational system. For practical purposes, this is the general concept of Indian education.

In early years of Indian affairs, the educational system consisted of schools operated by various religious organizations. In later periods, including the present time, government-owned and -operated schools have made up the educational system of the BIA for Indians.

This chapter is about the schools operated by religious societies in the early days.

TREATY PROVISIONS FOR INDIAN SCHOOLS

During preliminary treaty negotiations in 1791, Cornplanter, Half Town and Great Tree, spokesmen for the Seneca tribe, appealed to Washington to send missionaries to "teach our children to read and write, and our women to spin and weave."[1]

The first President assured the Seneca spokesmen that the new government desired and was willing to provide for the education of the tribal members whenever and wherever the tribe decided it to be done.

The anticipated treaty was not negotiated, but the willingness and the commitment of the federal government to provide for the education of Indians was incorporated in many treaties made after that.[3]

On December 2, 1794, at Oneida, New York, a treaty was concluded with the Stockbridge, Oneida and Tuscarora Indians. That treaty included for the first time a pledge by the United States to provide a specific kind of education to Indians. The government agreed to build 3 grist mills and saw mills, to employ one or two suitable persons to manage them and to keep them in repair. In addition, these employees had the job of instructing some young men of the 3 nations in the "arts of the miller and sawyer, and to provide teams and utensils for carrying on the work of the mills."[4]

On August 13, 1803, the Kaskaskia Indians made a treaty with the U.S. This was the second treaty providing for on-the-job training and the first to provide for classroom instruction. In the treaty, the government agreed to provide $100 annually for 7 years for a priest who, in addition to his church duties, would "instruct as many of the children as possible in the rudiments of literature."[5]

Many treaties negotiated in the following years stipulated that the federal government provide for the education of tribal members. Some of them provided for on-the-job type of training; others for academic education. A few of the treaty provisions are illustrative.

In a treaty with the Delaware Indians in 1804, the government agreed to provide $300 for 5 years to be used in the teaching of agriculture and mechanics.[6]

The Chippewa, Ottawa and Pottawatomie Indians obtained, in 1821, the pledge of the government to provide $1,000 for 15 years for a blacksmith and a teacher.[7]

In 1826, the Miami tribe was promised $2,000 for "as long as Congress thinks proper" for education and for the support of the infirm.[8]

In its treaty of July 15, 1830, with the Sacs and Foxes, various bands of Sioux, Omahas, Ioways, Ottoes and the Missourias, the federal government committed itself to provide $3,000 annually for 10 years for the education of the children of the tribes.[9]

For schools among the Pawnee Indians, $1,000 for a period of 10 years was stipulated in a treaty concluded in 1833.[10]

The Chickasaw Indians were promised, upon their removal in 1834, that the government would advance money to purchase territory west of the Mississippi for establishing mills, shops and schools and for employing competent persons to operate them.[11]

In 1836, the government agreed to establish schools for the Wyandot Indians.[12]

According to the treaty of 1846 with the Comanche, Cadoe, Wichita and other bands, school teachers were to be provided at the discretion of the President.[13]

To establish schools for the education of their children and to instruct them in agriculture and mechanics, the Blackfoot Indians were promised, in 1855, $15,000 annually for 10 years.[14]

The Menomonee Indians included a stipulation in their treaty of 1854 that the government establish a manual-labor school.[15]

In 1855, the government agreed in a treaty to establish 2 schools with necessary buildings, books and other school supplies and equipment and to employ 3 teachers to instruct the Yakima Indians.[16]

Toward the latter part of the 1850's, treaty provisions for education were broadened by phraseology known as the six-to-sixteen clause. The Indians agreed to compel their children between the ages of six and sixteen to attend school, and the government committed itself to provide schools, teaching materials and 1 teacher for every 30 students. The language in Article 6 of the treaty of 1868 with the Navajo tribe illustrates the six-to-sixteen clause.

... In order to insure the civilization of the Indians entering this treaty, the necessity of education is admitted, especially of such of them as may be settled on said agricultural parts of this reservation, and they therefore pledge themselves to compel their children, male and female, between the ages of six and sixteen years to attend school; ...; and the United States agrees that, for every thirty children between said ages who can be induced or compelled to attend school, a house shall be provided, and a teacher competent to teach the elementary branches of an English education shall be furnished ....[17]

Education was not provided for in all treaties. But stipulations for some kind of education were included in 100 or more treaties. They provided for technical education in agriculture and mechanical arts, reservation schools, boarding schools, or schools, teachers and education generally.[10]

In addition to treaties, countless congressional laws were enacted to establish and support schools and provide education to Indians.

LEGISLATION PROVIDING FOR INDIAN EDUCATION

The first identifiable authority for providing education to Indian boys and girls was a resolution of the Continental Congress on July 12, 1775. The resolution appropriated $500 for the education of Indian youth at Dartmouth College, New Hampshire.[19]

Under the constitutional government, the first evidence of expenditures of appropriated monies for the education of Indians was a statement rendered December 31, 1789, covering $20,000 provided by the act of August 20, for expenses of negotiating with Indian tribes. The statement of expenditures contained an item of $425.51 for

... Expenses incurred in equipping George M. White Eyes, an Indian youth of the Delaware tribe, in order to return to his own country, he having been educated by order, and at the expense of the United States ....[20]

The school attended by the youth and the amount provided for his education by the United States were not stated.

On March 1, 1793, Congress passed the act which included for the first time a provision to promote civilization among the friendly tribes of Indians. Some years later, Congress passed the act of March 3, 1819, which still "stands as the organic legal basis for most of the educational work of the Indian Service."[21] The act states that:

... For the purpose of providing against the further decline and final extinction of the Indian tribes, ... and for introducing among them the habits and arts of civilization, the President ... to employ capable persons of good moral character, to instruct them in the mode of agriculture suited to their situation; and for teaching their children in reading, writing, and arithmetic ....[22]

The act provided a permanent annual appropriation of $10,000 for the educational work among Indians. When the act passed, some of the missionary societies were operating schools among Indians. The President determined the object of the act would be best accomplished by grants-in-aid to the societies.[23] Grants were not restricted to only those societies that were educating Indians at the time. They were made available to societies or individuals who thereafter organized institutions for the education of Indians. The act and its grants-in-aid brought about a system of Indian education which existed for approximately 90 years. The core of the education was a network of schools called mission schools.

GROWTH OF MISSION SCHOOLS

Mission schools operated among Indians many years before the act of March 3, 1819. In fact, some of them were commenced along with establishment of the first colonial settlements. But the grants-in-aid bolstered mission schools, and they began to multiply and spread out among more and more Indian tribes.

In a report made in 1820, Secretary of War Calhoun gave an account of the mission schools in operation and those contemplated for the future.

He reported 2 schools in operation among the Cherokees. One at Brainard was attended by about 100 youths of both sexes. It was operated by the American Board of Foreign Missions, and its instruction was on the Lancastrian plan. The other school was at Spring Place. The United Brethern, or Moravians, were in charge of it. Two other schools were contemplated in the Cherokee nation; one by the American Board and the other by the Baptist Board for Foreign Missions. Plans also were under way to establish 2 schools among the Cherokee Indians on the "Arkansaw."

The Choctaws and Chickasaws, Secretary Calhoun reported, had a strong desire to have schools, and the American Board for Foreign Missions was interested in the project. The Six Nations in New York had made considerable improvement, he said, and plans were to push ahead with schools there as quickly as possible. Civilization among the Wyandots, Senecas and Shawanese at Upper Sandusky and among the Wapakonetts was moving forward under the superintendence of the Society of Friends.

From these beginnings the educational system of the religious societies began to grow. In 1823, there were 21 schools receiving government aid.[24] Two years later the first annual report of the BIA stated that thirty-eight schools were in operation, attended by 1,159 Indian children ....[25]

In the following decade, more mission schools were established. In 1834, a congressional committee found 60 schools in operation among the Indian tribes. They were attended by 2,049 students.[26] During the ensuing 10-year period, in the seeming aftermath of the removal policy, the number of schools among Indians declined. Student enrollment dropped also. In 1842, the schools in operation dropped to 38, and the enrollment fell down to 1,283 students.[27]

The work of the various religious societies in providing education to Indians reached its peak in the late 1850's and early 1860's. About that time, the federal government began operating schools.

ADMINISTRATION OF MISSION SCHOOLS

Although part of the money for the operation of mission schools was provided by the BIA, the educational work was the responsibility of the religious organizations. Local administration and operation of the schools were among the duties of the clergymen who headed the missions. They were assisted by teachers, matrons and other personnel assigned to the missions. No one nation-wide course of study or plan of operation existed for mission schools. But a degree of similarity resulted because of the eligibility requirements for the governmental financial support.

TYPES OF SCHOOLS

Mission schools of the period were known as day schools and boarding schools. Day schools were attended by students who returned to their nearby homes at the close of the school day. Boarding schools provided housing and meals to Indian students whose homes were located too far away to return each day.

Mission schools were coeducational. The schools furnished food, clothing and other necessities for the Indians. Students other than Indians were admitted to the schools, since missions were, for practical purposes, parts of Indian agencies. The greatest number of Indian students during a school term was usually no more than 25 or 30, and they were distinguished by their high rate of absenteeism. In the mission schools, courses of study paralleled somewhat those of the contemporary schools in the general population. However, time and reappraisals of the needs of Indians brought about gradual changes, and institutions known as manual-labor schools came into being.

Male students at manual-labor schools devoted the greater portion of their school days to live experiences in farming and other rural pursuits. Girls learned how to cook, sew and perform other household functions. A description of manual-labor schools, fundamental in a history of Indian affairs, was penned, as follows:

... Our school is in the field and in the shop, and in the house far more than in the school-room, and embraces all classes old and young, male and female. The field is the plantation, at first principally intended for the growth of vegetables, which the Indians cultivate under our direction. This is in addition to their own private patches of corn and potatoes. The shop and the log-houses they build for themselves, and when built, it is still the various articles of household furniture, or farming implements, which they are taught to supply for themselves and the house, and the domestic life; wherein cooking, washing and ironing, sewing, knitting and preparing their own clothing, are the things taught.

The school of the field, the shop, and domestic life, occupies old and young six hours per day; whereas the learning of letters in the school-room does but two, and is confined to the English tongue. We would endeavor to make the men, in order effectually to make them Christians ....[28]

Manual-labor schools stressed the practical aspects of living and sacrificed the three "R's." They emphasized the jobs of building homes, shops and furniture, and making the land produce crops and support livestock. Good housekeeping practices were also high priority items on the training list for girls. Reading, writing and number skills were relatively unimportant at manual-labor schools.

MISSION SCHOOL SCHEDULES AND TEXTBOOKS

A day at a boarding school was quite long. It began in the early morning and ended late at night. A description of a day's activities by one of the reporting school officials is quite informative. The report stated:

... Rise, in summer at half-past four, and in winter at five o'clock a.m.; prayers at half-past five in summer and six in winter; work from breakfast to half-past eight; school at nine; dinner at twelve; school at half-past one; work from half-past four to six; prayers at eight o'clock p.m., and the children immediately to bed ....[29]

This description identifies a 3-hour frame of time for school in both morning and afternoon, making up a 6-hour school day. Waking hours for students ran from 4 a.m. to 8 p.m., amounting to a 16-hour day.

Published textbooks of the day were used in the classrooms. They included McGuffy's Eclectic Readers, Pictorial Primer by Sanders, Bentley's Pictorial Spelling Book, Smith's Quarto Geography and First Book in Geography, Parley's New Geography and Arithmetic for Little Learners by Ray.[30]

STUDENT PROGRESS AT MISSION SCHOOLS

Students in some of the schools were divided into classes according to teacher judgment of their abilities and needs. They were advanced upon the recommendations of teachers, classroom tests and independent examinations. The practice at one school was described, as follows:

... The teaching business lasts six hours daily, Saturday and Sunday excepted, and there is monthly an examination held by Rev. T. B. Menet, followed by the reading of an account of each one's conduct, constancy, and progress, which account is sent to parents when deemed expedient ....[31]

Ultimate success of mission schools was measured by the number of students who became Christians and the extent to which they adopted and entered into the American way of life. Reports suggest that many students became farmers and cattlemen, established homes and reared families.[32] Other reports name specific Indians who became preachers among their own people, teachers at mission schools and students at some of the colleges.[33]

TERMINATION OF GOVERNMENT AID TO MISSION SCHOOLS

The period of approximately 25 years following the Civil War was marked by Indian wars and settlement of the west. Mission schools during those years remained relatively constant in number. In 1888, 71 mission schools received aid from the federal government. Enrollment at these schools totaled 4,308 and average attendance was 3,284.[34] The religious groups that operated the schools were the Bureau of Catholic Indian Missions, the Boards of Home and Foreign Missions of of the Presbyterian Church, American Missionary Association (Congregational), Lutherans, Friends, Unitarians, Mennonites and Episcopalians.[35]

In 1888, aid to religious denominations totaled $259,119.73.[36] This amount contined to be granted for the succeeding 4 years. In 1893 and the 2 following years, the amount was reduced. The reduction commenced a downward trend that continued until 1897. In that year, Congress declared it to be a settled policy of the government to make no further appropriations for the education of Indians in sectarian schools.[37]

Public funds in aid of mission schools for Indians were reduced gradually thereafter and ultimately discontinued in 1900.[38] Tribal funds were used in support of mission schools, however, until 1905.[39] Since that time, the schools have been financed by the religious organizations.

1. Lowrie and Clark, op. cit., Indian Affairs, Vol. I, p. 209.

2. Ibid., p. 166.

3. Felix S. Cohen, op. cit., p. 239.

4. U.S. Congress, "Treaty with Oneida, Tuscarora, and Stockbridge Indians," December 2, 1794; 7 Stat. 47.

5. U.S. Congress, "Treaty with Kaskaskia Tribe," August 13, 1803; 7 Stat. 78.

6. U.S. Congress, "Treaty with Delaware Tribe," August 18, 1804; 7 Stat. 81.

7. U.S. Congress, "Treaty with Ottowa, Chippewa, and Pottawatomie Nations," August 29, 1821; 7 Stat. 218.

8. U.S. Congress, "Treaty with Miami Tribe," October 23, 1826; 7 Stat. 300.

9. U.S. Congress, "Treaty with Confederated Tribes of the Sacs and Foxes; the Medawah-Kanton, Wapacoota, Wahpeton and Sissetong Bands or Tribes of Sioux, the Omahas, Ioways, Ottoes and Missourias," July 15, 1830; 7 Stat. 328.

10. U.S. Congress, "Treaty (articles of agreement and convention) with Confederated Bands of Pawnees--Grand Pawnees, Pawnee Loups, Pawnee Republicans, Pawnee Tappaye," October 9, 1833; 7 Stat. 448.

11. U.S. Congress, "Treaty (articles of agreement and convention) with Chickasaw Nation," May 24, 1834; 7 Stat. 450.

12. U.S. Congress, "Treaty with Wyandot Tribe," April 23, 1836; 7 Stat. 502.

13. U.S. Congress, "Treaty with Comanches and other Tribes (I-onOi, Ana-da-ca, Cadoe, Lepan, Long-wha, Keechy, Tah-wa-carro, Wi-chita, and Wacoe Tribes), May 15, 1846; 9 Stat. 844.

14. U.S. Congress, "Treaty with Blackfoot Indians," October 17, 1855; 11 Stat. 657.

15. U.S. Congress, "Treaty with Menomonees," May 12, 1854; 10 Stat. 1064.

16. U.S. Congress, "Treaty with Yakimas," June 9, 1855; 12 Stat. 951.

17. U.S. Congress, "Treaty with Navajo Tribe," June 1, 1868; 15 Stat. 667.

18. Felix S. Cohen, op. cit., p. 239.

19. U.S. Congress, op. cit., Senate Document No. 95, p. 161.

20. Lowrie and Clark, op. cit., p. 64.

21. Felix S. Cohen, op. cit., p. 239.

22. U.S. Congress, "An act making provision for the civilization of Indian tribes adjoining the frontier settlements," March 3, 1819; 3 Stat. 516.

23. U.S. Congress, op. cit., House Document No. 46, p. 16.

24. Ibid.

25. Rept. Com. Ind. Aff., 1825, p. 90.

26. U.S. Congress, op. cit., House Report No. 474, pp. 69-70.

27. Lawrence F. Schmeckebier, op. cit., p. 40.

28. Rept. Com. Ind. Aff., 1854, p. 65.

29. Ibid., p. 34.

30. Ibid., p. 44. Other texts in use are named in Rept. Com. Ind. Aff., 1857, p. 242, p. 259, p. 251.

31. Ibid., 1853 , p. 48.

32. Ibid., 1853, p. 37, pp. 85-86; 1854, pp. 54-55.

33. Ibid., 1853, p. 51; 1854, p. 121; 1855, p. 140.

34. Ibid., 1888, p. xi.

35. Ibid., p. xiv.

36. Ibid., p. xi.

37. U.S. Congress, "An act making appropriations for the current and contingent expenses of the Indian Department and for fulfilling treaty stipulations with Indian tribes for the fiscal year ending June 30, 1898, and for other purposes," June 7, 1897; 30 Stat. 62.

38. Lawrence F. Schmeckebier, op. cit., p. 85; Felix S. Cohen, op. cit., p. 242.

39. Ibid., Felix S. Cohen, p. 242.

CHAPTER 12

EARLY EDUCATION OF AMERICAN INDIANS AT GOVERNMENT SCHOOLS

The exact date the BIA began building and operating Indian schools is not too clear. In the annual report for 1854, the Commissioner of Indian Affairs tabulated the schools in operation among Indians. Most of the schools at that time were operated by various religious organizations. In the listing, however, 2 Menonomee schools at Keshena, Wisconsin, and 8 among the Creek Indians were identified as government schools. This was the first annual report to reveal BIA-operated schools.[1] Subsequent annual reports indicate the development of Indian schools by the BIA.

Two types of schools developed. One type was located near centers of Indian populations on reservations or adjacent to Indian agencies. They were reservation schools. The other type was off-reservation, or nonreservation, schools. These schools were established in close proximity to non-Indian cities or towns located at some distances from reservations.

This chapter traces the development of reservation and off-reservation Indian schools in the early periods, indicates the interrelationship of the schools, suggests the training at the schools and goes into some of the problems encountered by the BIA in its operation of the schools.

GOVERNMENT RESERVATION SCHOOLS

In 1860, the BIA established a school at Fort Simcoe, Washington, on the Yakima Indian Reservation. This school is said to be the first Indian school built and operated by the BIA.[2] In the following years, other schools were constructed and operated by the BIA.

In 1867, at Leech Lake, Minnesota, a school was organized and put into operation for the Chippewa Indians. A year later, a school came into existence for the Sac and Fox Indians in Oklahoma. The next year, 1869, the Kaw Indians, also in Oklahoma, were provided a school. All these schools were built, organized, opened and operated by the BIA. They were classified as reservation boarding schools, the principal kind of schools established by the BIA in the decade of the 1860's.

For the following 30 years, the BIA continued to establish boarding schools on various Indian reservations. Growth in their number and where they were located among the states with Indian reservations are illustrated by Table I. The table shows the number of schools established during each decade from 1870 to 1899, and a total of 71 for the 30-year period. In 1900, the BIA opened 5 more schools, so at the turn of the century, 76 reservation boarding schools were operated by the BIA.

In addition to boarding schools, the BIA established a considerable number of day schools among the Indian tribes. No records are available to show the dates they were opened and where they were located. But by 1900, the BIA was operated 147 day schools on Indian reservations.[3]

From these beginnings, reservation schools grew in number in the years thereafter.

GOVERNMENT OFF-RESERVATION SCHOOLS

In the early 1870's, thinking began to develop that reservation day and boarding schools were not the full answer to the problem of Indian education. Something else was needed to equip the Indians with necessary competencies and to update them to their changed situation in the world. Inability of reservation schools to achieve success with Indians was summed up by an Indian agent when he stated, "On the reservation no school can be so conducted as to remove children from the influence of the idle and vicious who are everywhere present." Pointing up the need for supplemental educational opportunities, he went on to say, "Only by removing them beyond the reach of this influence can they be benefited by the teaching of the schoolmaster."[4]

Table I

GOVERNMENT RESERVATION BOARDING SCHOOLS[a]

Number Established and Distribution Among States 1870-1899

States	1870-79	1880-89	1890-99
Arizona	1	4	3
California		2	1
Idaho	1	2	
Indian Territory	1		
Iowa			1
Kansas	2		
Minnesota	2		3
Montana		3	1
Nebraska	1	1	
Nevada		1	1
New Mexico		1	1
North Carolina			1
Oklahoma	5	1	5
Oregon	3	2	1
South Dakota	2	3	3
Utah		1	1
Washington	1		1
Wisconsin	1		2
Wyoming	1		
	24	21	26

[a]Compiled from: Rept. Com. Ind. Aff., 1901, pp. 21-23.

These kinds of thoughts became more prominent and universal as time passed, and BIA officials went to work searching for a way to solve the problem. They came up with plans that ultimately resulted in setting up and developing off-reservation schools.

In 1878, the BIA enrolled 17 Indian captives at Hampton Institute in Virginia, a school founded by S. C. Armstrong for the education of Blacks. One object of this enrollment was to find out how well Indians fresh from Indian wars would get along among non-Indians and in non-Indian surroundings. They proved Indians were capable of making necessary changes and of learning in classrooms, so in the following years, more Indians were enrolled at Hampton Institute. By 1883, a total of 109 Indians from different tribes attended school there.[5]

Booker T. Washington, in his autobiography, Up From Slavery, praised Indian students for their conduct and ability to adjust to the school situation and benefit from it. In doing that, he may well have been the first person to recognize Indians are not below other races in intelligence.

In the same year that Indian students were admitted for the first time to Hampton Institute, Congress authorized the use of the abandoned Army installation at Carlisle, Pennsylvania, as a boarding school for Indians.[6] The task of organizing the Indian school fell upon Captain R. H. Pratt, and the school was opened on November 1, 1879. Many other off-reservation schools were established for Indian students in the following years. Expansion of off-reservation schools is illustrated by Table II, showing the locations of the schools and the dates of openings.

Table II

EARLY GOVERNMENT OFF-RESERVATION SCHOOLS[a]

Locations and Dates of Openings

Locations	Dates of Openings
Carlisle, Pennsylvania	November 1, 1879
Chemawa, Oregon	February 25, 1880
Chilocco, Oklahoma	January 15, 1884
Genoa, Nebraska	February 20, 1884
Albuquerque, New Mexico	August --, 1884
Lawrence, Kansas (Haskell Institute)	September 1, 1884
Grand Junction, Colorado	--------, 1886
Santa Fe, New Mexico	October --, 1890
Fort Mohave, Arizona	December --, 1890
Carson, Nevada	December --, 1890
Pierre, South Dakota	February --, 1891
Phoenix, Arizona	September --, 1891
Fort Lewis, Colorado	March --, 1892
Fort Shaw, Montana	December 27, 1892
Perris, California	January 9, 1893
Flandreau, South Dakota	March 7, 1893
Pipestone, Minnesota	February --, 1893
Mount Pleasant, Michigan	January 3, 1893
Tomah, Wisconsin	January 19, 1893
Wittenberg, Wisconsin	August 24, 1895
Greenville, California	September 25, 1895
Morris, Minnesota	April 3, 1897
Chamberlain, South Dakota	March --, 1898
Fort Bidwell, California	April 4, 1898
Rapid City, South Dakota	September 1, 1898

[a]Compiled from: Rept. Com. Ind. Aff., 1904, p. 39.

STRUCTURE OF EARLY INDIAN EDUCATION

The relationship of day schools to reservation boarding schools, and of both of these to off-reservation schools, made up the structure of early Indian education administered by the BIA.

Day schools were somewhat in the nature of recruiting stations for the boarding schools, particularly reservation boarding schools. The Commissioner of Indian Affairs in 1883 explained that many children who could not be induced to go away from home to boarding schools on the reservations would "stray" into day schools located nearby their homes and when their minds were awakened, would gladly accept the better opportunities offered them at boarding schools. Reservation boarding schools received a good share of their students from day schools by this method.[7]

Reservation boarding schools were upward bound steps to off-reservation schools. The interrelationship of the different classifications of schools was described by the Commissioner of Indian Affairs, as follows:

... The reservation boarding school proposes to take the pupils from the camp or day school, and through six or seven years lay the groundwork of future advancement in the schools away from the reservation. After completing a reasonable term, unless the boy or girl shown an aptitude for further advancement, and is willing to leave the reservation, he or she is returned home and the vacant place filled with fresh material ....[8]

An important aim of off-reservation schools was to equip students with abilities for them to find their places in the "mainstream of the American society." However, according to the Commissioner, students who didn't wish to leave or stay away from their reservations, or who were unable to benefit from off-reservation school programs were returned to their homes.

PROGRAMS AT GOVERNMENT INDIAN SCHOOLS

Educational programs at government Indian schools were similar to the programs at the manual-labor schools of the missions. Industrial training, or another like term, was used, however, to describe the programs.[9] The Commissioner of Indian Affairs in 1901 likened off-reservation schools to reform schools and indicated that strict military discipline was maintained. He stated that vocational training was the major priority at the schools, and academic studies took a back seat. His own words are quite descriptive and what he said is significant to a study in history of Indian education. So it is well to quote him in some detail. He wrote:

> ... The class of largest Government Indian schools is located off the reservation, and usually near large cities and centers of wealth and culture. These schools are supported by transfer from the reservation day and boarding schools, although many children are taken directly from the camps. They correspond more nearly with the great industrial and reform schools of the states. Military discipline is maintained and thorough obedience to civil authorities inculcated. Literary training is subordinated to that for the industries. The majority is equipped with shops for shoe and harness making, carpentry, blacksmithing, wagon-making, and the teaching of other useful trades. Several have large domestic buildings adapted for the teaching of elementary and scientific cooking to the girls. These establishments are modeled after the most approved methods ....[10]

Success in the training of students was measured by the number of acres cultivated, the amount of produce grown, the number of wagons, shoes, harnesses and other articles made and the dairy products obtained or manufactured. Virtually every annual report of the Commissioner of Indian Affairs from about 1880 to 1920 included a statement which detailed the crops and other products obtained from the farms, gardens and dairies at Indian boarding schools of the time.

At some of the off-reservation schools, new and renovative programs were devised to help Indians close the gap from their native lifestyle to the non-Indian way of living. One of the more notable of these was the "outing system." This program originated at the Carlisle Indian School. Briefly, it consisted in allowing students to spend one or more years of their school life away from the school in select non-Indian homes. Pupils continued to be technically under the supervision of the off-reservation schools, but they attended local district schools along with non-Indian students. They lived at non-Indian homes and were required to render various services for which they received reasonable wages. They paid for their clothing and other expenses from these earnings. Off-reservation schools taught students how to buy and how to manage money. The schools also encouraged the students to save part of their earnings in banks.

The "outing system" was based upon the idea that it was of utmost importance for Indian students to associate with non-Indians. Contact with and living as non-Indians were judged to be the best way for Indians to learn how to think and reason in the manner of the dominant society. Under the outing system the Indian pupil was surrounded by all the civilizing influences of a good home, stated the Commissioner of Indian Affairs. An Indian student in the "outing system," the Commissioner explained lived the life of and mingled with white children of his own age, adopted their ideas, and formed similar hbaits. Male students were required to take part in all farm operations. Girls worked in the home doing household jobs. In these schools of experiences, students could learn how to operate their own farms and manage their own homes.[11]

The "outing system" was discontinued in the early 1900's. But it was revived in modified form in the 1960's. With its rebirth, it received the new name of student placement or student employment assistance.

The broad program of education at early BIA-operated Indian schools continued without drastic modification throughout many following years. As late as 1944, for example, a typical school day schedule included about a half a day academic study and a half a day live experience in agriculture, farm and domestic work.[12]

In the first years of the 1950's, a movement commenced to provide more time for students to study academic subjects. As it gained momentum, school farms, dairies and other learning facilities of a rural nature passed from the schenes of Indian schools. Courses in practical arts and vocational education became integral parts of school offerings.

COURSES OF STUDY

The first course of study for government Indian schools was developed in 1890. Schools were divided into the primary grade and the advanced grade for the course of study, and each grade covered 4 years rather than the usual 1 year.

In each year of the primary grade, students were required to take English language, reading, writing, numbers and general exercises, such as singing, calisthenics, marching or another action exercise. Form and color, penmanship, drawing and geography were added in the second year. Students were introduced to arithmetic in the fourth year of the primary grade.

In each year of the advanced grade, the required academic studies were reading, orthography, arithmetic, form and color, penmanship, drawing, language, geography, general exercises and observation lessons, such as nature study. The course of study included U.S. history, physiology and hygiene in the third year. In the fourth year, civil government and music were added to the list of subjects.

Published textbooks of the day were recommended for use, and the Rules for Indian Schools provided that "at the close of each term pupils should be examined in all the studies pursued and promotions should be made on the basis of these examinations."[13]

In 1901, another course of study was developed so that each school would know what to teach and pupils transferred from one institution to another could be properly graded.[14] The 1890 course of study was scrapped. The new course of study included 31 subjects among which were agriculture, baking, basketry, blacksmithing, carpentry, cooking, dairying, engineering, gardening, harnessmaking, housekeeping, laundering, printing, painting, sewing, shoemaking, tailoring and upholstering. Practical lessons in each subject were outlined in the course of study to give teachers a definite idea of the work that should be done in the schools to advance pupils as speedily as possible to usefulness and citizenship.[15] The division of schools into primary and advanced grades was discontinued. For each subject, lessons were outlined for each year, commencing with the first year and continuing, in some cases, through the seventh year. This was the first uniform course of study in Indian schools. English, mathematics and social study courses were included among the 31 subjects composing the course of study. The subjects were set up in such a way that the same material was taught on the same day at the same hour to all students enrolled in any given subject at all Indian schools across the land.

A revision of the course of study was made in 1910, and the following years brought other modifications.

In 1936, the uniform course of study was eliminated from Indian schools. Progressive education was adopted as the basic philosophy of Indian education and the guide for classroom work. Each school set up its own course of study adapted to the needs and interests of its students. In the classrooms, each teacher selected goals to be achieved and planned the content of the courses taught. In addition, each teacher set out, step by step, the knowledges and skills pupils needed to accumulate to achieve the goals.[16] This system was in effect for approximately 20 years.

The concept of a uniform course of study was reinstated in 1953 when <u>Minimum Essential Goals for Indian Schools</u> was produced. This course of study outlined for each subject the separate and specific learnings for students in the beginning year and in each of its levels numbered one through nine. These itemized learnings were judged by the administrators of Indian education to be the essential minimum every Indian student who enrolled in a particular subject needed to know. The goals included recommended teaching methods, together with listings of instructional materials.

In 1962, a committee of Indian school employees was organized "to develop curriculum guides to meet the changing composition of today's school enrollment."[17] Guides collectively captioned <u>Steps to Learning</u> were outcomes of the committee's work. The <u>Minimum Essential Goals for Indian Schools</u> were declared obsolete.

<u>Steps to Learning</u> was essentially a listing of basic understandings students needed in the various subjects at the different grade levels. The format of the guides was 3 columns for (a) basic understandings, (b) suggested activities and (c) resource materials. Subjects composing this course of study were language arts, social studies, science, arithmetic and guidance. For each subject a list of basic understandings was developed in the 3-column format.

Basic understandings were listed in sequential order across all grade levels. Activities varied with the needs of students depending upon maturity, achievement ability, and vocational goals in life. The "depth variables" activities would enable a student at any particular grade level who was achieving on a lower-grade level to study the same basic understandings ....[18]

<u>Steps to Learning</u> applied to grades 7 through 12. The "depth variables" permitted students to go on from any point they had previously reached, and also to go back and catch up on learnings they had missed in their previous lives.

APPROPRIATIONS FOR INDIAN SCHOOLS

An act of Congress passed in 1819 provided $10,000 annually for the civilization of Indians. The appropriations was a permanent one, so each year $10,000 was automatically available to the BIA for that purpose. By that time, the words <u>civilization</u> of Indians were in the process of being replaced by <u>education</u> of Indians. Appropriations for education commenced and began to increase in the passing years, particularly to fulfill treaty obligations.

Congressional appropriations were not the only sources of funds for Indian education. Tribes entered into treaties that provided for the sale of their lands. Moneys paid by the government for these lands were often put into reserve accounts called tribal funds. These reserve accounts were maintained on the books of the U.S. Treasury, and they were under control of the Congress. Some of these funds were made available by Congress for Indian education. Also funds of missionary societies were devoted to the operation of mission schools, the principal educational facilities for Indians up to the late 1860's.

In 1855, the Commissioner of Indian Affairs summarized the expenditures for education during the preceding 10 years. He found that congressional appropriations totaled $120,107.14 for the 10-year period. In this same time span, tribal funds used for Indian education, he found, aggregated $824,160.61, and missionary societies expended more than $830,000 for the "christianization and civilization of the Indian tribes." Additionally, over $400,000 was "paid out by Indian nations among themselves" for educational purposes. Total outlay for educational programs in the ten years exceeded $2,150,000.[19]

Significantly, in the 10 years up to 1855, Indians contributed to their education about 10 times more than the federal government. The total they put into education was more than half the entire education expenditures in that 10-year period.

In 1870 Congress appropriated $100,000 for the fiscal year 1871 "for the support of industrial and other schools among the Indian tribes not otherwise provided for."[20] That was the first general appropriation for education and the largest sum appropriated up to that time. It signified the government had adopted a liberal policy for education of Indians.

Increasing appropriations in the following years are indicated by Table III. The table shows appropriated amounts for select years a decade apart and the increasing number of schools and enrollment.

Table III

EXPENDITURES FOR INDIAN EDUCATION[a]

Fiscal Year	Appropriations	Number of Schools	Enrollment
1877	$ 20,000	150	3,598
1887	1,211,415	227	10,520
1897	2,517,265	288	18,676
1907	3,925,830	341	25,802
1913	4,015,720	412	26,281

[a]Compiled from: Rept. Com. Ind. Aff., 1912, p. 216.

The amounts shown in Table III were funds provided to the BIA for its Indian education programs. Tribal funds are not included in the amounts. Additional moneys were appropriated for distribution to the mission schools, public schools and private schools where Indian students were enrolled.

In the 1920's and thereafter, particularly during the depression years, appropriations continued to increase. Analyses of the appropriations were quite difficult, however. The appropriation structure in those days was so complicated that a respected writer, attempting to analyze expenditures for Indian schools, declared in 1928, "It is impossible to compile a table showing all appropriations for education, as some of the appropriations, especially those for fulfilling treaty stipulations provide for education, support and other objects." Complete figures showing expenditures from all sources for Indian education are not available for the decades of 1920 and 1930.[21] But a reasonable idea was obtained by taking a look at the limitations placed on the per-capita expenditures for schools.

The act of June 30, 1919, limited expenditures to $225 per student in schools of 200 pupils or more and to $250 per student in schools with less than 200 pupils.[22] Transportation of supplies, costs of transporting the students to and from schools and salaries of superintendents were not included in the limitations.

These limitations were gradually raised. By 1944, per-pupil costs at small elementary schools and at high schools were about $395 and $480, respectively, including transportation and salaries of superintendents. Appropriations for 1944 for operating Indian schools amounted to $10,474,650.[23]

After WW II increasing efforts to provide educational opportunities for Indians were accompanied by increasing appropriations. These increasing efforts and appropriations continued as time went on. The importance of education as a function of the BIA was emphasized in January 1963, as follows:

... Education is by far the biggest single function of this Bureau both in terms of manpower and in dollars. Where funds for the construction of school-connected facilities are added to those for school operation and aid to local school districts, the total accounts for nearly 60% of the Bureau's appropriations ....[24]

In the fiscal year 1963, the total of appropriations for the BIA was $193,000,000. Sixty percent of that is $115,800,000, the amount expended for education of Indians. Ten years later, funds devoted to Indian education totaled over $174 million.[25]

For fiscal year 1975, the budget for Indian education amounted to $219 million. In that year, the education budget was about 1/3 of the total BIA budget, and about 1/3 of all BIA employees were involved in Indian education or school-related activities.[26]

ADMINISTRATION OF INDIAN SCHOOLS

When the BIA first went into the business of constructing and operating Indian schools, the Commissioner of Indian Affairs took on the job of general administration of Indian education.

In 1882, an Inspector of Indian Schools was employed to inspect all Indian schools, develop plans to carry out treaty stipulations for Indian education and submit estimates of what it would cost to provide education to Indian youths for whom no educational opportunities existed.[27] In the following year, the title was changed to Superintendent of Indian Schools.[28] The fundamental nature of the duties, however, remained the same.[29]

Five years later, in 1888, when BIA schools were on a fast increase, a position to head Indian education was established.[30] The new position took the old title Superintendent of Indian schools.[31] In the following years, other positions were set up to help administer the schools and programs of Indian education.

By 1890, an organization known as the Indian School Service had developed in the BIA. It was a tri-level unit which consisted in the Superintendent of Indian Schools, located in Washington, D.C., supervisors of education, stationed at various locations across the country, and the personnel at Indian schools on and off the reservation.

Duties of the Superintendent of Indian Schools included visiting all Indian schools and reporting to the Commissioner of Indian Affairs any defects in administration and what was lacking for the most effective advancement of the pupils.

Supervisors of education were to visit reservation boarding and day schools, consult with teachers, give them instructions in methods of teaching and report defects in the schools and their operations to the Superintendent of Indian Schools.

At each Indian reservation, the Indian agent was the top man in matters pertaining to the schools. However, he had little to do with school operations and was forbidden by BIA rules to give directions to school employees. These were jobs for the superintendent of reservation schools.

The reservation school superintendent had general control of the schools on reservations. He was responsible for discipline, classification of pupils and distribution of duties among employees. He also performed the work of the principal teacher if no such position was provided for a school.

The principal teacher arranged classes, scheduled hours of study and recitation, supervised the literary work, taught classes assigned to him by the school superintendent and substituted for teachers temporarily absent. An industrial teacher performed similar duties in the industrial department of schools.

Superintendents at off-reservation schools reported directly to the Commissioner of Indian Affairs.[32] Superintendents of reservation schools reported to Indian agents.

This basic administrative structure has endured throughout the years. Position titles have changed and details incident to the broad functions of administration of Indian schools have expanded, resulting in the development of a sizeable suborganization in the BIA. The suborganization was known first as the Indian School Service. Eventually, it became the Branch of Education. In a reorganization of the BIA in 1965, the Branch of Education was upgraded to the Division of Education. It was later reshuffled in a subsequent reorganization and titled the Office of Indian Education Programs.

DIFFICULTIES IN OPERATION OF INDIAN SCHOOLS

Disappointments and difficulties marked the development and operation of Indian schools.

When the BIA first took over education on reservations, abandoned Army posts and old mission buildings often served as school houses. They were generally "ill-arranged, ill-ventilated, dilapidated and overcrowded buildings."[33] Difficulties in trying to hold classes in run-down buildings were accompanied by other troubles.

Supplies and equipment were wanting in quality and quantity.[34] Teachers and other school personnel, until put under Civil Service rules, frequently were political appointees, poorly qualified and lacking interest in the job of teaching Indians.[35] To these disappointments was added the customary irregular attendance of students. Almost every Indian agent and school administrator was aware of the high rate of student absentism and was looking for ways to get students to attend school every day.[36]

Many of these difficulties and disappointments continued on through the years. In fact, it was not until well into the 1900's that some of them noticeably changed.

During the decades of the 1950's and 1960's, modern structures began to replace buildings long since condemned, and renewable old schoolhouses started to get face-liftings. Entire new school complexes were constructed at some of the reservations to accommodate increases in school-age children. Supplies and equipment were upgraded at almost all schools so students could obtain instruction and training along modern lines.

Some of the problems, however, have been only partially solved. One of these is the irregular attendance of students.

At off-reservation boarding schools, irregular attendance is somewhat more manageable than at reservation schools. When a student sluffs a class at some of the off-reservation schools, the teacher reports the absence and a search is made of the campus, the buildings, the nearby town and elsewhere to find the student and get him to class. This way of securing regular attendance is feasible at off-reservation schools. It isn't too practicable, however, on reservations because students generally live at some distances from schools. So students enrolled at reservations schools can usually come and go whenever they wish.

Another problem that survived across the years is the lack of professionalism among employees in Indian education.

Teachers and other school personnel, when initially appointed, must meet minimum qualification standards set by the U.S. Civil Service Commission. But no further professional training or education is required for advancement, other than years of experience on the job. A teacher can rise to the highest positions in Indian education without any more formal training than he had when first employed. This is much less than he would need to occupy a similar position in public schools. For example, a superintendent, principal or other administrator need not possess more than a bachelor degree. As a matter of fact, a number of administrative positions at Indian schools are filled by employees who do not have master or doctoral degrees. Likewise many education employees up the line in Area Offices and the national office of the BIA in Washington, D.C. have only bachelor degrees. At some of the off-reservation schools, high administrative positions are filled by employees who do not possess even so much as a bachelor degree. Since it is not a requirement, administrators seldom go back to school to update themselves in the latest developments in education, and Indian education, consequently, lags behind in providing the schooling needed by the students.

Other troubles hung on for many years.

One of these is the never-ending bickering about whether to keep off-reservation schools open or to close them down. This quarrel started soon after the first students enrolled at them, and it hasn't let up much since then. Some of the thinking behind this issue is significant in the history of Indian affairs and for that reason should be reviewed.

A line of early argument to close down off-reservation schools was that the schools were basically detrimental to the ultimate good of the students. At early ages, children were taken from their parents, hauled away to remote places and denied the privilege of growing up in their native environments. They were robbed of their language and their culture in these schools, the argument ran, and were split from family ties. Yet the schools did not equip them for effective life in the non-Indian society. So they were suspended between the two worlds and cultures.

This line of argument was quite attractive. It characterized the BIA as heartless and merciless, interested only in forcing Indian children into molds and reshaping them into non-Indians. And, even so, the BIA failed. The argument seldom failed to touch and stir compassionate reaction. Time tested, it is heard even today as ample justification for closing down off-reservation schools.

The counter argument has been that in 1894, Congress passed an act prohibiting the removal of Indian children beyond the limits of their reservations without the consent of their parents or guardians.[37] A few years later, in 1909, another act was passed which provided that no Indian students under the age of 14 could be transported at government expense beyond the limits of the state or territory where their parents reside.[38] These acts brought about the rules of the BIA that Indian students must apply for admission to off-reservation schools, and consent of parents or guardians is a must before the students are enrolled.

Early Indian schools did forbid the speaking of native language and did discourage students in practices of their native culture, the counter argument goes on, but that was changed more than 50 years ago. The richness of Indian language and culture is recognized in the educational system, and students are not denied this treasure.

Varying opinions of the persons appointed Commissioner of Indian Affairs have kept the issue of off-reservation schools alive. Some of them were fully sold on these schools as the more effective means to bring about the acculturation of Indian students. Others claimed off-reservation schools failed in fulfilling expectations.[39]

One Commissioner expressed his idea about the ineffectiveness of Indian schools in the east, such as the Carlisle Indian School, in rather picturesque language. He pretty well revealed the sentiments of those who wanted the schools closed, so he is worth quoting at length. He wrote:

... The energy of the American people has made the great West as grand as the great East. As high a type of civilization has been developed, and the efforts of the Indian Office is proving successful in bringing at least a portion of this civilization to the Indian in his home. The idea of bringing East the entire 30,000 red children now in school and of educating, civilizing, and settling them in the East is a fantastic dream which has not been and cannot be realized. A fair trial of twenty years has been given this theory, and the paucity of results is amazing.

... It is a waste of public money to bring the average Indian to an eastern school, educate him for years upon the theory that his reservation home is a hell on earth, when inevitably he must and does return to his home. It is not only a waste of money, but an injustice to the Indian ....[40]

The Commissioner urged the speedy closing of a number of off-reservation schools. He suggested that the "best" of such schools be retained and that "sufficient day and boarding schools should be established on the reservations or near the homes of the Indians to carry civilization to their doors."[41]

Wavering opinions of different Commissioners coupled with authority to give realness to their thinking caused instability of off-reservation schools and fluctuations in their number.

The drive to establish off-reservation schools began in 1878 with the enrollment of Indian students at Hampton Institute. It moved forward for about 20 years. At the end of that time, 25 off-reservation schools were in operation. But that didn't last too long.

The Commissioner in 1904 couldn't see too much value in these schools, particularly those in the east. He touched off a move toward the close-down of some of them by consolidating the Perris, California, school with Sherman Institute at Riverside in the same state.

Enrollment at Hampton Institute came to an end in 1912.[43] The Carlisle Indian School was closed during WW I when the facilities were reconverted back to Army purposes. Other schools were closed in the following years. By 1927, off-reservation schools had been reduced to 18.[44]

In the following year, a new school was opened at Fort Wingate, New Mexico, a short distance from the boundary of the Navajo reservation. In that year, too, the Institute of Government Research issued a report, commonly called the "Meriam Report," recommending further decreases in the number of off-reservation schools and restricting their enrollment to pupils above the sixth grade.[45] Approximately half the remaining original off-reservation schools were closed during the following 15 years.

A congressional subcommittee, in 1944, however, recommended that the BIA establish more off-reservation schools. Its recommendation included a criticism of the BIA, as follows:

... The Indian Bureau is tending to place too much emphasis on the day school located on the Indian reservation as compared with the opportunities afforded Indian children in off-the-reservation boarding schools where they can acquire an education in healthful and cultural surroundings without the handicap of having to spend their out-of-school hours in tepees, in shacks with dirt floors and no windows, in tents, in wickiups, in hogans, or in surroundings where English is never spoken, where there is a complete lack of furniture, and where there is sometimes an active antagonism or an abysmal indifference to the virtues of education.

Your committee inspected off-the-reservation or boarding schools at Riverside, Oklahoma; Pierre and Flandreau, South Dakota. In each of them we found Indian children receiving praiseworthy education and living in desirable conditions. We believe these schools and similar institutions should be expanded and emphasized ....[46]

In 1949, Intermountain School was established at Brigham City, Utah, for Navajo students.

The Institute of American Indian Arts was opened in 1962 at Santa Fe, New Mexico, and in the same year, a demonstration school was organized at Concho, Oklahoma.

In 1972, the BIA opened the Southwestern Indian Polytechnic Institute at Albuquerque, New Mexico.

A year later, the then-nominee to the position of Commissioner of Indian Affairs stated, "the future of off-reservation boarding schools is a diminishing one." He went on to say that off-reservation schools should be phased out.[47] At that time, Intermountain School was scheduled to be closed down by 1975.

1. Rept. Com. Ind. Aff., 1854, pp. 112-113.

2. Lawrence F. Schemeckebier, op. cit., p. 65.

3. Rept. Com. Ind. Aff., 1901, pp. 22-23.

4. Rept. Com. Ind. Aff., 1883, p. 9.

5. Ibid., p. 165.

6. Lloyd E. Blauch, Educational Services for Indians, Staff Study No. 18. Prepared for the Advisory Committee on Education (Washington: Government Printing Office, 1939), p. 34.

7. Rept. Com. Ind. Aff., 1883, p. xxxii.

8. Rept. Com. Ind. Aff., 1901, pp. 20-21.

9. Rept. Com. Ind. Aff., 1883, p. xxxi. Other reports during the period under consideration use the term industrial training schools in reference to boarding schools. The superintendent at Fort Yates, South Dakota, however, labeled the school an agricultural boarding school. (Ibid., p. 311.)

10. Rept. Com. Ind. Aff., 1901, p. 19.

11. Rept. Com. Ind. Aff., 1902, p. 395.

12. U.S. Congress, Investigate Indian Affairs, Hearings Before a Subcommittee on Indian Affairs, House of Representatives, 78th Congress, 2nd Session (Washington: Government Printing Office), pp. 216-217.

13. Rept. Com. Ind. Aff., 1890, pp. clxvi-clxxxv.

14. Rept. Com. Ind. Aff., 1901, p. 418.

15. Ibid., p. 419.

16. Bureau of Indian Affairs, Education Division, Education for Action (Chilocco, Oklahoma: Chilocco Printing Department, 1944), p. 140.

17. Hildegard Thompson, "BIA Curriculum Guide for Overage High School Youth," Indian Education, No. 393, October 15, 1963, p. 2.

18. Ibid.

19. Rept. Com. Ind. Aff., 1855, pp. 17-18.

20. U.S. Congress, "An act making appropriations for the current and contingent expenses of the Indian Department and for fulfilling treaty stipulations with various Indian tribes for the year ending June 30, 1871, and for other purposes," July 15, 1870; 16 Stat. 335.

21. Lawrence F. Schmeckebier, op. cit., pp. 223-224.

22. U.S. Congress, "An act making appropriations for the current and contingent expenses of the Bureau of Indian Affairs, for fulfilling treaty stipulations with various Indian tribes and for other purposes, for the fiscal year ending June 30, 1920," June 30, 1919; 41 Stat. 3.

23. U.S. Congress, Investigate Indian Affairs, op. cit., pp. 113-114.

24. Bureau of Indian Affairs, Fact Sheet on BIA Programs and the American Indians (Printed on letterhead, undated), p. 1.

25. Department of the Interior, News Release, Office of the Secretary, August 8, 1972.

26. Bureau of Indian Affairs, Indian Record (Undated, no publisher indicated), 1974 Review, p. 2.

27. Rept. Com. Ind. Aff., 1888, p. xxi.

28. U.S. Congress, "An act making appropriations for the current and contingent expenses of the Indian Department, and for fulfilling treaty stipulations with various Indian tribes, for the year ending June 30, 1883, and for other purposes," May 17, 1882; 22 Stat. 68.

29. U.S. Congress, "An act making appropriations for the current and contingent expenses of the Indian Department, and for fulfilling treaty stipulations with various Indian tribes, for the year ending June 30, 1884, and for other purposes," March 1, 1883; 22 Stat. 433.

30. U.S. Congress, Senate Document No. 95, op. cit., p. 172.

31. U.S. Congress, "An act making appropriations for the current and contingent expenses of the Indian Department, and for fulfilling treaty stipulations with various Indian tribes, for the year ending June 30, 1889, and for other purposes," June 29, 1888; 25 Stat. 217.

32. Rept. Com. Ind. Aff., 1890, p. cxlvii-cxlx.

33. Rept. Com. Ind. Aff., 1883, p. xxxvii.

34. Rept. Com. Ind. Aff., 1887, p. 27.

35. Lawrence F. Schmeckebier, op. cit., pp. 70-76.

36. Rept. Com. Ind. Aff., 1883, p. xxxii.

37. U.S. Congress, "An act making appropriations for current and contingent expenses of the Indian Department and for fulfilling treaty stipulations with various Indian tribes for the fiscal year ending June 30, 1895, and for other purposes," 28 Stat. 286, August 15, 1894.

38. Felix S. Cohen, op. cit., p. 242.

39. Rept. Com. Ind. Aff., 1901, p. 39.

40. Rept. Com. Ind. Aff., 1904, pp. 32-33.

41. Ibid., p. 33.

42. Ibid., p. 39.

43. Evelyn C. Adams, American Indian Education, Government Schools and Economic Progress (Morningside Heights, New York: King's Crown Press, 1946), p. 52.

44. Institute of Government Research, The Problem of Indian Administration (Baltimore: The Johns Hopkins Press, 1928), p. 403.

45. Ibid.

46. U.S. Congress, Investigate Indian Affairs, op. cit., p. 341.

47. Daily Oklahoma, Nominee to BIA Cool on Boarding Schools, November 15, 1973.

CHAPTER 13

THE GENERAL ALLOTMENT ACT

The ending of Indian wars and the making of treaties and agreements started the thrust to relocate Indians upon their reservations. By the close of the American Frontier, most of the Indians had gone, forcibly or voluntarily, to areas set aside for their use and occupancy. At the Indian reservations, activities of the BIA continued to grow and expand as Congress passed laws for the economic, social, cultural and political rehabilitation of tribal members. From that time on, congressional laws have been the dominant source of growing Indian affairs, based mainly upon the guardian and ward relationship.

One of the congressional laws became the mainspring for further and more BIA activities. It was enacted on February 8, 1887, and was known familiarly as the General Allotment Act. It was also called the Dawes Act, taking the name of the Congressman who sponsored it. The act brought about BIA policies and subsequent legislation for approximately the next 50 years.

This chapter is about the General Allotment Act, the activities of the BIA originating from the act, the growth of the BIA because of it and the effect of the act and its administration upon the Indians.

AIMS AND PURPOSES OF GENERAL ALLOTMENT ACT

The General Allotment Act came about as the outcome of serious thinking about how to get Indians to apply their wisdom, individual initiative and self-responsibility to education, farming, stockraising, homemaking and other endeavors that characterized the settlers. Up to that time, efforts to civilize, or Americanize, them had pretty much failed, so they were not attaining the fullness and abundance offered by their new way of life. The General Allotment Act promised to change that failure to success.

The Commissioner of Indian Affairs in 1887 colorfully summarized the past failure and assurance of future success. Because of its importance in the history of the BIA, what he said is worth quoting at some length. He wrote:

... That hitherto, under tribal relations, the progress of the Indian toward civilization has been disappointingly slow is not to be wondered at. So long as tribal relations are maintained so long will individual responsibility and welfare be swallowed up in that of the whole, and the weaker, less aspiring will be the victims of the more designing, shrewd, selfish, and ambitious head-men ....

... He was taken a hostile barbarian, his tomahawk red with the blood of the pioneers; he was too wild to know any of the arts of civilization .... Hence some such policy had to be resorted to to settle the nomadic Indian and place him under control. The policy was a tentative one, and the whole series of experiments, expedients, and makeshifts which have marked its progress have looked toward the policy now made possible and definitely established by the allotment act ....[1]

When reservations were set aside for the use and occupancy of Indians, they were tribal or communal properties. No particular tribal member claimed any specific area on a tribal reservation. The entire reservation belonged to all the tribal members as community property. The tribe remained a unit, knitting the individuals together. Tribal relations, however, smothered the progress of Indians toward civilization, according to the Commissioner in 1887, and swallowed up individual responsibility.

The act of February 8, 1887, aimed to change this. It provided that in the discretion of the President, Indian reservations be surveyed, divided into tracts and put into individual ownership by allotment of tracts to the tribal members.

Each head of a family was to be allotted one quarter of a section of land, each single person over 18 and each orphan under 18, one-eighth of a section, and each other single person, one-sixteenth of a section. If the reservation were not large enough for these allotments, the size was to be reduced prorata.[2]

Lands remaining after allotment to all tribal members were declared surplus to the tribes. The act provided that surplus lands could be sold to the U.S. by the tribes. It required the U.S. to open the purchased surplus lands to homestead entry and settlement by non-Indians.

Funds derived from the sales of surplus lands were held in trust by the U.S. Treasury for the separate tribes to whom the different reservations belonged. They were called tribal funds. Interest at the rate of 3% was specified to be paid on these funds. The interest was subject to appropriation by Congress for the "civilization" of the Indians.

Tracts of land allotted to individual Indians were called allotments. Patents to allotments were to be held in trust by the U.S. in the name of the individual Indian allottees for 25 years. Indians were not allowed to sell their tracts during the trust period.

The act contemplated that an Indian getting an allotment would also acquire a pride of personal ownership by having a tract of land he could call his own. This would motivate him to exploit his land by farming and stockraising and to build and make a home for himself on the land. During the trust period, he would learn how to maximize the use of his land so that he could share in the wealth and prosperity of America.

At the end of the trust period, the act further contemplated, the individual Indian would have proved himself capable in the pursuits of his changed world. As a testimony to his capability, he would receive a certificate of competency and a patent in fee simple to his allotment of land. Thereafter he would be a citizen of the U.S. and cease to be a ward of the government.

When all Indians became citizens, the Indian problem would end.

ACTIVITIES OF THE BIA IN LAND MATTERS

In carrying out the provisions of the General Allotment Act, the BIA became eventually the manager of Indian lands, attending to all the details stemming directly from the act and all the offshoots springing from operation of the act.

The President put the program under way by selecting 27 reservations for allotment, and the BIA added 6 special agents to its staff. They were assigned to the Crow, Winnebago, Siletz, Lake Traverse, Yankton and Absentee Shawnee and Pottawatomie reservations. For some of the other reservations, the BIA entered into contracts with private individuals for the work. A special agent was also employed at the national BIA office to approve and certify the allotments made by the special agents and private contractors at the reservations.[2]

Surveying, dividing the lands into farming and grazing tracts and allotting the tracts to individual Indians were the main jobs of the special agents and individuals who contract ed to do the work. In time this work expanded to other reservations, and a new organizational unit came into existence in the BIA to perform the work. Special agents were absorbed into the new unit, and contracting with individuals to perform the jobs was discontinued.

Allotment of tracts to individual Indians sparked a number of other BIA projects.

One of the earliest of these additional activities was construction of irrigation systems for delivery of water to the separate tracts of allotted farming lands. Originally, these systems were confined to reservations. At many places, however, they were extended to the surplus lands homesteaded or otherwise acquired by settlers and others. After constructing the projects, the BIA took on the job of maintaining and operating the systems.

Another job of the BIA was to assist the Indian allottees in becoming farmers and livestock-men. To do this, the BIA procured equipment and material to fence tracts, clear the land and prepare it for cultivation. In addition, the BIA purchased seeds, implements, livestock, feed and other farming and stockraising articles and distributed it to the allottees. BIA employees called farmers showed Indians how to plow, sow and reap harvests.

Those were the principal duties stemming directly from the General Allotment Act. Other work had to be done as side effects of the act began to appear.

Not too long after allotments were made, it was discovered that some of the allottees were unable to work their land because they were physically or otherwise disabled. To overcome this situation, Congress passed an act in 1891. The act authorized the Secretary of the Interior to lease the tracts belonging to allottees whose age or disability prevented them from occupying or improving their allotments.[3] Moneys received from the leased lands were to be held in trust for the use and benefit of the individual allottees.

The Secretary of the Interior delegated this authority to the Commissioner of Indian Affairs, and the BIA, by this delegation, took over the task of leasing Indian lands. In most cases, the lessees were non-Indians.

The authority in the act was widened gradually by subsequent legislation and finally included all Indian lands. Thus the function of appraising land for rental value, preparing advertise-ments for bids, accepting bids and going over them, drawing up leases, collecting rents from lessees and administering the trust rental income developed into important activities of the BIA. In short, the BIA entered the real estate and banking business, especially on Indian reservations.

Another act came into being soon after passage of the General Allotment Act. This act was necessary to settle doubts about authority to determine heirs of allotted land. The General Allotment Act inferred that the Secretary of the Interior had the power. But inference was not enough. The act of May 27, 1902, was passed to confer the power definitely upon him.[4]

In time, this authority was delegated to the Commissioner of Indian Affairs. Gradually, the necessary staff to handle probates developed in the BIA. The work grew during the passing years with the increasing deaths of original allottees and the heirs.

Leasing Indian lands and determining heirs of allotted lands were 2 important activities in the BIA originating from the side effects of the General Allotment Act. Sales of Indian allot-ments became another important function of the BIA.

The General Allotment Act prohibited Indian allottees from selling their tracts of land during the trust period. When allottees died, their tracts passed on to their heirs in undivided interests. For various reasons, heirs were unable to make use of the inherited allotments. In-dian agents and other administrators didn't care to see the land remain idle, so they succeeded in getting the matter corrected by a subsequent act.

The act was passed on May 27, 1902. It authorized the sale of tracts belonging to heirs of allottees or of other heirs.[5] Five years later, on March 1, 1907, Congress passed another act to provide for the sale of tracts belonging to original allottees.[6] These 2 acts gave to the BIA the jobs of appraising allotments to determine sales prices, conducting sales, collecting sales income and distributing the money collected to the Indian landowners.

ACTIVITIES IN CULTURAL AND POLITICAL MATTERS

In carrying out the provisions of the General Allotment Act, Indian agents became the govern-ing authorities on reservations. Tribal units and tribal governments ceased to be recognized. In many cases, they faded into the past.

The Indian agent at the Fort Apache Indian Agency in 1902 described what was going on among Indians in general when he wrote, "An encouraging feature worthy of note is that most of these Indians are abandoning government by chiefs, councils and bands, and instead they are rapidly accepting the Government of the United States; the chief has lost most of his influence."[7]

The Commissioner of Indian Affairs in 1887 proclaimed, in effect, that no progress would be possible among Indians until tribal relations ceased to exist. Breaking up the political and social systems of Indian tribes became a policy and activity of the BIA.

The BIA set up goals to destroy the power of Indian chiefs, to splinter tribal cohesiveness, to fragment tribal relations and to break up the cultural matrix that was Indianhood.

Believing no synthesis of Indian and non-Indian cultures was possible, the Commissioner of Indian Affairs, during the latter part of 1901, issued a circular which became known as the "short-hair order." Addressed to Indian agents as instructions, the circular fully discloses the policy of the BIA on native Indian customs and practices and its vigor in wanting to stamp them out. The circular is so significant in describing the course of the administration of Indian affairs that it is worthy to be quoted in full. The circular reads:

Sir: This office desires to call your attention to a few customs among the Indians which it is believed should be modified or discontinued.

The wearing of long hair by the male population of your agency is not in keeping with the advancement they are making, or will soon be expected to make, in civilization. The wearing of short hair by the males will be a great step in advance, and will certainly hasten their progress toward civilization. The returned male student far too frequently goes back to the reservation and falls into the old custom of letting his hair grow long. He also paints profusely and adopts all the old habits and customs which his education in our industrial schools has tried to eradicate. The fault does not lie so much with the schools as with the conditions found on the reservations. These conditions are very often due to the policy of the Government toward the Indian, and often perpetuated by the agent's not caring to take the initiative in fastening any new policy on his administration of the affairs of the agency.

On many of the reservations the Indians of both sexes paint, claiming that it keeps the skin warm in winter and cool in summer, but instead this paint melts when the Indian perspires and runs down into the eyes. The use of this paint leads to many diseases of the eyes among those Indians who paint. Persons who have given considerable thought and investigation to the subject are satisfied that this custom causes the majority of the cases of blindness among the Indians of the United States.

You are therefore directed to induce your male Indians to cut their hair, and both sexes to stop painting. With some of the Indians this will be an easy matter; with others it will require considerable tact and perseverance on the part of yourself and your employees to successfully carry out these instructions. With your Indian employees and those Indians who draw rations and supplies, it should be an easy matter, as noncompliance with this order may be made a reason for discharge or for withholding rations and supplies. Many may be induced to comply with the order voluntarily, especially the returned students. The returned students who do not comply voluntarily should be dealt with summarily. Employment, supplies, etc., should be withheld until they do comply and if they become obstreperous about the matter a short confinement in the guardhouse at hard labor with shorn locks, should furnish a cure. Certainly all the younger men should war short hair, and it is believed by tact, perseverance, firmness, and withdrawal of supplies the agent can induce all to <u>comply</u> with this order.

The waring of citizens' clothing, instead of the Indian costume and blanket, should be encouraged.

Indian dances and so-called Indian feasts should be prohibited. In many cases these dances and feasts are simply subterfuges to cover degrading acts and to disguise immoral purposes. You are directed to use your best efforts in the suppression of these evils.

On or before June 30, 1902, you will report to this office the progress you have made in carrying out the above orders and instructions ....[8]

Rations and supplies were stipulated in treaties as partial payment for lands relinquished by tribes. They were intended to aid the Indians in a transition from their customary hunting to farming and stockraising. But under the General Allotment Act, rations were an economic weapon to the BIA. The weapon was used to force Indians to abandon their political institutions, their tribal relations, their native customs, dress, traits and other characteristics. If Indians failed or hesitated to do this, Agents were instructed, in effect, to starve them into submission. Indian employees who failed to comply were discharged or jailed.

The Commissioner of Indian Affairs in 1933 interestingly summarized the activities of the BIA in the cultural and political lives of Indians under the General Allotment Act. He wrote:

... To another, to exterminate the entirety of the Indian heritage became the central purpose of Indian affairs. Extermination was applied beyond the tribe and its government to the local community governments out of which the tribes were compounded, and beyond local governments to the family .... As tribe and local community crumbled under the pressure, remote authority had of necessity to be extended past the group to the individual and this authority was applied horizontally and vertically ....[9]

In addition to activities in the political and cultural lives of the Indians, the BIA continued many of the programs commenced in earlier days. Some of these were enforcement of law and order, construction and operation of schools and hospitals, building and maintaining roads and trails. The number of farmers, stockmen, teamsters, teachers, doctors, nurses, policemen and other personnel increased at the reservations and on up the line to give realness to the on-going projects and the new policies and programs initiated under the act of February 8, 1887.

ORGANIZATIONAL DEVELOPMENT

As the programs of the General Allotment Act were getting under way, the organization of the BIA began to expand. At first, the expansion was somewhat haphazard. But as time went on, positions were set up purposely to overcome troubles or accomplish specific tasks, and the structure of the BIA began to be refined for specialization of work.

Scandals of corruption and inefficiency in the BIA were not hushed for long after President Grant put in the system of appointing Indian agents selected by religious denominations. Further work was necessary to rid the BIA of mismanagement. Some of this work was keeping closer tab on what Indian agents and other administrators were up to among Indians.

This way of checking out Indian affairs brought about one of the first important changes in the structure of the BIA. A suborganization titled the Office of Inspector was set up in 1873. It had 5 inspectors whose duties were to visit Indian superintendencies, agencies and subagencies, take a hard look at management practices and the extent of compliance with laws, rules and regulations and bring about whatever adjustments were necessary.[10]

In 1879, Congress authorized the Secretary of the Interior to appoint special agents to perform duties similar to those of inspectors.[11] This legislation, by the use of the term special agents, made inspections more prominent and had the psychological effect of making Indian agents and other administrators think twice before getting into corrupt activities. As the system earned an important reputation, the need for superintendencies of Indian affairs lessened. With the passing of time, these superintendencies gradually vanished from the scene of Indian affairs.

Another important measure was taken to help tidy up the Indian field service and keep Indian agents and others free of temptations to become corrupt.

School superintendents were made subject to the Civil Service Act and were required to furnish bond for faithful performance of duties. After this went into effect, the management of agencies and reservation affairs was gradually taken away from Indian agents and given to school superintendents. This reassignment of duties continued until Indian agents were placed under civil service rules and required to furnish bonds.

Other changes in structural organization were generated by the nature of BIA activities and the growing volume of details.

In the early days of Indian affairs and reservations, the Commissioner of Indian Affairs and the Indian agents personally handled much of the work. But as BIA activities expanded by the implementation of the General Allotment Act, the volume of work grew to proportion too great for them to manage alone. Increasingly, too, the work became the kind that required specialists or persons with particular training and experience. To take care of these developments, responsibilities were divided. This brough about functional suborganizations called divisions and services in the BIA.

One of the earliest of these was the Finance Division. It was set up to handle technicalities of the budget process. An Accounts Division came into existence relatively early also to keep records of funds and accountable property. Other suborganizations followed. Growing Indian affairs caused increasing mails, filing, statistics and similar work. This created the need for an administrative suborganization titled the Records and File Division. Much of Indian affairs related to land, and many matters were legal in nature. For these functions, a Land and Law Division was organized.

A major division of duties occurred soon after the BIA began to construct and operate schools. Overall management of the school system was transferred from the Commissioner of Indian Affairs to a Superintendent of Indian Schools, a position established in 1882. In time, a functional suborganization called the Indian School Service developed.[12]

As a result of these early divisions of duties, the BIA in 1885 consisted in 5 suborganizations called divisions. These divisions were (1) Finance, (2) Land and Law, (3) Accounts, (4) Education and (5) Records and Files.[13] Other suborganizations were set up as BIA activities continued to grow.

In 1886, Congress created the Office of Assistant Commissioner of Indian Affairs to perform, among others, the duties of chief clerk for the BIA.[14] After the General Allotment Act was passed in 1887, the job of allotting lands to Indians was assigned to special agents who composed the Allotment Service.[15] Other matters related to land, such as leasing and land usage, formed the functions of a Land Division. This division was broken out and separated from the Land and Law Division.[16] In 1902, a chief engineer was appointed, and in time the position headed the Indian Irrigation Service.[17] The search for better management of forests on Indian reservations led to the establishment of a Forestry Division in 1910.[18] Other divisions emerged as Indian affairs continued to move in the direction of specialization.

Technicians who composed the staffs of divisions found, as time went on, that they had to be located near Indian reservations to perform their duties adequately and responsibly. To accommodate their findings, the U.S. was divided into geographical districts. Each district included a number of Indian reservations, and a headquarters called a district office was set up at a large city within the geographical area of each district. District offices were staffed with personnel skilled in the technical activities at Indian reservations, and they traveled to the reservations as required and necessary to do the work.

Before too long, however, district office technicians found they were not able to keep up with the increasing work by traveling to reservations. So Indian agents were authorized to set up positions and recruit employees whose main jobs paralleled the functions of divisions at the district and national offices.

As technicians became employed at Indian agencies, the work of the staff at district offices was more administrative and supervisory. District office personnel spent their time and efforts in developing plans, conducting studies, providing liaison between the national office and the Indian agencies and exercising general supervisory authority over the work at Indian reservations.

This newly-developed tri-level structure of the BIA and the administrative relationship existing between them continued with relatively minor changes during the era of the General Allotment Act.

RESULTS OF GENERAL ALLOTMENT ACT

The act of February 8, 1887, contemplated that Indians would acquire pride of personal ownership in land allotments and become contributing and self-supporting citizens by farming and livestock operations. A number of developments, however, prevented or impeded their progress.

Allotments were made to all tribal members regardless of their ages or physical abilities. Children, the old folks, the crippled and the otherwise disabled Indians could not work their allotments. Indians physically capable of farming or livestock operations encountered many difficulties.

The General Allotment Act wasn't supported adequately by funds for seeds, implements and equipment needed for successful farm and livestock operations. An observer of Indian affairs noted as early as 1889 that one of his Indian friends "had indeed a vast but unusual possession; a large land estate but without team, implements, money, houses, or experience, and consequently, without power to utilize a foot of it."[19]

This failure in the allotment system was observed by many others. But not much was done to overcome it. Appropriations lagged far behind the increasing need for funds.

The first 12 years of the General Allotment Act were from 1888 to 1900. For those years, a total of $105,000 was appropriated for the purchase of farm supplies, equipment and other items. During the same period, a total of 64,853 allotments was made, comprising 7,862,495 acres of land.[20] The total amount appropriated was approximately $1.62 per allottee, or about 1-1/3 cents per acre of allotted land.

In the following years, appropriations increased somewhat, particularly appropriations of tribal funds derived from the sale of surplus land. But they were not increased in proportion to the increasing need.

The quality and number of persons employed at the reservations to aid the Indians in becoming farmers and stockmen were neither adequate nor sufficient. A Land Planning Committee reported its study of this in the following words:

> ... Practical assistance to the Indians was limited to the appointment of Government "farmers" and "stockmen." As is well known, these employees were often poorly qualified and even if they had been able to stimulate and assist the Indians in farm work, their number was inadequate ....[21]

Administrators of Indian affairs who had the responsibility of allotting land tracts to Indians failed completely in taking account of the movement toward mechanization of farming which began more than 20 years before the General Allotment Act passed. The farming allotments they made were not large enough to make farming with the new gas-powered machinery economically profitable. Hundreds of acres could be farmed with machinery. A large amount of land had to be farmed to justify investment in machinery. On many reservations, however, allotments for farming were generally 20 acres. In some cases 40-acre and 60-acre farms were allotted. Since surplus lands were sold, it was impossible to increase the acreage of allottees to the size needed for mechanized farm operations.

Losses of land by Indians under the acts of February 8, 1807, May 27, 1902, March 1, 1907, and other acts and measures authorizing the sale or disposal of Indian lands are indicated by Table IV.

The table shows a total land loss of 87,623,456 acres. Details of the total loss are itemized in the table.

Table IV

INDIAN LAND SOLD AND ALIENATED 1887-1934[a]

Type	Acres
Surplus reservation land sold	22,694,658
Allotted land sold or alienated	23,225,472
Ceded reservation land	38,229,109
Miscellaneous losses	3,474,217
Total	87,623,456

[a]Compiled from: Indian Land Tenure, Economic Status, and Population Trends, p. 12.

These land losses reduced the area of Indian reservations from 130,730,190 acres to 43,035,734 acres.[22] In other words, Indians lost approximately 67% of their original reservation lands under the allotment system. Most of the land which remained in Indian ownership was economically unproductive or marginally productive.

Proceeds from sales of allotted lands weren't always spent on foot, clothing, homes and household articles. In 1901, the Indian agent at the Sauk and Fox Agency in Oklahoma, suggested what happened throughout the U.S. by reporting:

... Since July 1, 1900, there has been sold 16,438 acres of Absentee Shawnee and Potawatomi land, at from $2.50 to $40 per acre, amounting to $110,315.98. Of this sum, I feel safe in saying there is not $10,000 now in the hands of vendors, gamblers and saloons being recipients of the greater portion of it. Some few Indians have built homes for themselves, but such will not average over one per cent; the balance either expended what they received in dissipation, extravagant conveyances, or personal decoration. After the money is gone they live on their friends in affluence until compelled by circumstances to work or starve ....[23]

Indians whose allotments were sold became landless and, as such, could never achieve the aim of the General Allotment Act. By 1934, the number of landless Indians had swollen to approximately 100,000.[24] A year later, the Land Planning Committee reported "As a group, the landless Indians are the most maladjusted, helpless, and poorest of the entire Indian picture, which generally is one of deep poverty."[25]

Indians who were not landless found themselves trapped in a complexity known as fractionated heirship. A brief explanation of this heirship can show how it hindered Indians in their progress toward economic self-support.

Fractionated heirship had its beginning when the first original allottee died. His allotment became an estate, and when it was probated, his heirs received undivided interests in it. The undivided interests were expressed as fractions. For instance, when an allottee with 5 heirs died, the interest of each heir in the allotment was 1/5. The allotment remained intact, and the heirs claimed undivided interests in it. None of the heirs wanted to farm the allotment, and usually none of them had enough money to purchase the interests of the other heirs.

The complexity and intensity of fractionated heirship increased with the growing succession of heirs. Each succeeding heir inherited a smaller fractional interest. For example, if 1 of the 5 heirs died and he had 6 heirs, each heir would have a 1/6 undivided interest in the 1/5 interest, or a 1/30 undivided interest in the original allotment. Whenever any succeeding heirs died, fractional interests of their surviving heirs were calculated in this way.

Fractionated heirship has been carried so far at some of the reservations that heirs have undivided interests as small as 1/235,450 in a 20-acre allotment. That amounts to 3.7 square feet.

Indian lands in heirship status generally had to be leased out to non-Indians. Rent was collected by the Indian agents and distributed to the heirs in proportion to their undivided interests.

Soon after leasing Indian lands commenced, a policy was adopted by the BIA that worked a further hardship on heirs. The policy came into being when administrators of Indian affairs received the inspiration that Indian lessors ought to be charged a lease fee for all the work of the BIA in leasing the Indian land. A fee schedule was worked up starting with a minimum of 25¢ and graduating upward with increasing amounts of rent. The schedule applied to each heir and the amount of rent he was entitled to receive. The fee was deducted from each heir's share of rent, and the heir received whatever was left after the deduction.

The effect of this policy in many cases was that after the minimum 25¢ was deducted, nothing was left for the heirs. Sometimes the minimum fee was more than the heir's share of the rent. The BIA didn't adopt the policy of collecting the deficiency from the heirs.

Fractionated heirship is still one of the large problems in the administration of Indian affairs.

Results of the policy to exterminate or suppress native Indian customs and forms of government were described in the following words:

... Always through so many mediums, the Indian was told that as a race he was doomed to failure by social inferiority or impracticability. Always he was challenged to build a new personality out of no cultural heritage at all ....[26]

The General Allotment Act remained in effect for 47 years. In 1934, Congress passed an act that, in effect, repealed the General Allotment Act and introduced a new and different approach in administration of Indian Affairs.

1. _Rept. Com. Ind. Aff._, 1887, p. 6.

2. U.S. Congress, "An act to provide for the allotment of lands in severalty to Indians on the various reservations, and to extend the protection of the laws of the United States and the Territories over the Indians, and for other purposes," February 8, 1887; 24 _Stat._ 388. Allotments actually made ranged from 20 to 60 acres of farming land and from 160 to 320 acres of grazing land depending upon the size of the reservation allotted.

3. U.S. Congress, "An act to amend and further extend the benefits of the act approved February 8, 1887," February 28, 1891; 26 _Stat._ 794.

4. U.S. Congress, "An act making appropriations for the current and contingent expenses of the Indian Department and for fulfilling treaty stipulations with various Indian tribes for the fiscal year ending June 30, 1903, and for other purposes," May 27, 1902; 32 _Stat._ 245.

5. _Ibid._

6. U.S. Congress, "An act making appropriations for the current and contingent expenses of the Indian Department and for fulfilling treaty stipulations with various Indian tribes for the fiscal year ending June 30, 1908, and for other purposes," March 1, 1907 ; 34 _Stat._ 1015.

7. _Rept. Com. Ind. Aff._, 1902, p. 149.

8. _Ibid._, pp. 13-14.

9. John Collier, "Indians Come Alive," _The Atlantic Monthly_, 170:9, September 1942, p. 76.

10. U.S. Congress, "An act making appropriations for the current and contingent expenses of the Indian Department and for fulfilling treaty stipulations with various Indian tribes for the fiscal year ending June 30, 1874, and for other purposes," February 14, 1873; 17 _Stat._ 437.

11. U.S. Congress, "An act making appropriations for the current and contingent expenses of the Indian Department and for fulfilling treaty stipulations with various Indian tribes for the fiscal year ending June 30, 1879, and for other purposes," May 27, 1878; 20 _Stat._ 63.

12. _Rept. Com. Ind. Aff._, 1883, p. 315.

13. U.S. Congress, Senate Document No. 95, _op. cit._, p. 110.

14. U.S. Congress, "An act making appropriations for the current and contingent expenses of the Indian Department and for fulfilling treaty stipulations with various Indian tribes for the fiscal year ending June 30, 1887, and for other purposes," May 15, 1886; 24 _Stat._ 29.

15. _Rept. Com. Ind. Aff._, 1901, p. 728.

16. _Ibid._, p. 780.

17. _Rept. Com. Ind. Aff._, 1912, p. 6.

18. _Ibid._

19. Indian Rights Association, _Address by Professor Painter Before the Lake Mohonk Conference of the Indian Rights Association_ (Philadelphia: n.p.), August 18, 1889.

20. Land Planning Committee, _Indian Land Tenure, Economic Status, and Population Trends_ (Washington: Government Printing Office, 1935), pp. 28-32 and Table 6.

21. _Ibid._, p. 8.

22. _Ibid._, p. 13.

23. _Rept. Com. Ind. Aff._, 1901, p. 335.

24. Land Planning Committee, _op. cit._, p. 56.

25. _Ibid._, p. 14.

26. John Collier, _op. cit._, p. 78.

CHAPTER 14

THE INDIAN REORGANIZATION ACT

In the mid 1920's, thoughts began to develop and circulate that the General Allotment Act was more detrimental than beneficial to Indians and something ought to be done to stop some of the undesirable results. By the early 1930's, a new look about the whole sphere of Indian affairs had developed, and in 1934, Congress passed an act that virtually repealed the General Allotment Act and gave new direction to Indian affairs. The act was approved on June 18, 1934, and was called the Indian Reorganization Act.[1] Taking also the names of its sponsors, the act was known as the Wheeler-Howard Act.

In the general pattern of depression legislation, the Indian Reorganization Act was hailed as a New Deal for American Indians. Its proponents claimed it was built upon deep and enlightened insights about Indian affairs, in general, and Indians, in particular. The act promised to bring about self-sufficiency, economically and politically, among Indians and assure that Indianhood had a place and value in the American culture.

This chapter takes a look at the thinking behind the Indian Reorganization Act, indicates the purposes for the act, considers some of the programs under it and examines its effect among Indians.

UNDERPINS OF THE INDIAN REORGANIZATION ACT

A significant observation underlying the act of June 18, 1934, was that communally-owned reservations and tribal existence did not lessen or stifle individual effort and initiative among tribal members. When the General Allotment Act passed, 216 reservations were in existence. Of these, 118, including the Navajo reservation, were not surveyed and allotted. On the unallotted, or communally-owned, reservations, individual development and use of land had actually advanced. The classic example of land tenure and use was the centuries-old system of the United Pueblos.

Title to the land resides in the Pueblo people as a whole, but possession and use of the land is individual. A tribal member desiring land is assigned a tract by the tribal council. He or his family must farm the land or make beneficial use of it some other way. He is now allowed to sell it or dispose of it. For practical purposes of the Pueblo tribe, this is individual "ownership" of the land. The system is built upon the family as an economic unit, so when the assignee dies, the land passes into the "ownership" of the family, but never to outsiders.

On communally-owned reservations, title to the lands had been preserved for the Indians, and none of the lands were lost by sale of surplus areas or allotted tracts. This was an important underpin of the Indian Reorganization Act. A prediction in the early 1930's was that if the trend of land losses under the General Allotment Act continued, the third generation of Indians therefrom would be totally landless.

Another underpin of the act of June 18, 1934, was the value and necessity of the tribes and their governing bodies. These were entities to which Indians were culturally attuned. They should be promoted and developed, it was held, so they would be able to take over some of the management of Indian affairs on reservations and provide a stabilizing influence for individual Indians.

Behind the Indian Reorganization Act was the thought, also, that Indians, as citizens of the United States, were entitled to a fair share of the nation's educational heritage and the advances in health.[2]

Finally, it was held that the culture of the American Indians need not be sacrificed, but rather should be blended into the many cultures of America.

PURPOSES OF INDIAN REORGANIZATION ACT

The act of June 18, 1934, is a lengthy piece of legislation composed of terms and phraseology that usually characterize laws of the land. Its main purposes, however, were summarized by the chairman of the Committee on Indian Affairs, Senator Wheeler, a co-sponsor of the bill, in the following words:

> ... The purposes **of** the bill, briefly stated, are as follows:
>
> (1) To stop the alienation, through action by the Government or the Indians, of such lands, belonging to ward Indians, as are needed for the present and future support of these Indians.
>
> (2) To provide for the acquisition, through purchase, of land for Indians, now landless, who are anxious and fitted to make a living on such land.
>
> (3) To stabilize the tribal organization of Indian tribes by vesting such tribal organizations with real, though limited, authority, and prescribing conditions which must be met by such tribal organizations.
>
> (4) To permit Indian tribes to equip themselves with the devices of modern business organization, through forming themselves into business corporations.
>
> (5) To establish a system of financial credit for Indians.
>
> (6) To supply Indians with the means for collegiate and technical training in the best schools.
>
> (7) To open the way for qualified Indians to hold positions in the Federal Indian Service ....[3]

These purposes eliminated some of the work of the allotment system. But they gave rise to a number of new activities in the BIA and contributed to its further development.

PRELIMINARY ACTIVITIES

A special provision of the act of June 18, 1934, required that within 1 year an election be held on each reservation to determine whether or not the principles of the act were acceptable to the Indians. The act further provided that its principles would not apply to any reservation whose Indian population voted against it.[4]

In compliance with this special provision, administrators of Indian affairs held 9 preliminary regional conferences with Indians to acquaint the Indians with the purposes of the act and to ascertain their reaction to it. Following the regional conferences and under the general supervision of the reservation administrators, elections were held on 273 Indian reservations. The Indians at 196 of the reservations voted to accept the principles of the act.[5]

These favorable results were the green light for the BIA to go ahead with some of the other provisions of the act.

TRIBAL CONSTITUTIONS AND BYLAWS

Restoration of tribal governments, modified to agree with American democratic concepts, became a major function of the BIA. To get this job under way, the administrators composed constitutions and bylaws for each tribe that voted to accept the principles of the act. In broad context, the documents were similar. All of them contained the kinds of articles and provisions common to government constitutions. They differed in details to the extent necessary for application to each of the different tribes. For example, all the tribal constitutions provided for governing bodies. But they were not all called tribal councils. Another varying detail was the number of representatives specified for the governing bodies.

After developing constitutions and bylaws, the administrators met with tribal members and explained to them what the documents were all about, how they would be able to participate in the management of reservation affairs through elected representatives and what was necessary to get Indian self-government started. They then set up the machinery for the adoption of the instruments by popular ratification.

To be applicable, the document had to be ratified by a majority vote of the adult members of the tribe at an election in which at least 30% of the eligible voters cast a ballot. A ratified constitution authorized the tribal members to elect representatives from their tribe to make up a tribal council. The BIA helped in conducting the first elections of representatives and aided in organizing the tribal councils for their governing duties.

Promoting the first reservation self-governments kept the BIA busy for years that went into the 1940's. Up to that time, the Indians at 106 different reservations ratified the documents and organized tribal councils.

After a brief interruption for WW II, the BIA resumed the job of composing constitutions and bylaws for some of the remaining tribes. It also went about the job of obtaining ratification of them by tribal members and helping to get the governing bodies going. It also took on the job of updating the documents to enable tribes to cope more effectively and more adequately with the changing circumstances.[6]

The right to self-government through elected representatives was extended eventually to all tribes, including those who voted not to accept the principles of the Indian Reorganization Act. Many tribes that originally turned down the act ratified constitutions and bylaws and set up governing bodies when given the chance later. Among them was the Navajo tribe that established a 74-member tribal council for reservation self-government.

CORPORATE CHARTERS

Constitutions and bylaws were documents which provided for the tribes to organize for political purposes. In addition, the BIA developed corporate charters so tribes could form themselves into corporations to work on the economics of the reservations.

Charters were also similar in broad context, differing only in certain details for particular tribes. Purposes of tribal corporate existence were to further the economic development of the tribes, to secure assured economic injependence for tribal members and to provide for the proper exercise by the tribes of various functions performed by the BIA.

To get the tribes moving in the new economic direction, the BIA went to work to secure adoption of charters similar to the way it did for the constitutions. Practically all the tribes that ratified constitutions adopted corporate charters.

Constitutions and corporate charters provided for only very limited self-government. Both instruments were developed so that every action of material importance taken by governing bodies had to be approved by the Secretary of the Interior. At some of the reservations, superintendents dominated council meetings to assure that only actions that would be approved were taken up or even considered by the councils. At other reservations, superintendents handled the significant matters as official BIA business, and the tribal councils had little to do of any consequence. Superintendent was the new title under the Indian Reorganization Act for Indian agent.

A respected writer on Indian problems sees no way tribal councils can become the governing authorities on reservations. Tribal councils, he said, never can be fully self-governing. The reason for this, he explained is that the federal government is legally and ultimately responsible for all decisions and expenditures in Indian affairs, and the BIA cannot give up this responsibility to tribal councils. He went on to say that the requirement in the tribal consitutions for Secretarial approval of actions taken by tribal councils also makes self-government impossible.[7]

In the wake of the Civil Rights Act and the broad movements under it, tribal councils began to assert themselves more vigorously in reservation affairs. They have made progress in some of the activities. But up until 1975, the BIA was still seeing to it that tribal councils had very little to say about reservation budgets and appropriation requests although the instruments of self-government provided specifically for tribal participation in these important areas of reservation affairs.

PROMOTION OF CUSTOMS AND TRADITIONS

Indian lifestyles were strongly suppressed by policies of the allotment system. But the Indian Reorganization Act saw Indianhood as a valuable contribution to the larger culture of America. It frankly admitted that Indians could be Indians and, at the same time, become worthwhile and contributing citizens of the country.

The development of Indian arts and crafts was urged and made an acceptable endeavor at Indian schools and in Indian homes. The ban on the wearing of native costumes was lifted, and age-old rituals and ceremonials were reawakened in the tribal members. Pow-wows and other social gatherings began popping up on reservations, and Indians started to participate as Indians in local community celebrations near reservations.

Policies and programs of the General Allotment Act conditioned Indians to feel ashamed they were Indians. This was reversed by the Indian Reorganization Act. Nurturing pride in Indian heritage and culture became the theme of the new Indian policy. In this turn of events, Indian schools took an about face. Instead of trying to wipe out Indian culture, language and customs, they adopted the objective of giving students an understanding and appreciation of the cultural contributions their tribal arts have made to the literature, art, music and folklore of the U.S.[8]

The push of the greater minority movement in the 1950's and 1960's gave Indians a forward shove in this facet of Indian affairs. A Washington State University Indian student wore his warbonnet and Indian costume when he received his degree during graduation exercises in 1965. Indian candidates for graduation in 1968 had the BIA Institute of American Indian Arts in Santa Fe, New Mexico, start using Indian singers and a drum for the processional march. They've been a part of the marches since then. At colleges and universities across the country, Indian students formed Indian clubs, taking part in campus events as Indians and keeping other students aware of them as cultural identities. Indian students at some of the western colleges and universities arranged for an annual Indian Emphasis Week to acquaint the non-Indian students and people in the community with Indian dances, native foods, ceremonials and other Indian ways.

Beyond this, Indians are determined that public school teachers get some schooling in Indian culture. The National Congress of American Indians passed a resolution at the 1974 annual meeting in San Diego recommending that legislatures in states with significant Indian populations require the state departments of education to develop courses in history, tradition, customs, values, beliefs, ethics and contemporary affairs of Indians and include some of the courses among the certification requirements for teachers in primary and secondary schools.[9]

ECONOMIC REHABILITATION PROGRAMS

The Indian Reorganization Act spurred the BIA to renewed effort in promoting the economic development of tribes.

Land acquisition programs were initiated to broaden the greatly-reduced land bases of tribes. These programs included purchasing land adjacent to reservations and subjugating reservation areas to provide for more farms.

As a solution to the fractionated heirship status of land, consolidation of interests by exchange or purchase was undertaken to reestablish tracts of sufficient size for profitable farming and other purposes.

To finance Indians who wished to farm or raise livestock, the IRA established a fund known as the Revolving Credit Fund to be used for loans. A revolving cattle program was also initiated. It operated similar to the credit fund, but with cattle rather than money for loans.

A loan fund was established, also, to provide financial assistance to Indian students who were capable and desired to attend colleges or other institutions of higher learning.

In addition to the new programs, a number of earlier activities were broadened in scope. Irrigation systems were enlarged to accommodate new lands acquired or brought under subjugation. Extension services increased, and soil and moisture conservation programs were initiated, together with range improvement programs and other measures aimed at greater utilization of the reservation resources. Schools and hospitals increased in number and size to provide more adequate opportunities for better education and health among Indians.

The changing times gave still other activities to the BIA.

ACTIVITIES IN DEPRESSION YEARS

Commencing in 1934 and continuing through the depression years, Congress provided emergency funds for the BIA to develop among Indians the types of programs that were common under the broader plans for national recovery. Programs initiated and the work of the BIA in those years were described by the Commissioner of Indian Affairs in 1944, as follows:

... Funds were appropriated for the Indian C. C. C. and the Public Works Administration, and for road construction and for soil conservation. Those funds were all granted in flexible form and practically all of them were intended to be applied at the adult level and in the community. In the case of the C. C. C., the Indian Service obtained very broad authority for the utilization of C. C. C. money. We were not limited to the employment of youths only. We could employ Indians of any age. We were not under the Army. The management of the C. C. C. was liberal in construing our authorities ....[10]

The Commissioner described more fully the use of the funds provided during the depression years, particularly in relation to adult education. He said various emergency funds made it possible to start a program of adult education in terms of the realities of Indian life as lived locally. With the help of BIA employees, he said, Indians applied all the tactics of land utilization. They constructed buildings, handled machine tools, automotive equipment and other types of machinery. Some of them even learned about civil engineering, he reported. As many as 25,000 adult Indians at one time through successive years were involved in the programs.

Emergency-type programs were discontinued in WW II. Basic programs continued on a wartime basis and were pursued also without notable change in the years immediately following the end of the war.

ACTIVITIES DURING THE 1950'S AND 1960'S

During the decade of the 1950's, the dominant BIA policies were based on the thought that tribes who had reached a requisite degree of competency in self-government should be given complete management of their reservations and tribal affairs. In more familiar terms, this was called the termination policy. The object of the BIA was to terminate federal supervision over as many tribes as possible and to speed up the development of competencies in other tribes so that federal control of them could be terminated, too. This would end the guardian-ward relationship that existed for so many long years and was an increasingly expensive item in the federal budget.

This policy resulted in termination of federal supervision over the Menominee tribe of Wisconsin, the Klamath tribe in Oregon and various small groups of Indians in California and Utah. Among other tribes, certain of the BIA activities were transferred to other agencies. In 1953,

Indian hospitals and Indian health functions were transferred to the Public Health Service. In some parts of the country, particularly in the northwest, education was transferred to the states. These functions were no longer a responsibility of the BIA after they were transferred.

The avowed purpose of the terminations and transfers of activities was the eventual liquidation of the BIA. The end of the BIA would eliminate its cost in government operations.

Indians in general and many interested organizations and individuals were opposed to the termination policy. They began to gather the evidence to show that it was an unacceptable approach to the solution of Indian problems. One of the most influential in this behalf was a Task Force on Indian Affairs. Summarizing the effect of the policy among Indians, the Task Force observed and reported:

> ... Indians, fearful that termination will take place before they are ready for it, have become deeply concerned. Their preoccupation was reflected in vigorous denunciation of the so-called "termination policy" during the many hearings which the Task Force conducted with Indian leaders. No other topic was accorded similar attention. It is apparent that Indian morale generally has been lowered and resistance to transition programs heightened as a result of the fear of premature Federal withdrawal. Now, many Indians see termination written into every new bill and administrative decision and sometimes are reluctant to accept help which they need and want for fear that it will carry with it a termination requirement ....[11]

The Task Force was appointed by Secretary of the Interior Udall in February 1961, to look into Indian affairs. Consuming 5 months in its study, the Task Force appraised the termination policy and recommended that it be stopped. Placing greater emphasis on termination than on development, the Task Force reported, impaired Indian morale and produced a hostile or apathetic response which greatly limited the effectiveness of the Federal Indian program. The Task Force stated it was wiser to assist the Indians to advance socially, economically and politically to the point where special services were no longer required or justified. Then, the Task Force went on, termination could be achieved with maximum benefit to all concerned. If development rather than termination were emphasized, according to the Task Force, Indian cooperation which was essential for success could be expected.

In his annual report for 1961, the Commissioner of Indian Affairs announced adoption of the Task Force recommendations. He stated that a "New Trail" for Indians was the keynote of Indian affairs. The "new Trail," he said, contained the promise to Indians of equal citizenship rights and benefits, maximum self-sufficiency and full participation in American life. Commenting particularly on the termination policy, the Commissioner reported, "Probably the most important single recommendation was a shift in program emphasis away from termination of Federal trust relationship toward greater development of the human and natural resources on Indian reservations."[13]

STRUCTURAL CHANGES IN ORGANIZATION

The BIA developed into a refined tri-level organization in the allotment days. It consisted in the central office at Washington, D.C., several district offices located in different cities across the country and Indian agencies, off-reservation schools and a few detached offices at the local level. Overall management of Indian affairs was a responsibility of the central office. District offices exercised supervisory authority over the work at the Indian agencies and other local installations.

The tri-level structure was not changed under the BIA. But the responsibilities at each level were worked over, and that resulted in a redefined relationship between the levels of administration. General administration of Indian affairs at reservations was fixed on reservation superintendents. By this time the provisions of the Civil Service Act covered practically all positions in the BIA. Bonding of responsible jobs, such as reservation superintendents, coupled with improved accounting requirements and periodic audits had brought about a marked improvement in the conduct of reservation Indian affairs. School superintendents and all other personnel at agencies were made responsible to reservation superintendents.

The relationship of the central office to the Indian agencies was explained by the Commissioner of Indian Affairs in 1937, in the following words:

> ... The major principle of field administration is that the Superintendent of a jurisdiction is the responsible officer in that jurisdiction. He is responsible directly to the Commissioner of Indian affairs. There is no intervening administrative authority between him and the employees under his jurisdiction ....[14]

The Commissioner's explanation implies that no level of administration existed between the central office and the Indian agencies. That, however, was not the case. District offices were not abolished. They continued to be important in the administration of Indian affairs. But they became resource units. Their relationship was advisory and consultative to the reservation superintendents. They had no power to give directions to the superintendents or any other employees at the agencies.

Certain powers were delegated by the Commissioner of Indian Affairs to reservation superintendents. But the mass of administrative authority was reserved to and exercised by the central office in Washington.

This organizational arrangement was the structure of the BIA for about 15 years. During this time studies were conducted now and then to assess the efficiency of management operations. One of the studies was made by a congressional committee. A finding of the committee was that so much authority had been retained by the central office that superintendents and district offices were powerless in important matters directly affecting the development of tribes and their members.

For example, an Indian desiring a loan for over $1,000, was required to file an application with the superintendent. After due deliberation, the superintendent forwarded the application to the district office with his recommendation for approval. The district office, after considering the loan application and the superintendent's recommendation, sent the package with its recommendation for approval to the central office. When the central office finally got around to it in the backlog of work, the application was approved and returned to the district office for forwarding to the superintendent who notified the Indian applicant of approval.

The whole process consumed so much time that one disenchanted committeeman remarked the system ought to be revised and processing speeded up so an Indian who filed an application had a reasonable chance of getting the loan within his lifetime.[15]

In the late 1940's and early 1950's, decentralization of authority and responsibility was running a full course among private corporations. The concept found its way into the BIA.

The U.S. was redivided into areas. Districts and district offices were abolished. Installations called area offices were established in major cities within each area, and each area included a number of local installations. Administrative authority and responsibility, based upon the line-and-staff concept, ran from the Washington office to the area offices, and from the area offices to the Indian agencies and other local installations. Reservation superintendents became subject to control and direction of area offices.

Each area office was headed by an Area Director who was responsible to the Commissioner of Indian Affairs. A considerable amount of administrative authority was delegated by the Commissioner of Indian Affairs to the area directors.

Structural organization of the BIA by divisions was reexamined, and a pyramid of fewer divisions was built. The new divisions were placed under the general management of positions titled assistant commissioners at the central office and assistant area directors at the area offices. These positions were empowered with line authority for the respective division functions.

Divisions were composed of various branches at both the central and area office levels. Each branch was headed by a branch chief. An example is the Chief of the Branch of Personnel in the Division of Administration. Branch chiefs were staff to the heads of divisions.

Similar patterns of organization were established, when practicable, at Indian agencies and off-reservation schools. Certain functions, however, such as accounting, purchasing and other work classified undramatically as "housekeeping functions," were wiped out at local levels and centralized to area offices.

In the passing years, divisions and branches were structurally shuffled and reshuffled in frequent reorganizations. In the 1960's and 1970's, the reorganizations were so frequent that any chart of organization was practically obsolete by the time it was published. As a matter of fact, the BIA discontinued publication of organization charts for a few years. These were the years of the great surge in the minority movement. The BIA was one of the targets. Whenever it was hit--and that was quite often--its response was organization to better serve the Indian people.

In November 1973, the nominated Commissioner, Morris Thompson said, "It is unfortunage however that in recent months concern with reorganization and realignment appears to have been elevated to a high mission status." He vowed to put an end to all the shuffling and reshuffling and to settle the BIA down to its important jobs in Indian affairs.[16]

EFFECT OF IRA ON LAND PROBLEMS

The IRA prohibited allotment of land to individual Indians and made it virtually impossible for Indians to sell tribal lands and other lands, such as allotments, held in trust for them by the federal government. The restrictions were imposed to provide perpetual land bases on reservations for the future support of tribal members. The act contemplated a restoration of the land utilization plan said to be common to Indians, such as the system of the United Pueblos. These features were incorporated in tribal constitutions.

The Constitution and Bylaws for the Shoshone-Bannock Tribes of the Fort Hall Reservation, Idaho, approved April 30, 1936, is illustrative. Article VIII deals with the reservation lands. Section 12 defines tribal lands and specifies the uses of the lands, as follows:

... The unallotted lands of the Fort Hall Reservation, and all lands which hereafter be acquired by the Shoshone-Bannock Tribes or by the United States in trust for the Shoshone-Bannock Tribes, shall be held as tribal lands, and no part of such land shall be mortgaged or sold. Tribal lands shall not be allotted to individual Indians but may be assigned to members of the Shoshone-Bannock Tribes, or leased, or otherwise used by the Tribes as hereinafter provided ....

This section declares that all unallotted lands on the reservation and all lands acquired thereafter by the tribes are tribal, or communally-owned lands. It permits the tribes to assign tracts of land to individual tribal members.

Two types of assignment are permissable. One of them is called a standard assignment. Section 4 of Article VIII in the Shoshone-Bannock constitution is about standard assignments. It states the purpose and conditions of standard assignments in the following words:

... In any assignment of tribal lands which are now owned by the tribes or which hereafter may be acquired for the tribes by the United States or purchased by the tribes out of tribal funds, preference shall be given, first, to heads of families which have no allotted lands or interests in allotted lands.
. . . .
Assignments made under this section shall be for the primary purpose of establishing homes for landless Indians, and shall be known as standard assignments ....

To receive a standard assignment of land, an individual Indian is required to make application to the tribal council, showing his need for the land and the use he plans to make of it. If he receives a standard assignment and fails to use the land for a period of 2 years or uses it for unlawful purposes, his assignment is subject to cancelation by the tribal council.

When an Indian holding a standard assignment dies, the land reverts back to the tribe. However, his heirs or other individuals designated in a will or by a written request are given preference in reassignment, if they are otherwise eligible for a standard assignment.

Exchange assignments are provided in Section 6 of Article VIII of the Shoshone-Bannock constitution, as follows:

> ... Any member of the tribes who owns any restricted or unrestricted land or any interest therein may, with the approval of the Secretary of the Interior, voluntarily transfer his interest in such land to the tribes in exchange for an assignment to the same land or other land of equal value. If the assignee prefers, he may receive, in lieu of a specific tract of land, a proportionate share in a larger grazing unit.
>
> Assignments made under this section shall be known as exchange assignments ....

An Indian who inherited undivided interests in one or more allotments could consolidate his interests into one tract of land by an exchange assignment, if the exchange were agreeable to the Secretary of the Interior. Land acquired by exchange need not be operated, farmed or otherwise used by the assignee. It may be leased out to Indian cooperative associations, tribal members or non-Indians. When the assignee of an exchange assignment dies, the land is treated in probate the same as if it were allotted land.

The land articles and sections in the constitution of the Shoshone-Bannock tribes are representative of the kind of articles and sections in other tribal constitutions.

EFFECT OF IRA ON FINANCIAL PROBLEMS

The Act of June 18, 1934, authorized an appropriation of $10,000,000 for an Indian revolving credit fund. The fund was established nationally in the BIA for tribes and tribal corporations to borrow to establish revolving credit funds of their own at the reservations.

To obtain a loan, a tribal council had to sign a loan agreement and pledge adequate security or sign a promisory note. The loan agreement provided for a nominal rate of interest, originally 1%. The tribal council was required to include a statement with the loan agreement showing what the borrowed money would be used for.

One of the uses of borrowed funds was to relend the money to tribal corporate enterprises, to cooperatives or associations formed by tribal members and to individual Indians. Tribes could derive from 1% to 3% interest on the loans it made. Borrowers from the tribal revolving credit fund were required to sign loan agreements and promisory notes, pledge adequate security and detail the use planned for the money.

The theoretical operation of the revolving credit fund system can be shown by illustration.

Suppose an Indian tribe wanted a loan to set up a reservation loan fund so its members could borrow money to go into the farming or livestock business.

The tribal council applied for the loan, signed a loan agreement and a promisory note. The application was made, technically, to the Secretary of the Interior, but, for practical purposes, to the BIA through the reservation superintendent.

When the loan was approved, a portion of the national revolving credit fund was set aside for the use of the tribe. In the accounting processes, the amount of borrowed money was taken out of the national fund account and put into an account for the tribe at the Indian agency.

The tribe had to use the money for the purpose stated in the loan agreement. In this illustration it is assumed the funds were to be reloaned to individual members of the tribe.

A tribal member needing a loan filed an application with the reservation superintendent. When approved, the application effected a transfer of the borrowed account from the tribe's account to the borrower's account. The loan had to be used for the purpose stated on the application.

Carrying the illustration further, suppose the borrower's purpose for the loan was to get into the farming business. With the borrowed funds, he purchased equipment, seeds and other necessary articles, under the supervision of the superintendent or one of his subordinates. For these transactions, the superintendent issued government checks. Essentially, the checks were drawn on the account of the borrower and were posted as withdrawals on his account.

In time, the crops matured, and the borrower sold some of his harvest. From the proceeds of the sale, he repaid the loan in accordance with the terms of his loan agreement.

Money repaid was put back into the tribe's account and could be used in making other loans. This particular feature of the system allowed for the expansion of credit and was the reason for calling the fund a revolving credit fund. The money could be loaned, repaid, loaned again, repaid and the process continued over and over again.

The tribe was required to repay its loan in accordance with the terms of its loan agreement. The money repaid went back into the national fund and was available for relending to the same or to other tribes.

A revolving cattle program was also initiated. It operated in the same way as the revolving credit fund. However, instead of a loan of money, a borrower received cattle from the tribal herd. He repaid his loan in kind.

Table V shows the extent to which Indian participated in the revolving credit fund system during the first 10 years of its operation.

Table V

LOANS UNDER REVOLVING CREDIT FUND SYSTEM[a]
Totals to June 30, 1944

Type of Loans	Amount	Percent
Individual Indian loans	$4,569,285	63.93
Corporate enterprises	2,057,468	28.79
Indian cooperatives	520,412	7.28
Totals	$7,147,165	100.00

[a]Compiled from: Annual Report of Revolving Credit
Operations, 1944.

Congress authorized the amount of $10,000,000 for the capital of the fund. Actually, though, it had appropriated to June 30, 1944, only $4,273,400. Table V shows loans expanded to almost double the amount of the appropriated funds. Loans to individual Indians accounted for more than half the loan expansion.

Over the years since 1944, the financing of tribes, their enterprises, their cooperatives and their members increased. In 1963, the Commissioner of Indian Affairs reported that up to then about $23.7 million had been appropriated for the "BIA credit program." Loans totalling more than $48 million had been made since the program commenced. $30.5 million was repaid, and $236,000 was canceled, he said. The balanced was outstanding and not due.

Prior to 1961, the average amount of loans to tribes from the fund was about $1.5 million a year. In the next 2 years, loans to tribes swelled to nearly 4 times that. About $2 million was loaned to tribal organizations for relending to individual members. Approximately $3.5 million was loaned to tribally-owned enterprises, such as sawmills, livestock herds, pasture improvements and the operation of salmon canneries in Alaska. Another $350,000 was used to attract industries to establish plants on or near reservations.[17]

The Commissioner's report of 1963 covered other methods of credit. Among these was the use of monies, called tribal funds, belonging to the Indian tribes. Nearly $26 million of tribal money was being used in tribal credit programs at the close of fiscal year 1962. More tribal funds would be available for credit operations in the future, the report stated, as judgments were awarded by the Indian Claims Commission in compensation for tribal claims against the U.S.[18]

The report disclosed, too, the financial assistance of commercial banks and other lending institutions. "Financing of Indian enterprises from such sources had nearly quadrupled over the past decade," the report stated, "rising from $22 million in 1952 to $85 million in 1962."[19]

In November 1973, an American Indian National Bank was opened at Washington, D.C. It is owned, operated and controlled by Indian businessmen and stockholders. The bank was organized to attract money belonging to Indians that usually goes into the checking and savings accounts of local banks across the country where Indians reside. With the pooled funds of individual Indians and tribes, the American Indian National Bank promised to become another available source of money for use in credit operations of Indian tribes and their members.[20]

1. An act to conserve and develop Indian lands and resources; to extend to Indians the right to form business and other organizations; to establish a credit system for Indians; to grant certain rights of home rule to Indians; to provide for vocational education for Indians; and for other purposes, June 18, 1934; 48 Stat. 984.

2. The act of June 2, 1924 (42 Stat. 253), conferred U.S. citizenship on all Indians born within the territorial limits of the U.S. Previous to the act, only those Indians who had followed the method provided in the General Allotment Act were citizens of the U.S.

3. U.S. Congress, Senate Report No. 1080, 73rd Congress, 2nd Session, To Conserve and Develop Indian Lands and Resources (Wheeler-Howard Bill), May 10, 1934, p. 3.

4. By the act of June 15, 1935, the time for calling elections was extended 2 years (49 Stat. 78).

5. U.S. Congress, Investigate Indian Affairs, op. cit., p. 20.

6. Rept. Com. Ind. Aff., 1963, pp. 45-46.

7. E. Schusky, The Right to be Indian (San Francisco: The Indian Historian Press, Inc., 1970), p. 43.

8. 62 IAM 401.01, July 13, 1951.

9. National Congress of American Indians, Resolutions, 31st Annual Convention (Washington: NCAI, November 13, 1974), p. 23.

10. U.S. Congress, Investigate Indian Affairs, op. cit., p. 3.

11. Report to the Secretary of the Interior by the Task Force on Indian Affairs (Mimeographed pamphlet), July 10, 1961, p. 5.

12. Ibid., p. 8.

13. Rept. Com. Ind. Aff., 1961, p. 277.

14. U.S. Congress, Investigate Indian Affairs, op. cit., p. 107.

15. Office of Indian Affairs, Order No. 481, Field District Plan, June 21, 1937, p. 2.

16. Statement of Morris Thompson Before the Senate and Insular Affairs Committee November 14, 1973, IERC Bulletin 1:8, December 1973 (Albuquerque: Indian Education Resources Center), p. 2.

17. Rept. Com. Ind. Aff., 1963, pp. 32-33.

18. Ibid., p. 32.

19. Ibid.

20. Circular letter of AINB dated March 1974.

CHAPTER 15

ORGANIZATION STRUCTURE OF BUREAU OF INDIAN AFFAIRS

The structure of the BIA developed over many years into a 3-level organization consisting in a central office, several area offices and a number of local installations known as Indian agencies, off-reservation schools and irrigation projects.

This chapter examines in detail the organizational structure at each administrative level of the BIA. Structures are described as they existed in the mid 1960's, and corresponding charts of organization are presented. Changes in structural detail have occurred since that time as the result of administrative ideas about how best to accomplish the work in Indian affairs. In the early 1970's, these changes were frequent.

Because changes do occur, it is not possible to present organization charts that would be always right up to date. Up-to-the-moment charts are not necessary for illustration. The charts and descriptions in this chapter are sufficient to illustrate the structure at each level and the relationship of the levels to one another.

The basic structure and the administrative relationship between them do not change. Reorganizations put in and take out suborganizations and shuffle them around. But the 3-level structure survives.

BUREAU UNDER DEPARTMENT OF THE INTERIOR

The BIA is a suborganization of the Department of the Interior and is under the general supervision of the Assistant Secretary of the Interior--Public Land Management. The position of Assistant Secretary has been described as follows:

> ... The Assistant Secretary exercises Secretarial direction and supervision over the Bureau of Indian Affairs , Bureau of Land Management, Nation Park Service, Office of Territories, The Alaska Railroad, and the Bureau of Outdoor Recreation ....[1]

The Commissioner of Indian Affairs is responsible to the Assistant Secretary for the execution of congressional laws, Department of the Interior orders, rules and regulations and policies related to the administration of Indian affairs. To carry out this function, the Commissioner is assisted by heads of suborganizations that compose the central office of the BIA in Washington, D.C.

ORGANIZATION OF CENTRAL OFFICE

An organization chart of the BIA appears as Figure 1. The chart shows the structure of the central office, consisting in various offices and divisions. It also illustrates the line of authority and responsibility from the area offices to the local installations. The chart is dated August 28, 1964.

The broad scope of Indian affairs is indicated by the titles of the offices, divisions and branches.

The Office of the Commissioner consists in the Commissioner of Indian Affairs, an Assistant to the Commissioner and an Assistant Commissioner Legislation.

Under the Office of the Commissioner are the Public Information and Reports Office, the Deputy Commissioner and the Associate Commissioner.

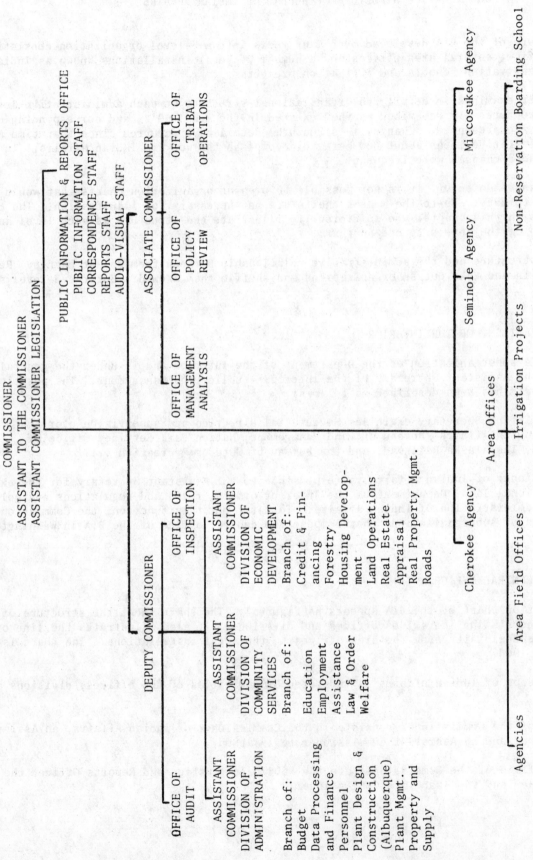

FIGURE I - ORGANIZATION BUREAU OF INDIAN AFFAIRS

112

The Public Information and Reports Office is made up of the Public Information Staff, the Correspondence Staff, and Reports Staff and the Audio-Visual Staff.

The Associate Commissioner is responsible for the operations of 3 suborganizations called the Office of Management Analysis, the Office of Policy Review and the Office of Tribal Operations.

Under the Deputy Commissioner are the Office of Audit, the Office of Inspection and 3 Divisions, each of which is headed by an Assistant Commissioner. The 3 Divisions are the Division of Administration, Community Services and Economic Development. The Program Planning Staff is a part of the Division of Economic Development.

Divisions are composed of branches. For instance, the Division of Community Services is composed of the Branch of Education, the Branch of Employment Assistance, the Branch of Law and Order and the Branch of Welfare. These branches and the branches that compose the 2 other divisions are shown on the chart.

Each branch is headed by a position called Chief, such as the Chief, Branch of Forestry and Chief, Branch of Personnel. Branch chiefs and heads of offices are technical experts in the areas of Indian affairs and management they head. The names of the branches and offices suggest their broad functions. For example, the Branch of Education is headed by a professional educator and handles the education activities of the BIA.

The Office of the Commissioner has under it, also, the Cherokee Agency, the Seminole Agency, the Miccosukee Agency and the Area Offices.

Indian agencies, area field offices, irrigation projects and off-reservation boarding schools are shown on the chart to be under the administrative direction of the area offices.

The chart clearly shows the BIA as a tri-level organization consisting in the central office, the area offices and the local installations.

ORGANIZATION AT AREA OFFICES

To illustrate the organizational structure of area offices, the chart of the Gallup Area Office, largest of such offices, appears as Figure II.

The chart shows the organization as it existed prior to a reorganization which took place in the last half of the 1960's. The reorganization brought about a new area office, called the Albuquerque Area Office, renamed the Gallup Area Office to the Navajo Area Office and redefined geographical jurisdictions of the two area offices. The fact that charts are outdated by reorganizations indicates usually that structural changes were necessary for functional realignment. Organization changes in response to changing or increasing activities and in the interest of efficiency. The chart shown as Figure II, however, is adequate for illustrative purposes. It ties in with the chart of the central office shown as Figure I.

In essence, the organization of the Gallup Area Office is similar to the central office organization. The Office of Area Director consists in the Area Director, a Relocation Specialist, an Assistant to the Area Director, 2 Administrative Assistants, a Secretary and a Clerk-Stenographer.

Under the Area Director are 3 divisions corresponding to the central office divisions. The various branches of the Area Office divisions also correspond to the branches of the central office. The different Indian agencies and the non-reservation boarding school under the jurisdiction of the Area Director are named on the chart.

Although it is not indicated on the chart, each of the divisions is headed by a position titled Assistant Area Director. Titles of the heads of branches differ. For example, the Branch

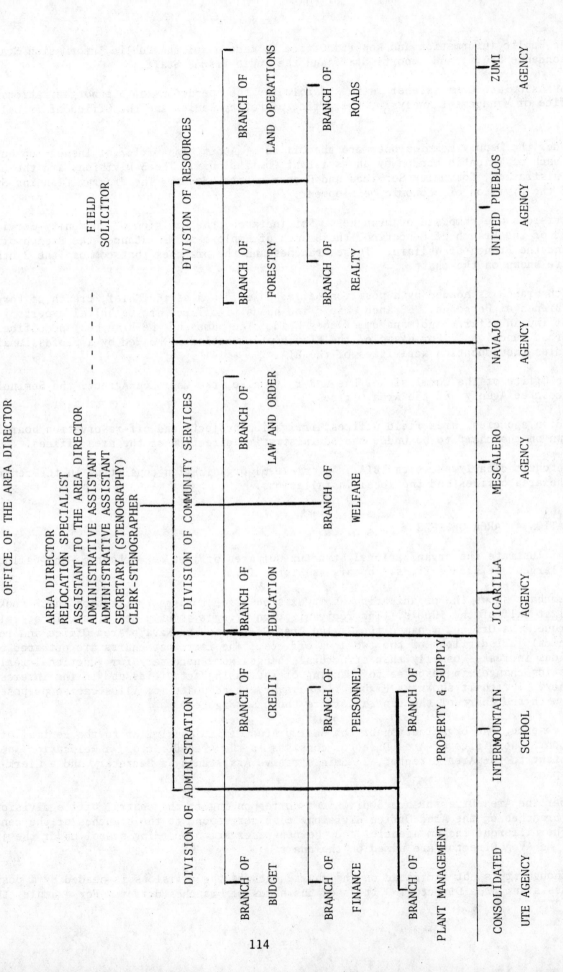

OFFICE OF THE COMMISSIONER

OFFICE OF THE AREA DIRECTOR

AREA DIRECTOR
RELOCATION SPECIALIST
ASSISTANT TO THE AREA DIRECTOR
ADMINISTRATIVE ASSISTANT
ADMINISTRATIVE ASSISTANT
SECRETARY (STENOGRAPHY)
CLERK-STENOGRAPHER

FIELD
SOLICITOR

DIVISION OF ADMINISTRATION

BRANCH OF
BUDGET

BRANCH OF
CREDIT

BRANCH OF
FINANCE

BRANCH OF
PERSONNEL

BRANCH OF
PLANT MANAGEMENT

BRANCH OF
PROPERTY & SUPPLY

DIVISION OF COMMUNITY SERVICES

BRANCH OF
EDUCATION

BRANCH OF
WELFARE

BRANCH OF
LAW AND ORDER

DIVISION OF RESOURCES

BRANCH OF
FORESTRY

BRANCH OF
REALTY

BRANCH OF
LAND OPERATIONS

BRANCH OF
ROADS

CONSOLIDATED
UTE AGENCY

INTERMOUNTAIN
SCHOOL

JICARILLA
AGENCY

MESCALERO
AGENCY

NAVAJO
AGENCY

UNITED PUEBLOS
AGENCY

ZUMI
AGENCY

FIGURE II - ORGANIZATION GALLUP AREA OFFICE

114

of Finance is headed by an Area Finance Officer, and the Branch of Personnel is headed by a Chief, Personnel Branch.

Assistant area directors are line officers in matters involving the responsibilities of the divisions they head. The heads of branches are staff positions in the divisions.

ORGANIZATIONAL STRUCTURE OF NAVAJO AGENCY

The structure of the BIA at Indian agencies can be illustrated by the organization at the Navajo Agency as it existed before the reorganization of the Gallup Area Office. The organization chart is not included.

Overall responsibility for BIA activities on the Navajo Reservation is fixed upon a reservation superintendent whose official title is General Superintendent. The immediate staff of the General Superintendent is made up of assistant agency superintendents who head agency divisions paralleling divisions at the Gallup Area Office.

Agency divisions are similar in composition to the divisions at the Area Office. For example, the agency Division of Community Services has suborganizations corresponding to the branches of the Area Division of Community Services. Each agency suborganization is headed by a Director. An example is the agency Director of Schools.

Assistant agency superintendents for the Navajo agency are empowered with line authority. Agency directors are staff to them.

The Navajo Reservation is subdivided for administrative purposes into 5 subagencies. Each subagency is headed by a Subagency Superintendent. The organization of the subagencies corresponds as nearly as possible to the Navajo agency organization.

Subagency superintendents have been delegated line authority in the administration of Indian affairs pertaining to the subagencies.

Indian reservations other than the Navajo Reservation are not generally subdivided into subagencies. The reservation superintendent is responsible for Indian affairs for the entire reservation. With this exception, agency organizations are similar to the Navajo agency structure.

ORGANIZATIONAL STRUCTURE OF INTERMOUNTAIN SCHOOL

Before going into the organization structure, it may be well to comment briefly on the general nature of Intermountain School.

Largest of the schools operated by the BIA until 1970, Intermountain School is an off-reservation boarding school. Authorized enrollment is 2,150. For the most part, its students are academically one or more years behind non-Indian students of the same age who attend public schools. Students, therefore, are categorized as overage.

Intermountain School commenced operations in 1950 as a special program school for Navajo youngsters whose English-speaking ability and academic backgrounds were quite deficient. The School developed in the passing years to include an accredited high school. For several years, the School consisted in an elementary, junior high and senior high. However, beginning with the school year 1964-65, the 8-4 plan was adopted, and the designations junior and senior high were subsumed under the term high school.

The head of Intermountain School is titled School Superintendent, and the administrative relationship between the School Superintendent and the Area Director is the same as between the General Superintendent of the Navajo Agency and the Area Director. This relationship is stated in the Indian Affairs Manual as follows:

... Non-reservation Indian boarding schools shall be under the direction of the Area Director. Under the direction of the Area Director, Superintendents shall be responsible for the overall education program of the schools ....[3]

Overall education programs at off-reservation schools are considered to be all activities of the BIA at the schools. They include, in addition to classroom and related activities, such functions as plant operation, procurement of supplies and property management. These functions are not primarily among the responsibilities of reservation school superintendents. Superintendents of off-reservation schools are empowered with line authority for operation of the schools.

The organization chart for Intermountain School is shown as Figure III. The chart shows that the overall administration of Intermountain School is a function of the School Superintendent under the direction of the Area Director. Activities of the School are subdivided into 5 broad areas, as follows:

Branch of Instruction
Branch of Guidance
Branch of Administration
Student Enterprises
Student Placement

In the order appearing above, the heads of the subdivisions are the Principal, the Director of Guidance, the Administrative Manager, an Education Specialist (Student Enterprises) and an Education Specialist (Student Placement).

The dental clinic and the hospital are shown on the chart as USPS Health Center. The facility is located on the School campus and is administered by the U.S. Public Health Service. Its operation is not included among the administrative functions of the School Superintendent.

The organization for Intermountain School is interesting enough to be looked at in more detail.

The Branch of Instruction consists in an Academic Elementary Department, an Academic High School Department, a Home Economics Department, a Vocational Department and a Student Records Unit. Each department has a department head at the top. The Student Records Unit is headed by a registrar. Department heads and the registrar compose the immediate staff of the Principal.

Two suborganizations, called Elementary I and Elementary II, each under an assistant department head, compose the Academic Elementary Department. Elementary I provides educational programs for students in grades 5 and below. Sixth, 7th and 8th grade instructional programs are provided by Elementary II.[4]

The High School Department is subdivided into mathematics, science, English and social studies. For these subdivisions, there are 2 assistant department heads, one for mathematics and science and one for English and social studies.

The Vocational Department is subdivided into Industrial and Trades-Mechanical studies. For each, there is an assistant department head, known as a Section Head.

The Home Economics Department is not subdivided. Its organization, however, includes an assistant department head.

The school employs approximately 110 teachers. Most of them are under the supervision of assistant department heads.

The Branch of Guidance consists in 2 guidance departments corresponding to the 2 academic departments, a physical education department and a food services department. Both guidance departments and the physical education department are headed by positions titled department heads. A steward is in charge of the food services department.

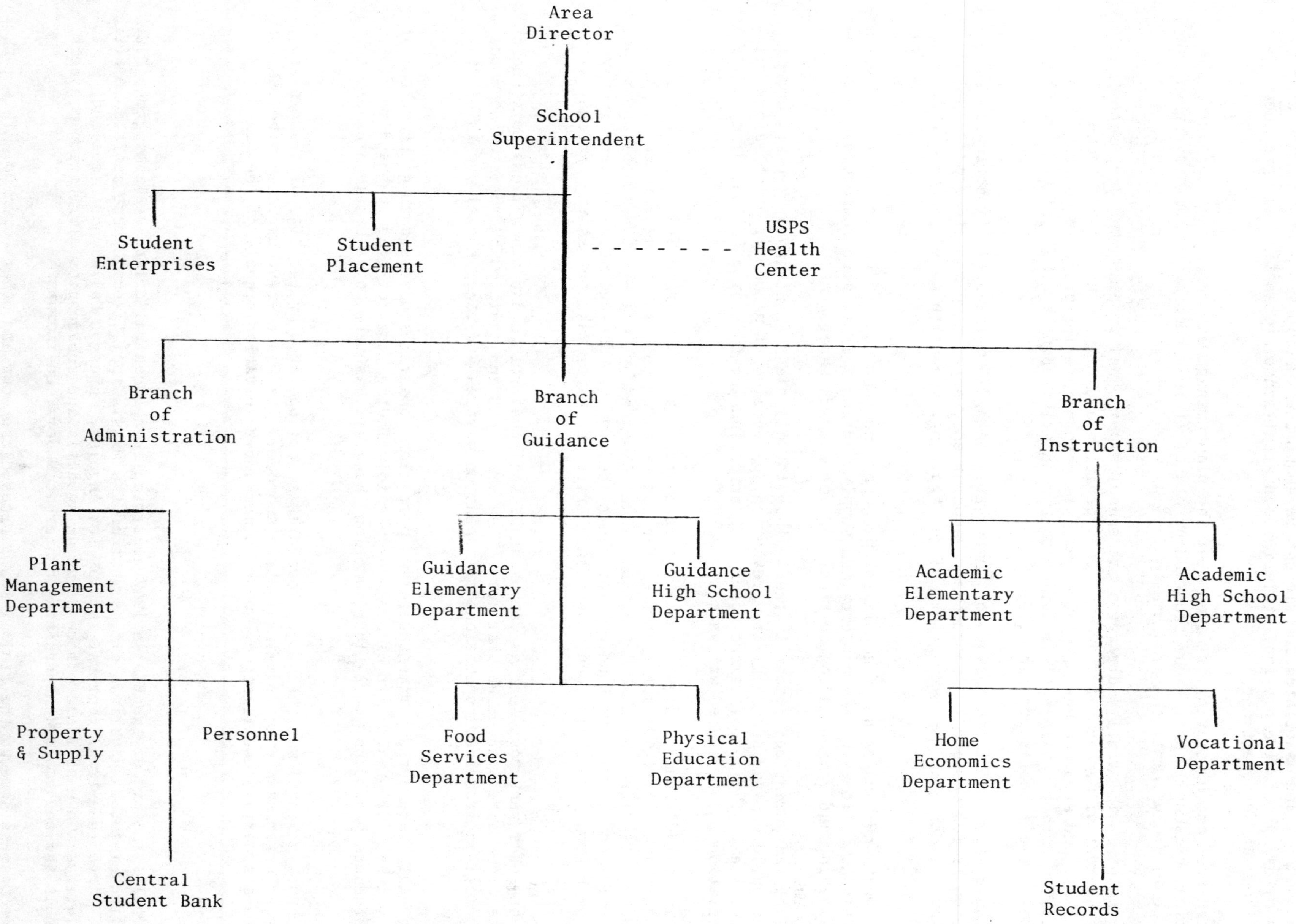

FIGURE III

ORGANIZATION FOR ADMINISTRATION - INTERMOUNTAIN SCHOOL

Student housing and associated activities are among the functions of the guidance departments. School-day physical education, athletics and after-school recreation are provided by the physical education department.

The branch of administration is made up of the plant management department, property and supply section, personnel section and the student bank. It is headed by an administrative manager. Stated in broad terms, the branch:

... Provides administrative direction the school's personnel program, the procurement and management of Government property, the operation and maintenance of plant and facilities, and student banking operations. Is responsible for preparing budgets and financial programs. Serves as assistant to the Superintendent in the over-all administration of the school's programs ....[5]

The suborganizations in the branch of administration perform the detail functions. The personnel section is responsible for recruitment, appointment, separation and other personnel actions and for directing and assisting in employee training, incentive awards, merit promotions and other programs.

Procurement and management of government property and supplies and control over vehicles are among the responsibilities of the property and supply section. It is also responsible for providing duplicating and communication services and for records management.

The plant management department is responsible for all plant maintenance, repairs and alterations to buildings and streets, fire prevention, protection of property, plant safety and custodial services. The school campus covers 300 acres and includes over 200 buildings, some of which are interlocked by covered walkways.

Accounts of individual students and of student groups are maintained by the student bank. Receiving and disbursing funds are a part of the functions of the bank. These funds are student monies on deposit with the bank. They are not funds provided by Congress for school operations. The bank receives deposits from students for their checking and savings accounts, and it pays out or disburses money to the students when they write checks or make out savings account withdrawal slips.

Quasi-business ventures, such as campus shops sell confections and other items to students. The ventures are called student enterprises. They are owned and operated by the student council, and profits derived from their operations are spent on parties and other social events of students.

The student placement department develops part-time jobs for students during the school year and summer months. Originally, it was responsible for finding jobs for graduates and for following up on students placed on jobs. That function, however, was taken over by the Area Office in 1960.

Intermountain School was the biggest boarding school operated by the BIA. Its administrative structure was larger than other off-reservation schools. Its basic structure, nevertheless, was common, with appropriate modification, to the other off-reservation schools of the BIA.

SUMMARY

The total structure of the BIA in 1967 consisted in the central office at Washington, D.C., 11 area offices located in various cities west of the Mississippi, 7 employment assistance offices situated at large industrial centers, such as Los Angeles, Chicago, Dallas and Cleveland, 97 local installations known as field offices, Indian agencies and subagencies, irrigation projects, Indian schools and one employment training center at Madera, California.[6]

As time passes, some of the field installations close down and others open up. This causes fluctuations in the numbers, but does not affect the tri-level structure.

1. Office of the Federal Register, National Archives and Records Service, General Services Administration, United States Government Organizational Manual, 1965-66 (Washington: Government Printing Office, 1966), p. 230. In the early 1970's a movement began to elevate the Bureau of Indian Affairs to Assistant Secretary of the Interior status, and a bill to accomplish this was introduced into Congress in early 1974.

2. At the time this book was being written, the Bureau of Indian Affairs was undergoing rapid reorganizations. The first of these occurred in 1965 when the Branch of Education was elevated to Division status. Other changes were made in the passing years. In 1973, an "Interim Chart" was published, dated August 10. The Chart shows that suborganizations called offices replaced divisions and some new offices were added. Divisions replaced branches, the chart shows, and branches were eliminated. The chart retains the basic structure of the Central Office as presented in this chapter.

3. Bureau of Indian Affairs, Indian Affairs Manual, Vol. VI, Part II, Chapter I, Section 102.03, September 28, 1951.

4. Intermountain School, General Information Bulletin, August 1967, p. 8.

5. Ibid., p. 12.

6. Bureau of Indian Affairs, Directory of Field and Central Offices, May 15, 1967 (Lawrence, Kansas: Haskell Printing Department, 1967).

CHAPTER 16

THE NEW TRAIL

The enduring purpose for federal government activities on Indian reservations is to promote the development of Indian tribes and their members so they may contribute to and share in and enjoy the abundance of American life. The General Allotment Act and the nearly 50 years of Indian affairs following it aimed to achieve that purpose. That was the reason also for the Indian Reorganization Act and the activities of the BIA since 1934.

Now and then over the years, the direction or major emphasis of Indian affairs was announced in a somewhat striking manner. At those times, the BIA stole the national spotlight for a few moments as it adorned the long-time purpose of Indian affairs with fetching terms. For instance, the activities of the General Allotment Act were proclaimed to be programs for the "emancipation" of the tribes. The Indian Reorganization Act, hurled by the Roosevelt thrust, was the "New Deal" for American Indians. Catch words were used again in 1961 when the BIA announced a "New Trail" for Indians.

The "New Trail" promised to lead the tribes and their members to maximum economic self-sufficiency, full participation in American life and equal citizenship responsibilities and privileges.

This chapter takes a ride on the "New Trail," looks at some of the trail markings and finally assesses how well it led to its promises.

REVERSAL OF TERMINATION POLICY AND PROGRAMS OF NEW TRAIL

During the 1950's, programs of the BIA were geared to eventually and the guardian-ward relationship. The ultimate objective was to rid the federal budget of the BIA expense by turning over reservation Indian affairs to the Indians and letting them manage their own affairs. The programs of those days were lumped into plans known as the "termination" policy.

In giving effect to this policy, the Klamath, Menominee and several Utah tribes were released from federal supervision. Several other tribes were scheduled to be released one by one over a period of years as the Secretary of the Interior determined that each had attained sufficient competency to manage its own affairs.

Tribes that saw what happened to Indians who were terminated wanted no part of the program. They made their opposition to the policy known to a Task Force on Indian affairs established in 1961 to come up with ideas about how to speed up achievement of the ages-old purpose for Indian affairs. The Task Force found that the fear of termination among tribes actually hampered the government in providing assistance and help sorely needed and wanted by the Indians.

Indian tribes had, in fact, turned down proposals for the development of reservation economics and for improvements in Indian education and health. The Indians felt that if they accepted any help it would trigger the mind of the Secretary of the Interior to decide summarily that they were willing and able to manage their own affairs. The Secretary of the Interior would then release them from federal supervision. This the tribes did not want. So they did not go along with some of the programs.

To overcome the resulting impasse, the Task Force recommended that the termination policy be abandoned and that renewed emphasis be placed on development of the human and natural resources of Indian reservations.

The BIA announced, in 1961, the end of the termination policy and its adoption of the Task Force recommendations. Constituting the "New Trail" for Indians, the Task Force recommendations included the following items:

1. More vigorous efforts to attract industries to reservation areas,

2. An expanded program of vocational training and placement,

3. Creation of a special Reservation Development Loan Fund and enlargement of the Indian Revolving Credit Fund,

4. Establishment of a statutory Advisory Board on Indian affairs,

5. Negotiation with States and counties, and resort to the courts, where necessary, to make certain that off-reservation Indians are accorded the same rights and privileges as other citizens of their areas,

6. Collaboration with States and tribes to bring tribal law and order codes into conformity with those of the States and counties where reservations are located,

7. Acceleration in the adjudication of cases pending before the Indian Claims Commission, and

8. More active and widespread efforts to inform the public about the status of the Indian people and the nature of their problems.[1]

It is not possible to go into all the programs of the New Trail nor to tie them down to the items listed. Some of the recommendations were given a great deal of attention. Others, very little. Some, too, were subsumed in governmental programs developed for the well-being of the whole nation. Nevertheless, a few of the more prominent activities can be looked at here.

AREA REDEVELOPMENT ACTIVITIES

The Area Redevelopment Administration was organized in the Department of Commerce on authority of the act of May 1, 1961. Soon after that, the Secretary of Commerce and the Secretary of the Interior agreed to let the BIA carry out provisions of the law that applied to Indian reservations and Indian tribe.

The agreement provided that the BIA develop criteria and formulate standards for Indian reservations to be designated "reservation redevelopment areas." This designation entitled the tribes to obtain financial assistance provided by the act. By August 1961, 48 reservation areas, including 4 in Alaska, had been classified as reservation redevelopment areas.

Having accomplished this, the BIA shifted its major emphasis to assisting tribes in planning the overall economic development programs required by the law. These plans pointed up existing economic conditions and problems on reservations, described potentialities for upgrading local economies and providing job opportunities, and proposed specific programs to achieve the potentials.[2]

Two years later the Commissioner of Indian Affairs summarized the results of the plans in terms of on-going activites, as follows:

... 675 Indians took part in 19 training programs of the Area Redevelopment Administration in Indian communities of 5 States, and an undetermined number of others participated in ARA training programs in non-Indian communities. Eighteen different occupations were involved in the 19 ARA Indian-community projects ....[3]

The Commissioner went on to say that the BIA and the ARA were working on off-reservation training programs and finding jobs in cities for trainees. An outstanding example of the cooperative effort, he mentioned, was the movement of 35 Indians from Arizona and New Mexico reservations to Los Angeles where they completed a basic electronics course and then moved directly into jobs.

In the following years, the BIA continued to implement reservation redevelopment programs. In time, however, these programs lost their separate identity in the broader program of vocational training.

INDUSTRIAL DEVELOPMENT

One of the markings on the New Trail was to exert more vigorous effort to attract industries to reservation areas. These industries would provide both immediate employment opportunities and on-the-job training to Indians.

In this program the BIA acted somewhat as a negotiator. It worked closely with tribal organizations to obtain the support of the tribes and their members for the industries. At the same time, the BIA maintained liaison with industrial concerns interested in new plant locations, pointing up the advantages of locating on or near reservations.

To help in this work, the Indian tribes agreed to put up money to construct buildings and obtain equipment for industrial companies that would lease the facilities for long periods of time. New plants opened up in this way also trained Indians in manufacturing processes when the BIA made contracts with the plants and paid them to train the Indians. Trained men and women were then able to take subsequent full-time jobs at the plants.[4]

The Commissioner of Indian Affairs in 1963 commented on newly-established plants. His remarks show quite clearly the work of the BIA in attracting new industries to reservations and the support of the tribes in the industrial development. For this reason, he is quoted somewhat at length, as follows:

... The most noteworthy new plant to begin operations in Indian country during fiscal 1963 was an electronics establishment on lands of the Laguna Pueblo west of Albuquerque, New Mexico. The tribal group agreed to construct a $440,000 building to house the operation and to lease it to the company. The BIA helped the arrangement in a liaison capacity and provided financial assistance through an on-the-job training contract. The plant is expected to provide jobs eventually to 200 or more Indian workers.

Arrangements were also completed in fiscal 1963 for a plant to manufacture hair curlers and similar cosmetic aids on the Cherokee Reservation in North Carolina. This will be the third industrial plant for that reservation. It is expected to employ about 200 at full operation ..., the tribe will construct a $250,000 building to house the operation and make building and equipment available to the company under a 25-year lease. The Bureau has agreed to help through an on-the-job training contract ...[5]

From beginnings such as these, the project of attracting new industrial plants to or near reservations began to expand. During July 1, 1963 to June 30, 1964, a total of 21 new plants commenced operations. Six months later, a study showed there were 55 private industrial and business enterprises established on or near reservations.[6] By 1967, that number had doubled, providing more than 9,000 jobs.[7] In addition, in 1967, Indians in on-the-job training at these plants numbered 1,344.[8]

The work of the plants ranged from diamond processing to the manufacture of underwear.

ADULT VOCATIONAL TRAINING

Adult vocational training began in 1956 with the enactment of the Indian Vocational Training Act. Each year thereafter, it became increasingly more important in the lives of the Indians. At the end of 7 years, the Commissioner of Indian Affairs reported:

... Fiscal 1963 was a peak year for vocational training of Indians. During the year, 2,911 trainees were enrolled in vocational schools across the country under the Bureau's program. This was 549 more than the 1962 total, or an increase of more than 20 percent. Of the 1963 trainees, 1,164 were carried over from the previous year and 1,747 entered training. When family dependents are included, 5,047 persons benefited from the 1963 operations ....[9]

By 1966, vocational training courses in 125 different occupations had been approved for Indians by the BIA. The courses were established at accredited schools in 26 states. Schools providing the vocational training were located in both urban centers and on or near reservations.[10]

Vocational training continued to expand. In the fiscal year 1968, approximately 8,000 Indians received adult vocational training, either school type or on-the-job.[11]

Adult vocational training was the spinoff to another program that gave employment to many Indians.

RELOCATION FOR DIRECT EMPLOYMENT

The Task Force of 1961 recommended expansion of a program commenced in 1952 to relocate Indians in urban centers where employment possibilities were more numerous and promising than at Indian reservations. The program was commonly called "relocation." Under it, the BIA provided financial assistance to Indians who desired to move away from their reservations to major cities, such as Los Angeles, Cleveland, Denver and certain other large cities, for direct employment on jobs.

Results of the program during 1963 were reported as follows:

... The total family units or unattached individuals assisted in this way was 1,696, compared with 1,866 for 1962; the total number of individuals involved was 3,318, compared with 3,494. The decreases reflected BIA's greater emphasis on vocational training as preparation for the steadier and better paying types of employment ....[12]

In addition to relocating Indians in urban centers for jobs, the BIA helped an additional 2,052 family heads or unattached individuals find jobs, temporary or permanent, on or near reservations. Many qualified for this employment through on-job training in industrial plants on reservations.

The Commissioner reported that more and more Indians were able to obtain adequate employment near the reservations and in urban centers because they had the kind of job skills industrial companies needed.

In the years following 1963, relocation for direct employment increased. The program defrayed the costs of transportation for Indian families or unattached individuals and provided for living expenses during the period of time considered necessary for the relocations to become self-supporting.

The program was in operation for 20 years during which more than 100,000 Indians were relocated in 8 major cities. In 1972, the Commissioner of Indian Affairs announced the abandonment of the program and said that the funds would be used for job programs on reservations. Relocation by then amounted to $40 million annually.[13] The program was not stopped, however. It remained in operation under the name of Employment Assistance.

ACCELERATED PUBLIC WORKS PROGRAM

For those Indians who did not choose to leave the reservations, a sizeable program called Accelerated Public Works Projects was initiated. This program had the two-fold purpose of providing at-home employment to Indians and of developing and improving the reservation.

The program had 4 principal reservation development and improvement objectives, as follows:

1. Upgrading Indian-owned timber stands,

2. Conserving of soil and water,

3. Improving reservation roads, and

4. Constructing community centers.

The work done on these objectives was described by the Commissioner of Indian Affairs in 1963. He stated that forests on Indian reservations were managed on the basis of sustained yield and well-balanced multiple use. Specific projects included the thinning of overcrowded young stands to promote better growth of select trees, pruning to produce knot-free timber of greater value, cleanup of roadsides to improve scenery and reduce fire hazards, construction of fire-reaks and providing campgrounds and other picnic facilities.

Soil and water conservation projects were designed to meet local needs and conditions. These projects were developed primarily to control soil erosion and to increase forage production. One kind of conservation involved the fencing of Indian rangelands to promote better use of the range. Another kind concentrated on brush and weed eradication and range reseeding. By eliminating low-grade plants that compete with grass, by uprooting noxious weeds and by other similar eradication measures, forage production was increased by as much as 15 to 20 times. Another type of conservation project carried out on many reservations was the construction of small dams to control floods and store water for livestock and recreational use.

Road projects ranged from improvement of trails used principally for the protection of forests to complete construction, surfacing and upkeep of reservation roads. In 1963, this kind of work was performed on 88 roads totaling 651 miles on 38 different reservations.

Construction of community centers was also an objective of the Accelerated Public Works Program. The Commissioner of Indian Affairs reported on this phase in 1963, as follows:

... Allocation of the APW funds also made it possible for the BIA to build long-needed community centers on many Indian reservations to house tribal gatherings and promote greater cohesion of tribal populations. Nine such constructions were undertaken in Alaska and 14 on Indian reservations in the other States. All but three were completed by year's end ....[14]

The BIA was allocated $12 million for the Accelerated Public Works Program. During the fiscal year 1963, 86 projects were under way on Indian reservations in 18 states. The projects provided over 17,000 man-months of employment for Indians. By the end of the fiscal year, over 5,500 Indians were working on reservation public works projects.

INDIAN-OWNED BUSINESS ENTERPRISES

In addition to public works type of economic development on reservations, the BIA conducted studies to explore the feasibililily of various kinds of business enterprises that might be developed by tribes, and it helped the tribes to start some of the businesses.

A number of initial studies were conducted to find out how practicable it would be to develop tourist attractions on reservations. These vacation areas were to be tribally-owned and operated and would create additional jobs for reservation Indians. They would also bring revenues into the tribal treasuries. Studies for tourist attractions were made on the Pyramid Lake Reservation in Nevada, the Warm Springs Reservation in Oregon, the Allegany (Seneca) Reservation in New York, the Crow Creek and Lower Brule reservations in South Dakota, the Hopi Reservation in Arizona, the Nez Perce Reservation in Idaho and the Navajo Reservation, particularly in the four-corners area.

Studies to determine the possibilities for tribal businesses were made also. For instance, on the Quinault Reservation in Washington and the Kotzebue area of Alaska, the feasibility of food processing industries was examined. The commercial utilization of forest products was studied on the Blackfoot and Rocky Boy's reservations in Montana, the Wind River Reservation in Wyoming and the Navajo Reservation.

Encouraged by the favorable findings of these initial studies, the BIA made appraisals for tribal enterprises on many other Indian reservations. In all, more than 80 of these studies were conducted during the 4-year period ending in 1964.

These studies became realities during the following years in a variety of tribal enterprises, particularly million- and multimillion-dollar luxury recreation facilities and vacation resorts. A few of them are illustrative.

Campsites, picnic grounds, boating and fishing facilities were set up on the Fort Apache Reservation in Arizona.

The Indians of the Cherokee Reservation in North Carolina constructed a motel, gift shop, restaurant and a dramatic playhouse.

An olympic-size pool, a convention center, a cabin-motel complex, a 9-hole golf course, trailer sites, riding and hunting trails were built by the tribes inhabiting the Warm Springs Reservation in Oregon.

On the Mescalero Reservation in New Mexico and the Rocky Boy's Reservation near Billings, Montana, the Apache tribe and the Chippewa and Cree tribes, respectively, established ski lifts, lodges and ski schools.

Motels, convention centers, campsites, gift shops, boating, horseback riding and fishing facilities, restaurants and other accommodations were opened on the Seminole Reservation in Dania, Florida, on the Miccosukee Reservation near Miami, on the Navajo Reservation in Arizona and on the Uintah and Ouray Reservation in Utah.

In fact elegant and plush vacation resorts and convention centers sprang up on many other Indians reservations across the country. To make it known that the facilities were available to tourists and for conventions, the BIA produced a pamphlet titled "Vacationing With Indians." The pamphlet described in detail the facilities available, their locations, fees charged and other pertinent material.

In addition to tourist attractions, some of the tribes went into production-type businesses.

One of the most noticeable of these was the Cherokee Nation Industries, Inc. This tribal-owned enterprise consists in 2 plants. One plant is located at Stilwell and the other at Tahlequah, Oklahoma. The Stilwell plant manufactures intricate electrical telephone relays for the Bell Telephone Company. At the Tahlequah plant, seat covers are made and carpents are cut into finished patterns for American Airlines planes. All of the more than 100 employees are also a part of the Indian owners of the plants.

Other tribes entered the business world by setting up service concerns and various other types of manufacturing plants. The Navajo tribe took over operation of a giant lumber industry on the reservation. In addition, it owns and operates an enterprise that makes maps for the U.S. Geological Survey. The Ute Indians on the Uintah and Ouray Reservation in Utah became owners and operators of a concern that makes prefabricated furniture. The Gila River Indian Enterprises in Arizona and the Cherokee Snowbird Sewing Enterprises at Robinsville, North Carolina are two Indian-owned and operated textile plants.

Many other businesses were established by the various Indian tribes. In 1973, the Secretary of the Interior reported there were 475 Indian-owned enterprises in existence on Indian reservations. "Some will fail," he stated, "but most will succeed."[15]

Examples of the various products manufactured by these concerns are panelized homes, prefabricated houses, mobile homes, metal furniture, tinned tubing, lumber, leathercraft, tool boxes, carpet yarn and matresses. Service enterprises include laundromats, filling stations, cafes, amusement centers and the like.

FORMAL EDUCATION

Education activities of the BIA comprise the largest collective function in terms both of manpower and dollars. Nearly 1/3 of the employees in the BIA are engaged in activities related to education. About 40% of these employees are teachers, administrators and other personnel directly involved with the students in the learning situation. About 1/3 of the annual multi-million dollar annual appropriations of the BIA is devoted to the construction of school facilities and operation of the school system.

The BIA philosophy of education is to help develop each personality to its full stature and maturity and to equip each Indian child with the abilities, skills and understandings which will permit him to live harmoniously, productively and happily in a changing democratic society.[16]

During fiscal year 1964, the BIA operated 263 schools, 82 of which were located in Alaska. Eight of these schools were classified as boarding schools, on and off reservations, 163 as day schools, 11 as trailer schools, 4 as instructional-aid schools and 5 as hospital schools. Enrollment at these schools totaled 46,090 students.[17]

In the decade preceding 1964 and on into 1973, the number of Indian schools declined slightly each year. Enrollment, however, increased during the period. This seeming incongruity reflects the efforts of the BIA to fill every available seat before building new schools.

Admission to Indian schools is governed by the general rule that the schools are for students of 1/4 or more Indian blood for whom no other educational opportunities are available. An exception to this rule is at the Cherokee Agency where enrolled children of less the 1/4 Indian blood are permitted to attend federal schools.

The bulk of Indian schools in 1964 were elementary schools, although 27 schools offered a full 4-year high school program and 14 provided training at the secondary level at less than the 4-year course. Three of the schools were technical institutions. They were Chilocco Indian School at Chilocco, Oklahoma, the Institute of American Indian Arts at Santa Fe, New Mexico, and Haskell Institute at Lawrence, Kansas. At these 3 schools, general high school academic offerings were available in grades 9 through 12, and vocational education was concentrated in grades 13 and 14.

Nearly two-thirds of all the Indian students enrolled in school attend public schools. One-third of the students attend Indian schools, and the greater number of these go to Indian schools located on the reservations. Off-reservation schools enroll about 20% of the students who attend Indian schools.

Off-reservation schools in operation during the 1964-65 school year are shown in Table VI.

Since the 1964-65 school year, there have been some changes in the off-reservation schools. Haskell Institute developed into a junior college, and the Southwest Indian Polytechnic Institute came into existence at Albuquerque, New Mexico. The Concho Demonstration School and the Cheyenne-Arapahoe School were consolidated and renamed the New Concho Indian School. The Wingate Vocational School became the Wingate Elementary and Wingate High School. These changes were the major ones that occurred in the 10-year period ending with the 1973-74 school year.

In the early 1960's, Indian high schools graduated an average of about 1,200 students each year. An official of the BIA reported in 1964 that "the number of students graduating from Bureau High Schools totalled 1,320 in school year 1963-64, an increase of 256 over the pervious year."[18]

About 10 years later, in the early 1970's, graduates from Indian high schools had increased to an average of over 1,900 annually. The number of graduates reported for 1970-71 school year was 2,090.[19] In the following school year, 1,958 students were graduated. A year later in the 1972-73 school year, the number of graduates dropped to 1,685.[20]

A report in 1969 by a Senate Special Subcommittee on Indian Education was quite illuminating about dropouts at Indian high schools. Findings of the subcommittee were that about 40% of the

Table VI

OFF-RESERVATION INDIAN SCHOOLS--1965[a]

Name of School	Location
Flandreau School	Flandreau, South Dakota
Wahpeton Indian School	Wahpeton, North Dakota
Pierre Indian School	Pierre, South Dakota
Haskell Institute	Lawrence, Kansas
Chilocco Indian School	Chilocco, Oklahoma
Cheyenne-Arapahoe School	Concho, Oklahoma
Concho Demonstration School	Concho, Oklahoma
Riverside Indian School	Anadarko, Oklahoma
Wingate Vocational School	Fort Wingate, New Mexico
Aneth Boarding School	Aneth, Utah
Albuquerque School	Albuquerque, New Mexico
Institute of American Indian Arts	Santa Fe, New Mexico
Intermountain School	Brigham City, Utah
Seneca Indian School	Wyandotte, Oklahoma
Sequoyah Vocational School	Tahlequah, Oklahoma
Phoenix Indian School	Phoenix, Arizona
Sherman Institute	Riverside, California
Chemawa Indian School	Chemawa, Oregon
Stewart Indian School	Stewart, Nevada

[a]Compiled from: Bureau of Indian Affairs, Fiscal Year 1964
Statistics Concerning Indian Education, pp. 16-20.

students in Indian schools on reservations drop out before graduation, and no more than about 28% of the Indian high school graduates go on to college.[21]

Five years later, in 1974, the Commissioner of Indian Affairs said that in 1970, 1/3 of all Indians 25 years and over had completed high school, up from less than 1/5, or 20%, in 1960. He also reported that the median years of education Indian people achieved in 1970 was higher by 1.4 years than the median of 8.4 years in 1960. In the 20-24 age group, he further said, the median years of education for Indians was 12.2, which was higher than the national median of 12.1 years.[22]

The BIA does not operate colleges. It does provide grants, loans and scholarships to Indian students and helps students to obtain aid from other sources. Financial assistance to Indian college students has been on the increase year by year. In 1969, 3,500 Indian students participated in the $3 million higher education fund of the BIA. By 1973, the number had swelled to 13,500 students and the amount had climbed to $20 million.[23]

Tribes contribute substantial amounts annually to help their members obtain the higher education. The scholarship program of the Navajo tribe, for example, rose from about $400,000 in 1963 to over $1 million in 1972. Approximately 1,000 Navajo students were enrolled in graduate and undergraduate courses in colleges during 1972. Practically every one of the Indian tribes dedicated a share of tribal funds to a scholarship program in 1972.[24]

The dropout rate among Indian college students is quite high. Only about 28% of the Indian students who begin college stay long enough to graduate, according to the Senate Special Subcommittee. No more than 1 in 100 go on to earn a master's degree.

ADULT EDUCATION

In addition to operating Indian schools, the **BIA** conducts an adult education program to assist adult Indians in upping their general education level and reducing the educational gap between Indian people and the general populations.

A pilot adult education program was commenced on the Fort Hall Indian Reservation in the mid 1950's. Judged a success, the program expanded by 1956 to include 5 other reservations. Two years later, and again in 1960, the adult education program spread to more Indians. The growth of adult education and how well Indians responded to it are indicated by the following report for fiscal year 1961:

> ... Adult education teaching units have been established upon the request and with the concurrence of the tribal governing bodies at 28 agencies and locations throughout the United States. These teaching units are now serving approximately 107 Indian communities and offer a wide variety of instruction. The programs range from reading and writing courses to instructing individuals and groups of Indian people in specific subjects and civic skills. Personnel of the adult education program are in the process of developing a series of in-service training guides which will be used to strengthen the instructional and other phases of the program. Throughout this past year there have been approximately 5,800 adult Indian participants or learners in this program. Of this number, several have completed the required studies for high school graduation, while others have been engaged in informal learning activities ....[25]

The popularity of adult education is attributed to its promise to provide the opportunity for adult Indians to acquire the necessary skills and understandings to live better and participate more effectively in their world of today. Courses the Indians express a desire to take are written into the schedules of classes. These include elementary reading and writing classes, citizenship training and classes in practical and business skills.[26]

The adult education program of the BIA continued to expand with the passing years. In the fiscal year 1973, nearly 11,000 adult Indians were enrolled in formal adult education classes on reservations.[27]

ADDITIONAL FUNDS FOR BIA ACTIVITIES

In some of the past years, whenever the BIA was criticized for its failure to bring about better economic, social, political and educational conditions among Indians, the response was generally that Congress didn't provide enough money to accomplish the improvement. Annual appropriations, the BIA claimed persistently, were barely sufficient to continue existing programs.

As the BIA travelled along the New Trail, it saw circumstances develop that opened up the vaults of many other agencies. So the BIA went into the vaults and came out with bundles of additional funds for its activities on Indian reservations.

The background of the BIA money situation in earlier years, the circumstances that developed and how the BIA took advantage of the situation are interesting highlights in Indian affairs and deserve a few moment's review here.

Previous to 1960, the BIA carried out its activities through appropriations made directly to it. Until that time in its long history, the BIA determined its programs, prepared budget estimates and obtained appropriations from the Congress through the appropriation process. With the exception of tribal funds which the Congress appropriated as part of the funds to pay for reservation programs, there were no other monies available to the BIA.

But this began to change in the early 1960's. The civil rights movement began to mushroom and, in a few short years, almost unbelievable attention was showered upon the various minority groups in the country. The Supreme Court issued opinions favorable to the causes of minorities.

The Equal Employment Act and other legislation was enacted by Congress to help improve the lot of the minority citizens. Businesses began to advertise their acceptance of the principles of equality by going out of their way to recruit minorities for jobs. Minority men and women were put under spotlights to model clothing and demonstrate other products for mail-order houses, large manufacturing businesses and other concerns. Newspapers and periodicals prominently displayed pictures along with by-line articles of their minority reporters and writers. Minorities began to pop up on TV programs as newscasters, performers and whatever.

Government agencies were not to be outdone in this shakeup of the nation's internal affairs. They started to search for minorities to fill some of their top positions. Several of the federal installations were successful in their searches. Others put minorities in training programs and saw to it that the trainees advanced up the pyramid to higher jobs.

In this wide sweep of events, something happened that was identifiably favorable to Indians. The Executive Office of the President set up an internal subunit and called it the "Indian Desk." Moreover, it placed an Indian in charge of the subunit. Before too long, "Indian Desk" subunits began to appear at more and more agency headquarter offices at the nation's capitol. Their function was to do whatever they felt was warranted to promote the welfare of the American Indians. This complex of moving events eventually served to open the way for the BIA to fatten its appropriations by obtaining monies from "Indian Desks." This development needs to be explained in a little more detail.

In 1961, the Area Redevelopment Act passed and the Secretaries of Commerce and Interior agreed to let the BIA perform much of the area redevelopment work among Indians. Additionally, and most importantly, the Department of Commerce transferred to the BIA the necessary sums of money to accomplish the work. This was one of the first times the BIA obtained funds from another agency to finance programs among Indians.

In time this kind of arrangement spread to other federal agencies, and funding for activities of the BIA increased year by year. By 1968, the BIA had agreements or understandings with the Departments of Agriculture, Commerce, Health, Education and Welfare, Housing and Urban Development and Labor, the Small Business Administration and the Office of Economic Opportunity. It even had an agreement with its own Department of the Interior! These agencies by that time were swelling the normal annual appropriations of the BIA by nearly $100 million.[28]

RESERVATION HOUSING PROJECTS

The way the BIA went about getting funds from the federal housing agency and applying it to reservation housing projects is another example of how additional funds were obtained for activities among Indians.

In the depression years, limited money was appropriated for Indian housing. But the BIA had not in all its long history established a housing program for Indians nor had it requested funds for the construction and repair of Indian homes.

In reiterating its commitment to the New Trail in 1962, the BIA reviewed its major accomplishments during the preceding year. Among other items, the Commissioner stated "Recent Bureau efforts to accelerate improvements in Indian housing have been directed mainly towards enabling reservation Indians to participate in the various Federal housing programs on the same basis as non-Indians."[29]

For this kind of participation, the BIA helped the Indian tribes to organize reservation housing authorities. It then assisted the tribal housing authorities in writing up the necessary justifications to obtain funds from the Federal Housing Administration and its successor, the Department of Housing and Urban Development.

Ninety tribal housing authorities were developed on Indian reservations in 23 different states by 1968.[30] These housing authorities were participating in 1 or more federal housing programs administered by the Department of Housing and Urban Development. Funds obtained were available to Indians for the construction of new homes on reservations.

A mutual-help kind of arrangement developed on Indian reservations. Indians who desired new homes acquired lots or set aside parcels of their allotted land for homes. They made down payments on their new homes by helping to build the homes or by doing other jobs. This was called a mutual-help project. Frequently, the mutual-help was a communal-type program in which several prospective new home owners pooled their labor to build several homes for themselves. Tribal housing authorities paid for the building materials.

In 1968, the Commissioner of Indian Affairs described the development of tribal housing projects, as follows:

... The Indian people are at a point where housing can be produced at a rapid rate. To illustrate, during the period fiscal year 1963-67, about 1,100 low-rent and mutual-help housing units were completed. In fiscal year 1968 alone some 1,300 such units were completed ....[31]

About the time tribal housing authorities were in the initial stages of development, the BIA came up with a new activity called the Housing Improvement Program. The major emphasis of the program was to renovate and repair existing homes, bringing them up to a higher plane. Additionally, some new homes were planned, particularly for those Indians who for one reason or another were unable to obtain homes through any other housing program.

Congress appropriated money directly to the BIA for the Housing Improvement Program for the first time in 1964. In the following 4-year period, with subsequent appropriations, about 700 new homes were built and approximately 2,000 existing homes were renovated or repaired.[32]

Construction, renovation and repair of Indian homes continued to increase in the following years under programs of both the tribal housing authorities and the BIA. In fiscal year 1970, more than 5,000 new homes were built and about 3,570 were remodeled or repaired. Pointing up the continued importance of the programs in the years to come, the BIA at that time estimated that between 7,000 and 8,000 new homes would be built during each of the following few years, and about 3,500 existing Indian homes would be repaired or renovated each year.[33]

1. Rept. Com. Ind. Aff., 1961, pp. 277-278.

2. Ibid., p. 286.

3. Rept. Com. Ind. Aff., 1963, p. 24.

4. Ibid., p. 25.

5. Ibid.

6. Bureau of Indian Affairs, American Indians and the Federal Government (Washington: Government Printing Office, 1965), p. 16.

7. Rept. Com. Ind. Aff., 1963, p. 10.

8. U.S. Senate, Hearings Before the Subcommittee on Indian Education of the Committee on Labor and Public Welfare, Ninety-First Congress, First Session (Washington: Government Printing Office, 1969), p. 1578.

9. Rept. Com. Ind. Aff., 1963, pp. 23-24.

10. Rept. Com. Ind. Aff., 1968, p. 9.

11. U.S. Senate, Hearings Before the Subcommittee on Indian Education of the Committee on Labor and Public Welfare, Ninety-First Congress, First Session, op. cit., p. 1579.

12. Rept. Com. Ind. Aff., 1963, pp. 24-25.

13. "U.S. Halts Relocation of Indians," The Washington Post, January 13, 1972, p. 1.

14. Rept. Com. Ind. Aff., 1963, pp. 26-27. All material in the section was taken from this reference.

15. U.S. Department of the Interior, Secretary of the Interior Morton Reports on Indian Matters (Washington: Office of Communications, March 1973), p. 1.

16. Hildegard Thompson, "That Which is Priceless--A Child," Indian Education No. 342, April 1, 1960, pp. 1-2.

17. Bureau of Indian Affairs, Fiscal Year 1964 Statistics Concerning Indian Education, op. cit., pp. 10-11.

18. Selene Gifford, "Educating the American Indian," School Life, 47:2, November 1964, pp. 10-12.

19. Bureau of Indian Affairs, Information About the Bureau of Indian Affairs (Washington: Informational Bulletin, n.d.), p. 3.

20. Bureau of Indian Affairs, Fiscal Year 1973 Statistics Concerning Indian Education, p. 4.

21. U.S. Senate, Indian Education: A National Tragedy--A National Challenge, 1969 Report of the Committee on Labor and Public Welfare, United States Senate, Made by its Special Subcommittee on Indian Education (Washington: Government Printing Office, 1969), p. 59.

22. Bureau of Indian Affairs, Indian Record (1974 Review), op. cit., p. 8.

23. U.S. Department of the Interior, Secretary of the Interior Morton Reports on Indian Matters, op. cit., p. 2.

24. Bureau of Indian Affairs, <u>1972 Scholarships For American Indians</u> (Albuquerque: Branch of Higher Education, 1972), pp. 11-12.

25. <u>Rept. Com. Ind. Aff.</u>, 1961, p. 291.

26. Bureau of Indian Affairs, Fiscal Year 1964 Statistics Concerning Indian Education, <u>op. cit.</u>, p. 4.

27. Bureau of Indian Affairs, Fiscal Year 1973 Statistics Concerning Indian Education, <u>op. cit.</u>, p. 41.

28. <u>Rept. Com. Ind. Aff.</u>, 1968, Table IV.

29. Bureau of Indian Affairs, Fact Sheet on BIA Programs and the American Indians, <u>op. cit.</u>, p. 3.

30. <u>Rept. Com. Ind. Aff.</u>, 1968, p. 9.

31. <u>Ibid.</u>, p. 10.

32. <u>Ibid.</u>

33. Bureau of Indian Affairs, Information About the Bureau of Indian Affairs, <u>op. cit.</u>, p. 5.

CHAPTER 17

INDIAN SELF-DETERMINATION

Tribes of Indians during the colonial period were dealt with by the federal government as nations, and this relationship continued throughout the early treaty period. But as the Union expanded farther and farther into the west, the notion gradually developed that tribes and their members were actually at the mercy of the invading non-Indians and it was the duty and responsibility of the federal government to protect, guide and care for them.

In line with this principle of responsibility, the idea was conceived, particularly as Indians were put on reservations, to develop federal programs for their economic, social and political reconstruction and to see that the programs were carried out. But the unwavering belief was that Indians were obstinately wild, and they were neither able nor willing to refashion their institutions to fit the modified situation. Some other medium was necessary to bring about alterations. This change-agent was the BIA.

PATERNALISM

The takeover of reservation affairs by the BIA was known as paternalism. The BIA assumed the role of a parental authority and regarded the tribes and their members as children. The parental authority decided what was good for the children and insisted that the children comply fully with its judgments and edicts. Tribes and their members were given no voice in the development of reservation programs. They were not consulted. They were not asked to contribute their thoughts. In fact, in the early stages of paternalism, the BIA clamped down on the influence of Indian leaders. In one way or another, the BIA crushed Indian political and social systems, robbed Indian leaders of their power and established itself as the authority on Indian reservations. Paternalism thus became firmly entrenched in Indian affairs.

In time, this type of reservation management was assessed and found to be wanting in several areas. So an attempt was made in the mid 1930's to free the tribes and their members from it. At that time, the federal government gave tribes the promise they would have some say about what was going to happen on their reservations. The government pledged the BIA would consult them about what programs ought to be undertaken on reservations.

That was a first try at aligning Indian affairs with Indian thinking. A little progress was made in this direction. But in more passing of time, the progress was considered to be too slow. Thoughts about speeding it up began to circulate.

Finally, in 1970, the President announced the federal government would open wider the way for the say-so of Indians in Indian affairs. He called his movement "Indian self-determination."

INDIAN SELF-DETERMINATION ANNOUNCED

On July 8, 1970, President Nixon proposed to the Congress a series of policies and goals for American Indians. In his opening remarks, he stated, "It is long past time that the Indian policies of the federal government began to recognize and build upon the capacities and insights of the Indian people."[1] He went on to say that a decisive breakaway from past policies and practices in the management of Indian affairs was much overdue. It was necessary now to create a system and develop the climate for the future of Indians to be determined by Indian acts and Indian decisions.

The President isolated termination from among the past policies. He spoke quite strongly against it, stating that it was wrong for a number of reasons. One of the wrongs, he said, was the false premise that the federal government could discontinue its trust responsibilities for Indians whenever it saw fit to do so. He declared the responsibilities were obligations and commitments of the federal government in Indian treaties and agreements, and they were not subject to cancelation at the option of the government. Going on, he said another wrong with termination was the practical results of it. Termination had proved to be clearly harmful to the Indians among whom it had occurred. Tribesmen who previously were oriented toward the BIA were unable to relate to other federal, state and local agencies when federal supervision ended. Scores of Indians sunk to the very depth of poverty, and many others suffered a myriad of different afflictions. A third wrong, the President pointed up, was that termination put so much fear in Indians that it made tribes and individual Indians regard with suspicion any steps proposed or taken by the federal government for their social, economic and political well-being.

After these and other prefatory remarks bringing out the ills of existing government policies and practices among Indians, the President proposed Indian self-determination in the following words:

> ... Federal termination errs in one direction. Federal paternalism errs in the other. Only by rejecting both of these extremes can we achieve a policy which truly serves the best interests of the Indian people. Self-determination among the Indian people can and must be encouraged without the threat of termination. In my view, in fact, that is the only way that self-determination can effectively be fostered.
>
> This, then, must be the goal of any new national policy toward the Indian people: to strengthen the Indian's sense of autonomy without threatening his sense of community. We must assure the Indian that he can assume control of his own life without being separated involuntarily from the tribal group. And we must make it clear that Indians can become independent of Federal control without being cut off from Federal concern and Federal support. My specific recommendations to the Congress are designed to carry out this policy ....[2]

These statements by President Nixon are significant enough to deserve a few moment's further exploration. He stated essentially that federal policy must be reshaped to allow Indians to decide their own destiny. The grant of this decision-making power would constitute a rejection of both long-standing paternalism and the more recent termination policy. At the same time, it would introduce self-determination among Indians. But these measures alone would not be sufficient inducement for Indians to take control of Indian affairs on reservations. The threat of termination as a psychological barrier must also be removed. In President Nixon's view, Indian self-determination and the fear or threat of termination are incompatible. Indians must be made to feel completely free to develop reservation programs and order their priorities without fear that the government might withdraw its support, financial or otherwise. Indians must be assured, too, he said, that tribal life is not jeopardized by their taking the initiative to determine the projects needed for their economic, social and political development. Beyond this, he intimated that Indian tribal organizations could develop in time to become the governing authorities on Indian reservations. When that occurred, however, Indians would not need to be fearful of termination because they would continue to be an important concern of the federal government and could receive financial aid from it independent of the BIA or any other agency.

The President specified areas of Indian affairs requiring action and commented at length upon them. He urged the Congress to enact legislation which would make his recommendations the law of the land.

EXECUTIVE RECOMMENDATIONS

The first of the President's recommendations was renunciation, repudiation and repeal of the termination policy. This could be accomplished by a concurrent resolution of Congress putting an end to House Concurrent Resolution No. 108 of the 83rd Congress. HCR 108 was the mandate of Congress for the BIA to begin to work itself out of business by terminating federal supervision and control over Indians. Repealing HCR 108, the President said, would "reaffirm for the Legislative branch--as I hereby affirm for the Executive branch--that the historic relationship between the Federal government and the Indian communities cannot be abridged without the consent of the Indians."[3]

With the termination policy legally out of the way, the President visualized that Indians would be more receptive to federal programs and services. But he proposed that reservation programs and services be administered by the Indians rather than by the BIA or any other federal agency. This would correspond to the way federal-support programs in non-Indian communities operated. In his own words, the President said:

> ... In the past, we have often assumed that because the government is obliged to provide certain services for Indians, it therefore must administer those same services ... But there is no necessary reason for this assumption. Federal support programs for non-Indian communities--hospitals and schools are two ready examples--are ordinarily administered by local authorities. There is no reason why Indian communities should be deprived of the privilege of self-determination merely because they receive monetary support from the Federal government. Nor should they lose Federal money because they reject Federal control ....[4]

The President recalled that Indian participation in reservation programs had for many years been a hope of the federal government. Yet, whenever a decision was necessary about whether the Indians should take over a program, it was the BIA and not the Indians who made the decision. This kind of practice must be stopped, the President said, so he proposed that the Congress empower tribal organizations to make the decision. With this kind of authority, the tribes would not have to take over control or operation of federal programs unless they voted to do so. Moreover, he indicated that tribal organizations might desire not to continue operating certain programs after a trial period. In such cases, the control and operation of the programs could be turned back to the BIA or other applicable agency. The President called this process the "right of retrocession."

Some cautions needed to be kept in mind, according to the President, to make the takeover of reservation programs by tribal organizations a success. Among these were assurance that technical assistance be provided to help tribal organizations in program operations, guarantee against the loss of tribal economic assets from operation of programs, funding on equal terms with other programs administered by the BIA or any other federal agency, protection against actions that might endanger the rights, health, safety or welfare of individuals, and providing for safeguards against mismanagement of federal funds.

When Nixon urged Indian self-determination, the idea that Indian tribes were able to manage Indian affairs was already a reality on several of the reservations. More than 60 Indian communities were at that time managing programs funded by the Office of Economic Opportunity. Many of these programs had been under tribal control for at least 4 years, and the results compared favorably with outcomes of the same types of programs administered by local groups in non-Indian communities.

In addition to this, the Salt River tribe and the Zuni tribe were well on their way to taking over complete control of the many programs that for long years had been administered by the BIA.

These examples of the effectiveness of Indian control and management of reservation programs were sufficient proof to the President that favorable results could rightly be anticipated among Indian groups exercising self-determination. He expressed full confidence in the tribal groups and underscored the necessity to revamp Indian policy by stating that "A policy which encourages Indian Administration of these programs will help to build greater pride and resourcefulness within the Indian community. At the same time, programs which are managed and operated by Indians are likely to be more effective in meeting Indian needs."[5]

OTHER EXECUTIVE PROPOSALS

Other proposals by President Nixon on July 8, 1970, and brief comments about them are:

1. Restore Blue Lake to Taos Pueblo. For 64 years these Indians had been trying to regain possession of the lake to preserve its natural state and to use it in expressions of their

135

religious faith. The lake and its surroundings had been designated a national forest in 1906 without the consent of the Indians and without payment to them.

2. Local School Control. The President stated he would establish a special education subcommittee composed of educators to provide technical assistance to Indian tribes wishing to establish school boards to direct their reservation school systems.

3. Amend Johnson-O'Malley Act. This act provides funds to public school districts enrolling Indian students who reside on Indian reservations or other tax-exempt land within their geographical boundaries. The funds go directly to the public school districts, and Indians have little to say about how the money is spent. President Nixon urged legislation requiring that these moneys be directed to tribes and Indian communities so Indians would be able to have a voice in shaping programs of public schools attended by their children, or so they could set up schools of their own.

4. Economic Development Legislation. The President proposed an Indian Financing Act to broaden the Revolving Loan Fund and create additional incentive for private lenders to loan more money to Indians for reservation economic projects. He suggested the Revolving Loan Fund be increased from the existing $25 million to $75 million and that $200 million be authorized to guarantee loans to Indians by private lenders.

5. Assistant Secretary for Indian and Territorial Affairs. This new position in the Department of the Interior was proposed to handle only Indian and Territorial affairs. These activities were under the Assistant Secretary for Public Land Management, and his responsibilities in other natural resource areas competed with his concern for Indians.

6. Other proposals were to increase funds for Indian health, to give more support to urban Indian centers, to establish an Indian Trust Counsel Authority to assure independent legal representation for the rights of Indians in the natural resources and to raise the standards of existing programs among Indians.

To get the Executive recommendations and proposals going would take the thinking and work of several different organizations and groups. Some of the recommendations had to be taken over by Congress for appropriate legislation. This would involve a great deal of work spread across many years. Other proposals had to be worked on by Indian tribes and their members. But with the shattering effects of termination still vivid, it would be necessary for the Indians to rebuild their confidence in the sincerity of federal programs. Certain actions to get the ball rolling, however, could be taken immediately within the Executive Branch under the general authority of the Presidency to conduct Indian affairs and under existing legislation.

INDIANS PLACED IN KEY POSITIONS

Congress passed several laws over many years of BIA operations to establish the national policy that qualified Indians be placed in BIA positions. Yet, very few Indians had risen in the BIA hierarchy. Previous to the 1960's, only one Indian held the post of Commissioner of Indian Affairs and less than a handful of Indians were heads of divisions and branches in the Washington BIA office. One or 2 Indians succeeded in becoming directors of area offices and hardly more than that held up-the-line jobs in area offices. A scattering of Indians were superintendents of Indian reservations and off-reservation schools. By and large, though, the BIA key posts at each of its 3 levels of operation were held by non-Indians.

Self-determination presupposed and necessitated that Indians be in high BIA positions to develop policies and programs for Indian reservations and to transmit the thinking and wishes of Indians to the President and Congress.

The Commissioner of Indian Affairs at the time Nixon made his proposals for Indian self-determination was Louis R. Bruce. Of Mohawk-Sioux lineage, he was the 3rd person of Indian descent to be appointed the head Indian affairs. It fell upon him to see that more Indians were in some of the top BIA positions.

To accomplish this, Commissioner Bruce reorganized the BIA national office and in the process created 20 new positions. Then he filled 15 of these top posts with Indians of different tribes and of varied orientations. The reorganization resulted from the Commissioner's study and consultation with various Indian groups. Indians placed in the positions were recommended to the Commissioner by Indian organizations and tribes.[6]

With the passing of time, the 15 appointed Indians became known by various names, such as "Bruce's Braves" and "The Activists." Officially, however, they composed a BIA executive committee whose duty, among others, was to come up with ideas about how to promote Indian self-determination.

Placing Indians in top spots went down gradually to the area offices and the local levels.

Achievements at the Washington and area levels were indicated in September 1972, by the Deputy Assistant Secretary of the Interior who reported that "Today a majority of the top BIA executive positions at the Washington level are filled by Indians, and the number of Indians serving as BIA area directors has risen from 1 out of 11, to 7 out of a possible 12."[7]

Putting Indians in top positions at the reservation level promised also great involvement of Indians at the grassroots. The Commissioner pledged that Indian tribes would be consulted for pertinent information to help in selecting personnel. Vacancies would be filled, he said, by choosing from a list of candidates nominated by the governing bodies of the applicable reservations. To assure that superintendents would promote Indian self-determination, the Commissioner stated their performance would be judged by the degree to which they meaningfully involved the Indians in the day-to-day operations on reservations.[8] The title reservation superintendent was changed to field representative.

INDIAN CONTROL AND OPERATION OF INDIAN SCHOOLS

Before leaving office in 1968, President Johnson directed the Secretary of the Interior to establish Indian school boards for federal Indian schools, to provide for the selection of school board members by Indians in the community and to provide the training necessary for the school boards to carry out their responsibilities.[9] This directive was the start of the movement for Indians to have some say in how the Indian school system was operated and what subjects were provided. The BIA became the principal instrument for putting the movement into motion and keeping it going.

A private educational services organization was recruited by the BIA to provide school board training and produce a handbook for community involvement in schools. In the summer of 1968, the organization conducted the first Indian school board workshop ever held in the long years of federal schooling among Indians. The workshop was attended by Indian members of the United Pueblos.

An outcome of the workshop was a school board handbook which became available to tribes across the country. The handbook was prepared to help Indians recognize that Indian schools are vital parts of Indian communities and to aid school board members in becoming education leaders.

School boards soon began to be organized on Indian reservations throughout the land, and at the end of the next 4 years, in 1972, all the more than 200 Indian elementary and secondary Indian schools had Indian advisory school boards or education committees.[10] In fact, education committees came into being among tribes of Indians that had no Indian schools on their reservations. This happened particularly in the northwestern part of the U.S. where the Indian students long since attended public schools. In some areas, Indians were elected to school board membership of public schools, and in 1 or 2 of these cases, they composed the majority membership of the school boards.

The establishment of Indian school boards began a couple of years prior to Nixon's announcement of Indian self-determination, but it was accelerated after the proposals. Beyond this, the way was opened for Indians to assume control of and operate Indian schools and the federal education programs. Various means to accomplish this were undertaken. Two of the more prominent steps are illustrative.

In 1968, by Executive Order, the President established a body called the National Council on Indian Opportunity. Composed of 8 Indians and 8 federal government members and chaired by the Vice President, the organization was a direct communication link between the Indian people and the very top of the federal government.[11] Two years after it was organized, the NCIO noted that "the low quality of Indian education stands in direct contrast to a key source of American progress--good education."[12]

Within its own organization, the NCIO formed a Special Indian Education Subcommittee composed of Indian educators to address the crucial matters of Indian education. The Subcommittee's duties were stated to be as follows:

... The Subcommittee will provide technical assistance to Indian communities wishing to establish school boards, will conduct a nationwide review of the educational status of all Indian school children in whatever school they may be attending and will evaluate and report to the President annually on the status of Indian education, including the extent of local control ....[13]

The subcommittee helped to produce the surge in Indian school boards. It was involved, too, in assessing the effectiveness of Indian education and keeping tab for the President on how much control and operation of federal Indian schools were taken over by Indians.

To obtain control and operation of a reservation Indian school system, a tribe had to enter into a contractual or similar relationship with the BIA. The agreement specified, in essence, that the tribal organization do whatever needed to be done to keep the school in operation, such as recruit personnel, develop curricula, procure equipment and supplies, provide for student transportation and the many other functions of school operations. Tribes didn't have to take over all operations, however. They could agree to manage any part of the school system, such as cafeteria operations or transportation. The BIA agreed to provide funds to the tribes for the education programs, or any part, taken over by the tribes.

This method was not entirely new when Indian self-determination was announced by the President. In the 1966-67 school year, the Navajo tribe contracted with the BIA to operate the Rough Rock Demonstration School. The next year, Indians of the Salt River Reservation contracted to operate the Blackwater Day School.

With these as successful experiments, the drive for more and more Indian control and operation of Indian schools was accelerated. In 1970, two additional local schools were turned over to the all-Indian school boards under contract with the BIA. They were the Stephen High School of the Crow Creek and Lower Brule Tribes in South Dakota and the Ramah School in New Mexico.[14]

At the beginning of the following year, several different negotiations were under way for Indian control and operation of educational functions. Contracts were in the making for tribal operation of 3 different schools on the Navajo Reservation and for 6 day schools in Iowa, Florida, Montana and Alaska. In addition to these, the Mescalero Apache Tribe and the Standing Rock Sioux Tribe were negotiating for the management of various educational programs administered by the BIA. The United Tribes of North Dakota and the Nebraska Indian Inter-Tribal Development Corporation were in the process of obtaining a contract specifying that they administer Johnson-O'Malley funds for Indian students attending public schools in those areas. The administration of the BIA Higher Education Assistance Program of Pueblo Indians and Navajo Indians was being contracted to the All-Indian Pueblo Council and the Navajo Tribal Council, respectively.

Indian control and operation of Indian schools continued to expand. Early in 1972, the Assistant Secretary of the Interior stated that 7 schools were being operated under contract to tribes and 8 more would be added by the end of the year. He also said the applicable tribes were in the process of contracting to operate 3 reservation junior colleges. The number of various educational programs operated by Indians, he reported, would increase from 45 to 75 during the year.[15]

A year later the BIA announced that tribal groups took over the operation of 3 dormitory schools and all or part of the education program at 21 other Indian schools in 1973.[16]

OTHER ACTIONS OF EXECUTIVE BRANCH

The executive committee which resulted from the reorganization of the BIA in the latter part of 1970 visited Indian tribes on practically every reservation during the following year. The object of the committee was to find out from Indians the kinds of programs desired on reservations and from this information to build the BIA eventually into an organization that would reflect the thinking and feelings of the majority of Indian people and respond as quickly and effectively as possible to Indian needs.

The committee developed 5 goals for the BIA. The goals were:

1. Transform the BIA from a management to a service organization.

2. Reaffirm the trust status of Indian land.

3. Make the BIA fully responsive to the Indian people it serves.

4. Provide tribes with the option of assuming greater responsibility relating to BIA program functions.

5. Work with Indian organizations to become a strong advocate of all Indian interests.

These goals were not entirely new to the BIA. Most of them were already being worked on. But the committee's restatement and formalizing of them into a list made them a blueprint for the BIA to keep in mind and refer to now and then.

Some of the goals were interrelated so that the achievement of one helped in attaining another. For instance, as takeover of BIA functions by Indians was occurring, the BIA inevitably was changing from a management to a service organization. How much of the management functions the BIA turned over to tribes showed how responsive the BIA was to the Indians it served. All the goals, however, would require persistent and long-range effort of the BIA before achievement of them were possible.

Other actions were taken by the Executive Branch to get Indian self-determination on the move. These actions were reinterpreting certain existing laws of Congress to open up opportunities for greater Indian participation and say-so in Indian affairs.

One of these laws was the Buy Indian Act of 1910. That act authorized the Secretary of the Interior to purchase, by contract, Indian-made products from Indian tribes. Up until 1970, the act had been interpreted to relate only to the purchase of Indian-made goods and whatever involvement of Indians the manufacture of Indian-made products entailed. To further the policy of self-determination, however, the meaning of the act was broadened when the act was looked at more closely and reinterpreted. First it was reinterpreted to mean that it authorized training and employment of Indians in manufacturing or making products. This reinterpretation allowed the BIA to use its funds in training programs and employment opportunities for Indians. Later, the act was reinterpreted more broadly to mean that it authorized Indian involvement in the conduct of Indian affairs.[17]

Another act widened in meaning by reinterpretation was the so-called Indian preference legislation. Actually, Indian preference was included in a series of acts. The first one was enacted in about the mid 1800's. It provided essentially that Indians be hired for vacant BIA jobs they were qualified to do. This preference provision was repeated in several other laws during the next 100 years and was expressly written into the Indian Reorganization Act of 1934.

For many years, particularly in the late 1930's and thereafter, the BIA held that Indian preference was restricted to initial hiring and Indian had no preference in promotions. The result of this interpretation was that very few Indians moved up the ladder to higher BIA positions even though they were qualified. Usually, they had to stay in the lower positions where they were first hired because they were not selected when they applied for vacant jobs up the pyramid.

In 1972, the Secretary of the Interior announced that the statutes dealing with Indian preference had been carefully reviewed and the conclusion reached that Indian preference was not restricted to initial appointment. It applied to the filling of all vacancies, whether by original appointment, reinstatement or promotion.[18] The intent of this interpretation was to widen the opportunity for qualified Indians to advance upward in the BIA jobs.

This interpretation didn't set too well with 4 non-Indian BIA employees. They took their objection to the U.S. District Court in Albuquerque, and the Court decided that preference given to Indians in BIA jobs violated the Civil Rights Act and the Equal Employment Opportunity Act.[19]

Based upon this ruling, the BIA stopped giving preference to Indians in initial hirings and other actions.

RESTORATION OF TAOS LAND

Congress pushed Indian self-determination forward by enacting into law some of the recommendations of the President.

Following his July 1970, address on Indian policy, President Nixon transmitted a package of legislative proposals to the Congress. Among them was the recommendation that the Blue Lake land be restored to the Taos Pueblo Indians.

The Blue Lake land was appropriated in 1906 as part of the Carson National Forest in New Mexico. Almost immediately thereafter, the Taos Indians started a fight to regain possession of it. The battle continued for the next 64 years and came to an end when the President signed into law a congressional act placing the land in trust for the Taos Indians.

The President signed the bill on December 15, 1970, in the presence of a delegation of Taos Pueblo Indians. The law provided that the Indians may use the land for religious ceremonies, for hunting and fishing, as a source of water, as forage for livestock and for other specific purposes. With the exception that the land was made subject to conservation practices prescribed by the Secretary of the Interior, the law provided that the 48,000 acres remain in natural condition forever and be administered as a wilderness under the Wilderness Act of 1964.[20]

Three years later Congress passed another act that signalled victory in a 10-year struggle of a different tribe of Indians.

MENOMINEE RESTORATION ACT

During the 1950's, the Klamath and Menominee tribes and several bands of Utah Indians were released from supervision of the federal government. Saying this another way, the historical relationship between the federal government and these tribes and groups of Indians ended. In the words of Congressman Lloyd Meeds of Washington, "The idea was to make Indians as much like white people as we could and then cut them off from the federal relationship."[21] Tribal organizations were dissolved and the members were adrift in the mainstream of American society.

The Menominee Indians opposed termination, but nobody listened to them. They did manage, however, in the next couple of years after they were turned loose to form an organization to preserve their remaining land as a unit and to go to bat for restoration to trust status. Their 10-year struggle ended on December 22, 1973, when President Nixon signed into law the Menominee Restoration Act. A Presidential statement was released the day the act was signed, declaring that the law represented a turning point in the history of Indian affairs. According to the President, the act was a clear reversal of the erroneous policy of forcibly terminating tribal status and ending the special relationship of the federal government and the Indians.

After the bill was signed, much work remained for the Menominee people. A new official body called the Menominee Restoration Committee was organized and an election scheduled to choose members for it. The work of the committee was to prepare a list, called a tribal roll, of tribal members and to set up the machinery for the adoption of a tribal constitution. A tribal council could then be elected to work on the health, education, unemployment, poverty and the many other problems.[22]

OTHER RESTORATIONS

In 1974, the Commissioner of Indian Affairs reported that 3,500 acres of land were returned to the Fort Mojave Indian Tribe. The land was taken from the tribe half a century ago when a faulty survey was made to establish the reservation boundaries.

Hunting, fishing and boating rights were returned to the Colville and Spokane tribes on Lake Roosevelt in Washington. The Indians lost these rights when the Grand Coolee Dam was built.

In addition, the Commissioner reported, the Chemehuevi Tribe of California regained trust title to land taken some years ago for the Lake Havasu Project. The land is an 18 mile shoreline strip along Lake Havasu, located about 40 miles southeast of Needles, California.

CONGRESSIONAL ACTION AT STANDSTILL

After the President transmitted the package of legislative proposals to the Congress in 1970, a number of bills were introduced in both the Senate and the House of Representatives. Some of the bills were enacted into laws. Examples are the Taos and Menominee acts, the Indian Education Act of 1972 and several laws dealing with specific issues of particular tribes.[23]

On several other crucial bills, however, Congress was not too swift. A good many of the bills died at the end of 1970. These bills and others were reintroduced in the first session of the next Congress in 1971. But they met a similar fate in that session.

The status of the legislation in 1972 was indicated by the Secretary of the Interior when he addressed a meeting of the National Tribal Chairmen's Association on August 7. He stated, "Today key portions of desperately needed Indian legislation are blocked in a committee of Congress."[24]

He pointed up that among these were the proposed Indian Financing Act, various economic development acts, the Trust Council Authority legislation, and the act to elevate the position of Commissioner of Indian Affairs to Assistant Secretary of the Interior. He expressed hope to the tribal chairmen that the bills would soon be passed to assure continued progress in Indian self-determination.

Early in 1974, the Indian Financing Act was passed and signed into law by President Nixon. The act authorized an additional $50 million for the Revolving Credit Fund. It also created a new Indian Loan Guaranty and Insurance Fund to make it easier for Indians to obtain loans from private non-Indian sources. Additionally, it established an Indian Business Development Program and authorized up to $10 million for it over the next 3 years. This program is to provide capital to Indians who want to set up or expand Indian-owned enterprises on reservations. The act merely authorized the programs. No money was appropriated by the act.[25]

THE INDIAN PRESS

Under the stimulus of civil rights and the self-determination policy, Indian groups began to spring up in practically every part of the country. In different ways and for different purposes, they developed and began to take an active part in Indian affairs.

In early 1970, a research was undertaken by a writer to analyze the currentness and relevancy of Indian newspapers and periodicals. The writer discovered there was no such thing as an Indian press corresponding to the American press. A few scattered publications by a handful of equally strewn Indians made up the channel of communications about the news and events in Indian country.[26]

But this began to change soon thereafter. In September 1970, a group of 12 Indian editors of assorted Indian newsletters, pamphlets and other publications assembled at Durango, Colorado. They organized the American Indian Press Association, and the new AIPA took on the job of getting Indian news to Indian people throughout the country.[27]

The AIPA is headquartered in Washington, D.C. It works for Indian publications similar to the way the Associated Press and the United Press operate for newspapers and other publications in the nation. The AIPA gathers news and other articles about Indian happenings and distributes the stories to its members, the local media among reservation and urban Indians across the U.S. One of its major jobs is to keep Indians informed and up-to-date about legislation and other Indian goings-on at the nation's capitol and throughout the country.

After the AIPA went into business, the number of newspapers, periodicals and other publications about Indians began to multiply rapidly. By 1973, they numbered more than 400, and they were published by Indian centers, Indian tribes, urban Indian groups, Indian communities and interested non-Indian groups and organizations.

A few of the Indian newspapers are The Navajo Times, a weekly of the Navajo Tribe; The Native Nevadan, published by the Intertribal Council of Nevada; River Times, originating at Fairbanks, Alaska, and the Anishinabe Journal, a publication of the White Earth Reservation in Minnesota.

Periodicals include The Sentinel, produced by the National Congress of American Indians, Washington, D.C.; The Indian Historian, published by the American Indian Historical Society, San Francisco, California; Indian Voice, a product of the Native American Publishing Company, San Jose, California; and Many Smokes, published quarterly at Reno, Nevada.

Many other publications keep the Indians abreast of important legislation, plans and programs of the federal government, developments and happenings on the various reservations and the many other facets of Indian affairs and daily life among Indians.

INDIAN ORGANIZATIONS

Traditionally, the unit to which the individual Indian looked was the tribe. And each tribe was more or less autonomous. In the Colonial period, the League of Six Nations was a reality. But other attempts by different Indians to form this type of socio-political alliance failed, particularly among the early eastern and southeastern tribes. In many later years, during the early days of Indian Territory, 5 different tribes joined together as the Five Civilized Tribes. Other than these, there were practically no other Indian associations in all the long history of Indians up to the close of the Frontier.

The creation of Indian reservations purposely split tribes and kept them from getting together for any kind of alliance. Early federal programs among reservation Indians broke up tribal units. In those days, associations of different tribes, or members of different tribes, was out of the question. This continued until about the early 1940's.

At that time, an organization called the National Congress of American Indians (NCAI) came into being. Its voting membership was open to all Indians of every tribe. Interested non-Indians, however, could become nonvoting members by a specified dues contribution. The general objectives of the NCAI were to seek legislation that would positively promote the welfare of Indians and to try to prevent laws that might be detrimental to the best interests of Indians.

Over the years, the NCAI had its ups and downs. It endured, nonetheless, and is the grand-daddy of modern Indian organizations, particularly national Indian organizations. The constitution and bylaws of the NCAI gets an update every couple or 3 years to define more specifically its goals and its internal structure. The latest revision was adopted at the 28th annual convention held at Reno, Nevada, on November 17, 1971. According to the document, the NCAI is dedicated to the following tasks:

1. To secure the rights and benefits to which Indians are entitled under the laws of the United States,

2. To enlighten the public toward a better understanding of Indian people,

3. To preserve rights under Indian treaties or agreements with the United States,

4. To promote the common welfare of American Indians, and

5. To foster the continued loyalty and allegiance of American Indians to the flag of the United States.[28]

The NCAI was the only Indian organization of its type previous to the civil rights movement. Since then, many different Indians have formed into both national and regional entities.

On the national level, there is the National Tribal Chairmen's Association composed, as its name implies, of the chairmen of the reservation tribal governing bodies. Other recently formed Indian organizations are the National Tribal Court Judges Association, the National Indian Education Association, The National Indian Youth Council, the American Indian Movement and the Institute for Development of Indian Law. The names of the organizations suggest generally what they are all about. But when necessary they get involved in other phases of the broad area of Indian rights and welfare.

Regional Indian organizations have emerged in many states where Indian reservations are located. Among these are the United Southeastern Tribes, Inc., in Florida; the United Council of Urban Indian Affairs, in Utah, and the American Indian Consultants, Inc., in Arizona. These examples are suggestive of many other Indian organizations that have arisen in other states where Indians are located. Each year adds 1 or 2 more local Indian organizations. For instance in 1973, Eastern Indians formed the Coalition of Eastern Native Americans to help in upgrading the conditions of the more than 100,000 Indians who live east of the Mississippi River.

Some of the Indian organizations are of so recent origin at the time of this writing that they are hardly beyond on "drawing board" phase. A few of them have managed to capture momentarily the national spotlight for a brief time, particularly the American Indian Movement in the Wounded Knee and other incidents. Others, such as the NCAI are starting to assert themselves more and more in Indian affairs, hopeful that the policy of Indian self-determination will admit their thoughts and ideas.

1. Richard Nixon, The White House to the Congress of the United States (Office of the White House Press Secretary, July 8, 1970), p. 1.

2. Ibid., p. 2.

3. Ibid., p. 3.

4. Ibid.

5. Ibid., p. 4.

6. "BIA Makes Sweeping Changes in Structure Policy in Move from Management to Service Organization," Indian Record, December 1970-January 1971 (Washington: Bureau of Indian Affairs), p. 2.

7. "Remarks of William L. Rogers, Deputy Assistant Secretary of the Interior for Indian Affairs at the Osage Tribal Centennial Celebration," Department of the Interior News Release, September 30, 1972, p. 3.

8. "BIA Makes Sweeping Changes in Structure Policy in Move from Management to Service Organization," op. cit., p. 2.

9. Bureau of Indian Affairs, School Board Handbook, 1969, p. ii.

10. "Morton Cites Progress in Achieving Indian Self-Determination," Department of the Interior News Release, August 8, 1972, p. 3.

11. "What is NCIO," NCIO News, 2:3, November 15-December 1971, p. 10.

12. "Council to Form Education Subcommittee," NCIO News 1:1, December 1970, p. 3.

13. "Vice President Names Special Indian Subcommittee," NCIO News, 1:3, February 1971, p. 2.

14. Bureau of Indian Affairs, Information About the Bureau of Indian Affairs, op. cit., p. 3.

15. "U.S. Indians Win More Self Rule," The New York Times, Thursday, January 13, 1972, Section C, p. 35.

16. Department of the Interior, Program for the Bureau of Indian Affairs, Fiscal Year 1973 (Mimeographed leaflet), p. 16.

17. Bureau of Indian Affairs, Information About the Bureau of Indian Affairs, op. cit., p. 1.

18. "Interior Expands Policy of Indian Preference in Bureau of Indian Affairs," Department of the Interior News Release, June 23, 1972.

19. "Indian Preference Stopped by Court," The Gallup Independent, Saturday, June 2, 1973, p. 1.

20. "Blue Lake Bill Signed, Taos Lands Restored," Indian Record, December 1970-January 1971, pp. 1 and 7.

21. "Menominees--Back on the Road to Strength as Congress Rights Wrong," Akwesasne Notes, Early Winter, 1973, p. 17.

22. "After Ten Years, Menominees to Reestablish Tribal Government," The Navajo Times, March 21, 1974, p. A-15.

23. Bureau of Indian Affairs, You Asked About Current Legislation, op. cit., January 1973, pp. 1-4.

24. "Morton Cites Progress in Achieving Indian Self-Determination," op. cit., p. 4.

25. Bureau of Indian Affairs, Indian Record, op. cit. (1974 Review), p. 4.

26. "The Indian Press: Alive and Well," Wassaja, February-March 1973, p. 7.

27. "Indian Editors Meet for Press Association," Indian Record, October 1970, p. 2.

28. National Congress of American Indians, Constitution and By-Laws, Preamble.

SELECTED BIBLIOGRAPHY

CONGRESSIONAL DOCUMENTS

American State Papers:

Vol. V, Class II, Indian Affairs, Vol. I, 1789-1815.

Vol. VI, Class II, Indian Affairs, Vol. II, 1815-1827.

Journals of the Continental Congress, 34 Vols., 1774-1789:

Vol. III, Reference to Treaty of Neutrality with Six Nations at Albany, August 1775; November 11, 1775, pp. 350-351; November 23, 1775, pp. 365-368.

Vol. XXV, Instructions to Commissioners on Negotiating for Peace With Hostile Indians of Northern and Middle Department, October 15, 1783, pp. 680-695.

Vol. XXXIII, Recommendations of Committee on Indian Affairs, particularly on Land Disputes Between Creek and Cherokee Indians, and States of North Carolina and Georgia, August 3, 1787, pp. 454-463.

_____, Instructions to Commissioners for Negotiating a Treaty Between Southern Indians and States of North Carolina and Georgia, October 26, 1787, pp. 707-714.

United States Congress:

Annals of Congress, 1789-91, 1st Congress, 1st Session, Message on Nature of Indian Treaties--President George Washington, p. 83.

_____, 1796-97, 4th Congress, 1st Session, Indian Trading Houses, pp. 229-230.

Executive Documents, 6th Congress, 1st Session, Report on Indian Trading Houses, April 22, 1800.

Annals of Congress, 7th Congress, 1st Session, Message on Indian Trading Houses; its extension; recommendations of prohibition of liquor from Indian Territory, January 28, 1802, pp. 150-151.

Executive Documents, 7th Congress, 2nd Session, Report on Indian Affairs--Treaties, Boundaries, Trading Houses, January 18, 1803.

Executive Documents, 11th Congress, 2nd Session, Report on Indian Trading Houses, April 14, 1810.

Executive Report, 14th Congress, 1st Session, Report on Indian Affairs, March 14, 1816.

House Documents, 14th Congress, 2nd Session, Report on Indian Trade, February 4, 1817.

Annals of Congress, 1817-1818, 15th Congress, 1st Session, Report on Establishment of Trading Houses and Encouragement of Education, Part I, pp. 800-801.

Senate State Papers, Report No. 47, 15th Congress, 2nd Session, Petition for the Civilization of the Indians--Society of Friends, December 23, 1818.

House Document No. 91, 15th Congress, 2nd Session, On the Civilization of Indian Tribes, January 15, 1819.

Senate Document No. 105, 16th Congress, 1st Session, On Abolition of System of Indian Trade, April 5, 1820.

House Document No. 46, 16th Congress, 1st Session, Report on Indian Affairs--Secretary J. C. Calhoun, February 16, 1820.

House Document No. 110, 17th Congress, 1st Session, Report on Indian Affairs--Secretary J. C. Calhoun, April 11, 1822.

House Report No. 104, 17th Congress, 2nd Session, Abolishing Indian Trading Establishments-- Committee on Indian Affairs, March 1, 1823.

House Document No. 47, 18th Congress, 1st Session, Statement on Disbursement for Civiliza- tion of Indians--Secretary J. C. Calhoun, January 24, 1824.

House Document No. 56, 18th Congress, 1st Session, Report on Indian Agencies--Secretary J. C. Calhoun, January 12, 1824.

House Report No. 92, 18th Congress, 1st Session, On Civilization of the Indian--Committee on Indian Affairs, May 25, 1824.

House Report No. 129, 18th Congress, 1st Session, Abolition of Indian Trading Establishments, May 25, 1824.

House Document No. 102, 19th Congress, 1st Session, Report on Preservation and Civilization of Indian Tribes--Secretary James Barbour, February 3, 1826.

House Document No. 124, 19th Congress, 1st Session, Report on Preservation and Civilization of the Indians--General Clark, Supt. Ind. Aff., March 1, 1826.

House Document No. 146, 19th Congress, 1st Session, On Establishment of a General Super- intendency of Indian Affairs in Department of War, May 20, 1826.

House Document No. 9, 19th Congress, 2nd Session, Message on Indian Affairs--President J. Q. Adams, December 11, 1826.

House Document No. 11, 20th Congress, 2nd Session, On Civilization of the Indians, December 8, 1828.

Senate Document No. 110, 21st Congress, 1st Session, Report on Indians, March 25, 1830.

House Document No. 127, 22nd Congress, 1st Session, Statement Relative to Indian Annuities, February 27, 1832.

Senate Document No. 24, 22nd Congress, 2nd Session, Indian Annuities Payable in 1833, December 20, 1832.

House Report No. 474, 23rd Congress, 1st Session, Regulating the Indian Department--Committee on Indian Affairs, May 20, 1834.

Senate Document No. 106, 25th Congress, 2nd Session, Report on Payment of Indian Annuities-- Secretary of War J. R. Poinsett, January 16, 1838.

House Document No. 247, 28th Congress, 1st Session, Report on Indian School Fund--Secretary William Wilkins, April 23, 1844.

Senate Document No. 1, 28th Congress, 2nd Session, Report on Indian Affairs, November 25, 1844.

House Document No. 2, 29th Congress, 1st Session, On Indian Affairs, November 24, 1845.

House Executive Document No. 1, 31st Congress, 2nd Session, Report on Indian Affairs, November 27, 1850.

Senate Executive Document No. 1, 32nd Congress, 2nd Session, Report on Indian Affairs, November 30, 1852.

House Report No. 133, 33rd Congress, 1st Session, Terms of Treaties with Indians, April 7, 1854.

House Executive Document No. 10, 34th Congress, 1st Session, On Amounts Due Indians, November 1, 1855.

House Executive Document No. 1, 34th Congress, 3rd Session, Indian Annuities, October 16, 1856.

House Executive Document No. 93, 35th Congress, 1st Session, Report on Indian Service-- Secretary Howell Cobb, March 26, 1858.

Senate Report No. 156, 39th Congress, 2nd Session, Report on Condition of Indian Tribes-- Joint Special Committee, January 27, 1867.

House Executive Document No. 130, 41st Congress, 2nd Session, On Annuities Withheld from Indian Tribes, February 8, 1870.

Senate Report No. 268, 41st Congress, 3rd Session, Citizenship of Indians, December 15, 1870.

Senate Report No. 336, 41st Congress, 3rd Session, Organization of Indian Territory, February 1, 1871.

House Report No. 39, 41st Congress, 3rd Session, Report on the Indian Department, February 25, 1871.

Senate Miscellaneous Document No. 44, 42nd Congress, 2nd Session, Report on Education of Indians--Secretary C. Delano, January 25, 1872.

House Document No. 89, 42nd Congress, 2nd Session, Minority Report Against Establishing Indian Territory, May 27, 1872.

House Report No. 98, 42nd Congress, 3rd Session, Investigation of Indian Frauds, February 22, 1873.

House Miscellaneous Document No. 167, 44th Congress, 1st Session, On the Management of the Indian Department, April 18, 1876.

Senate Report No. 744, 45th Congress, 3rd Session, Indian Territory, February 11, 1879.

House Report No. 29, 46th Congress, 1st Session, Indian Training Schools, June 14, 1879.

House Report No. 430, 46th Congress, 2nd Session, Police for Indian Reservations, March 9, 1880.

House Report No. 752, 46th Congress, 2nd Session, Industrial School for Indians, April 6, 1880.

Senate Executive Document No. 95, 48th Congress, 2nd Session, Special Report of 1888 on Indian Education and Civilization, Indian Education and Civilization, March 4, 1885.

Senate Report No. 1278, 49th Congress, 1st Session, Condition of Indians in Indian Territory, March 1, 1886.

Senate Report No. 281, 52nd Congress, 1st Session, Report on Indian Affairs, n.d.

House Miscellaneous Documents, Vol. 37, Part 2, 53rd Congress, 2nd Session, First Annual Message on Removal, p. 458.

House Report No. 222, 68th Congress, 1st Session, Granting Citizenship to Indians, n.d.

Hearings, Senate Subcommittee of Committee on Indian Affairs, 70th Congress, 1st Session, Survey of Conditions of the Indians in the United States, Parts I, II, III, IV, December 1928-January 1929.

_____, 71st Congress, 1st Session, Survey of Conditions of the Indians in the United States, Part V, July 1929.

_____, 71st Congress, 2nd Session, Survey of Conditions of the Indians in the United States, Parts 6, 7, 8, 9, 10, 12, 14, 19, 20, 22, January 1930-February 1932.

_____, 71st Congress, 3rd Session, Survey of Conditions of the Indians in the United States, Parts 11, 13, 16, 17, 18, 21, 24, January 1931-June 1931.

_____, 72nd Congress, 1st Session, Survey of Conditions of the Indians in the United States, Parts 23, 25, 26, 27, 28, 29, 32, July 1929-October 1933.

_____, 73rd Congress, 1st Session, Survey of Conditions of the Indians in the United States, Parts 31 and 33, November 1933-July 1934.

Hearings, Senate Committee on Indian Affairs, 73rd Congress, 2nd Session, To Grant to Indians Living under Federal Tutelage Freedom to Organize for Purposes of Local Self-Government and Economic Enterprises, etc., n.d.

Hearings, House Committee on Indian Affairs, 73rd Congress, 2nd Session, Readjustment of Indian Affairs, H. R. 7902, 1934.

Senate Report No. 511, 73rd Congress, 2nd Session, Report on Johnson-O'Malley Bill for Federal-State Cooperation in Education, Social Welfare, etc., of Indians, S. 2571.

Senate Report No. 1080, 73rd Congress, 2nd Session, To Conserve and Develop Indian Lands and Resources, S. 3645 (Wheeler-Howard Bill).

House Report No. 1804, 73rd Congress, 2nd Session, Readjustment of Indian Affairs, H. R. 7902 (Wheeler-Howard Bill), 1934.

Senate Report No. 900, 74th Congress, 1st Session, To Promote the Development of Indian Arts and Crafts and Create a Board to Assist Therein, S. 2203.

Hearings, House Committee on Indian Affairs, 74th Congress, 2nd Session, Condition of Indians in United States, H. R. 8360, 1936.

Hearings, House Subcommittee of Committee on Indian Affairs, 78th Congress, 2nd Session, Investigate Indian Affairs, 1945.

Hearings Before the Senate Committee on Interior and Insular Affairs, 89th Congress, 1st Session, Federal Indian Policy, 1957.

Report of the House of Representatives Committee on Interior and Insular Affairs, 89th Congress, 1st Session, Federal Opinion on the Need for an Indian Treaty Study, 1965.

Hearings Before the House of Representatives Committee on Interior and Insular Affairs, 90th Congress, 2nd Session, Rights of Members of Indian Tribes, 1968.

U.S. Senate, Hearings Before the Subcommittee on Indian Education of the Committee on Labor and Public Welfare, 91st Congress, 1st Session, 1968-1970, 9 volumes.

Senate Report No. 91-501, 91st Congress, 1st Session, Indian Education: A National Tragedy--A National Challenge, 1969.

CONGRESSIONAL LEGISLATION

An Act to establish an Executive Department to be denominated the Department of War, August 7, 1789; 1 Stat. 49.

An Act to provide for the Government of the Territory Northwest of the river Ohio, August 7, 1789; 1 Stat. 50.

An Act providing for the expenses which may attend negotiations or treaties with the Indian Tribes, and the appointment of Commissioners for managing the same, August 20, 1789; 1 Stat. 54.

An Act for establishing the salaries of the Executive Officers of the Government, with their assistants and clerks, September 11, 1789; 1 Stat. 67.

An Act for the Government of the Territory of the United States, south of the river Ohio, May 26, 1790; 1 Stat. 123.

An Act providing for holding a treaty or treaties to establish peace with certain Indian tribes, July 22, 1790; 1 Stat. 136.

An Act to regulate trade and intercourse with the Indian tribes, July 22, 1790; 1 Stat. 137.

An Act making alterations in the Treasury and War Departments, May 18, 1792; 1 Stat. 279.

An Act for establishing trading houses with the Indian tribes, April 18, 1796; 1 Stat. 452.

An Act to regulate trade and intercourse with the Indian tribes, and to preserve peace on the frontiers, May 19, 1796; 1 Stat. 469.

An Act to regulate trade and intercourse with the Indian tribes, and to preserve peace on the frontiers, March 30, 1802; 2 Stat. 139.

An Act directing the manner of appointing Indian agents, and continuing the "Act for establishing trading houses with the Indian tribes, April 16, 1818; 3 Stat. 428.

An Act fixing the compensation of Indian agents and factors, April 20, 1818; 3 Stat. 461.

An Act making provision for the civilization of the Indian tribes adjoining the frontier settlements, March 3, 1819; 3 Stat. 516.

An Act to abolish the United States' trading establishment with the Indian tribes, May 6, 1822; 3 Stat. 679.

An Act to provide for the appointment of a commissioner of Indian affairs, and for other purposes, July 6, 1832; 4 Stat. 564.

An Act to provide for the organization of the department of Indian Affairs, June 30, 1834; 4 Stat. 735.

An Act to regulate, in certain cases, the disposition of the proceeds of lands ceded by Indian tribes to the United States, January 9, 1837; 5 Stat. 135.

Joint Resolution No. I--Joint Resolution authorizing the Secretary of War to continue certain clerks employed in the office of the Commissioner of Indian Affairs, May 2, 1840; 5 Stat. 409.

An Act making appropriations for various fortification, for ordnance, and for preventing and suppressing Indian hostilities, September 9, 1841; 5 Stat. 458.

Joint Resolution No. IV--Joint Resolution to continue two clerks in the business of reservations and grants under Indian treaties, May 18, 1842; 5 Stat. 583.

An Act authorizing the sale of lands, with the improvements thereon erected by the United States, for the use of their agents, teachers, farmers, mechanics, and other persons employed amongst the Indians, March 3, 1843; 5 Stat. 611.

An Act to amend an Act entitled "An Act to provide for the better organization of the Department of Indian affairs," and an Act entitled "An Act to regulate trade and intercourse with the Indian tribes, and to preserve peace on the frontiers," approved June 30, 1834, and for other purposes, March 3, 1847; 9 Stat. 202.

An Act authorizing persons, to whom reservations of land have been made under certain Indian treaties, to alienate the same in Fee, March 9, 1848; 9 Stat. 213.

An Act to establish the Home Department, and to provide for the Treasury Department an Assistant Secretary of the Treasury, and a Commissioner of the Customs, March 3, 1849; 9 Stat. 395.

An Act to authorize the appointment of Indian agents in California, September 28, 1850; 9 Stat. 519.

An Act to provide for the appointment of a Superintendent of Indian Affairs in California, March 3, 1852; 10 Stat. 2.

An Act to confirm the sale of the reservation held by the Christian Indians, and to provide a permanent home for said Indians, June 8, 1858; 11 Stat. 312.

An Act to confirm the land claim of certain Pueblos and towns in the Territory of New Mexico, December 22, 1858; 11 Stat. 374.

An Act to establish two Indian Agencies to Nebraska Territory, and one in the Territory of New Mexico, June 25, 1860; 12 Stat. 113.

An Act to provide for a Superintendent of Indian Affairs for Washington Territory and additional Agents, February 8, 1861; 12 Stat. 130.

An Act to amend an Act entitled "An Act to regulate trade and intercourse with the Indian tribes, and to preserve peace on the frontiers," approved June 30, 1834, February 13, 1862; 12 Stat. 338.

An Act to protect the property of Indians who have adopted the habits of civilized life, June 14, 1862; 12 Stat. 427.

An Act to provide for the appointment of an Indian agent in Colorado Territory, July 1, 1862; 12 Stat. 498.

An Act relating to trust funds of several Indian tribes invested by the Government in certain State bonds abstracted from the custody of the late Secretary of the Interior, July 12, 1862; 12 Stat. 539.

An Act for the removal of Winnebago Indians, and for the sale of their reservation in Minnesota for their benefit, February 21, 1863; 12 Stat. 658.

An Act for the removal of the Sisseton, Wahpaton, Medawakanton, and Wahpakoota Bands of Sioux or Dakota Indians, and for the disposition of their lands in Minnesota and Dakota, March 3, 1863; 12 Stat. 819.

An Act to aid the Indian refugees to return to their homes in the Indian Territory, May 3, 1864; 13 Stat. 62.

An Act to vacate and sell the present Indian reservations in Utah Territory, and to settle the Indians of said Territory in the Uinta Valley, May 5, 1864; 13 Stat. 63.

An Act to aid in the settlement, subsistence, and support of the Navajoe Indian captives upon a reservation in the Territory of New Mexico, June 30, 1864; Stat. 323.

Joint Resolution No. 1--A resolution authorizing the President to divert certain funds heretofore, appropriated, and cause the same to be used for immediate substance and clothing, & c., for destitute Indians and Indian tribes, December 21, 1865; 14 Stat. 347.

An Act to transfer to the Department of the Interior, certain powers and duties now exercised by the Secretary of the Treasury in connection with Indian affairs, July 27, 1868; 15 Stat. 228.

An Act to provide for the removal of the Kansas tribe of Indians to the Indian Territory, and to dispose of their lands in Kansas to actual settlers, May 8, 1872; 17 Stat. 85.

An Act regulating the mode of making private contracts with Indians, May 21, 1872; 17 Stat. 136.

An Act to provide homes for the Pottawatomie and Absentee Shawnee Indians in the Indian Territory, May 23, 1872; 17 Stat. 159.

An Act to confirm to the Great and Little Osage Indians a reservation in the Indian Territory, June 5, 1872; 17 Stat. 228.

An Act to establish a reservation for certain Indians in the Territory of Montana, April 15, 1874; 18 Stat. 28.

An Act providing for the sale of the Kansas Indian lands in Kansas to actual settlers, and for the disposition of the proceeds of the sale, June 28, 1874; 18 Stat. 272.

An Act to authorize the sale of the Pawnee reservation, April 10, 1876; 19 Stat. 28.

An Act appropriating $50,000 for subsistence supplies for Apache Indians in Arizona Territory and for the removal of the Indians of the Chiricahau Agency to San Carlos Agency, May 9, 1876; 19 Stat. 41.

An Act to legalize certain patents issued to members of the Pottawatomie tribe of Indians, June 14, 1878; 20 Stat. 542.

An Act to confirm certain instructions given by the Department of the Interior to the Indian agent at Green Bay Agency, in the State of Wisconsin, and to legalize the acts done and permitted by said Indian agent pursuant thereto, March 31, 1882; 22 Stat. 36.

An Act to provide additional industrial training schools for Indian youth, and authorizing the use of unoccupied military barracks for such purposes, July 31, 1882; 22 Stat. 181.

Joint Resolution No. 8--Joint resolution appropriating $100,000 for the support of certain destitute Indians, February 8, 1884; 23 Stat. 267.

Joint Resolution No. 14--Joint resolution authorizing an expenditure of money for Indian educational purposes, February 25, 1884; 23 Stat. 268.

An Act providing for allotment of lands in severalty to the Indians residing upon the Umatilla Reservation, in the State of Oregon, and granting patents therefor, and for other purposes, March 3, 1885; 23 Stat. 296.

An Act to provide for the allotment of lands in severalty to Indians on the various reservations, and to extend the protection of the laws of the United States and the Territories over the Indians, and for other purposes, February 8, 1887; 24 Stat. 388.

An Act to enable the Secretary of the Interior to pay certain creditors of the Pottawattomie Indians out of the funds of said Indians, April 4, 1888; 25 Stat. 79.

An Act to divide a portion of the reservation of the Sioux Nation of Indians in Dakota into separate reservations and to secure the relinquishment of the Indian title to the remainder, April 30, 1888; 25 Stat. 94.

An Act for the protection of the officials of the United States in the Indian Territory, June 9, 1888; 25 Stat. 178.

An Act in relation to marriage between white men and Indian women, August 9, 1888; 25 Stat. 392.

An Act to accept and ratify an agreement made with the Shoshone and Bannack Indians, for the surrender and relinguishment to the United States of a portion of the Fort Hall Reservation, in the Territory of Idaho, for the purposes of a town-site, and for the grant of a right of way through said reservation to the Utah and Northern Ry. Co., and for other purposes, September 1, 1888; 25 Stat. 452.

An Act for the relief and civilization of the Chippewa Indians in the state of Minnesota, January 14, 1889; 25 Stat. 642.

An Act in relation to dead and fallen timber on Indian lands, February 16, 1889; 25 Stat. 668.

An Act to accept and ratify the agreement submitted by the Shoshones, Bannocks, and Sheepeaters of the Fort Hall and Lemhi Reservation in Idaho May 14, 1880, and for other purposes, February 23, 1889; 25 Stat. 687.

An Act to provide for the settlement of the titles to the lands claimed by or under the Black Bob band of Shawnee Indians in Kansas, or adversely thereto, and for other purposes, March 1, 1889; 25 Stat. 768.

An Act to provide for the sale of lands patented to certain members of the Flathead band of Indians in Montana Territory, and for other purposes, March 2, 1889; 25 Stat. 888.

An Act to authorize the President to confer brevet rank on officers of the United States army for gallant services in Indian campaigns, February 27, 1890; 26 Stat. 13.

An Act to authorize the Secretary of the Interior to procure and submit to Congress a proposal for the sale to the United States of the western part of the Crow Indian Reservation, in Montana, September 25, 1890; 26 Stat. 468.

An Act to amend and further extend the benefits of the act approved February 8, 1887, entitled "An act to provide for the allotment of land in severalty to Indians on the various reservations, and to extend the protection of the laws of the United States over the Indians, and for other purposes," February 28, 1891; 26 Stat. 794.

An Act to provide for the adjudication and payment of claims arising from Indian depredations, March 3, 1891; 26 Stat. 851.

An Act providing for the completion of the allotment of lands to the Cheyenne and Arapahoe Indians, January 28, 1892; 27 Stat. 1.

An Act to provide for the disposition and sale of lands known as the Klamath River Indian Reservation, June 17, 1892; 27 Stat. 52.

An Act to legalize the deed and other records of the Office of Indian Affairs, and to provide and authorize the use of a seal by said office, July 26, 1892; 27 Stat. 272.

An Act authorizint the Secretary of the Interior to correct errors where double allotments of land have erroneously been made to an Indian, to correct errors in patents, and for other purposes, January 26, 1895; 28 Stat. 681.

An Act to provide for the entry of lands formerly in the Lower Brule Indian Reservation, South Dakota, February 13, 1901; 31 Stat. 790.

An Act providing for a monument to mark the site of the Fort Phil Kearny massacre, April 29, 1902; 32 Stat. 175.

An Act fixing the punishment for the larceny of horses, cattle, and other live stock in the Indian Territory, and for other purposes, February 2, 1903; 32 Stat. 793.

An Act to authorize the sale of a part of what is known as the Red Lake Indian Reservation in the State of Minnesota, February 20, 1904; 33 Stat. 46.

An Act to authorize the cutting of timber, the manufacture and sale of lumber, and the preservation of the forests on the Menominee Indian Reservation in the State of Wisconsin, March 28, 1908; 35 Stat. 51.

An Act to provide for determining the heirs of deceased Indians, for the disposition and sale of allotments of deceased Indians, for the leasing of allotments, and for other purposes, June 25, 1910; 36 Stat. 685.

An Act to provide a suitable memorial to the memory of the North American Indians, December 8, 1911; 37 Stat. 46.

An Act conferring jurisdiction on the Court of Claims to hear, determine, and render judgment in claims of the Sisseton and Wahpeton bands of Sioux Indians against the United States, April 11, 1916; 39 Stat. 47.

An Act to authorize the establishment of a town site on the Fort Hall Indian Reservation, Idaho, May 31, 1918; 40 Stat. 502.

An Act granting citizenship to certain Indians, November 6, 1919; 41 Stat. 350.

An Act authorizing certain tribes of Indians to submit claims to the Court of Claims, and for other purposes, May 26, 1920; 41 Stat. 623.

Joint Resolution relative to payment of tuition for Indian children enrolled in Montana state public schools, February 13, 1922; 42 Stat. 364.

An Act providing for the reservation of certain lands in New Mexico for the Indians of the Zia Pueblo, April 12, 1924; 43 Stat. 92.

An Act to authorize the Secretary of the Interior to issue certificates of citizenship to Indians, June 2, 1924; 43 Stat. 253.

An Act providing for the final disposition of the affairs of the Eastern Band of Cherokee Indians of North Carolina, June 4, 1924; 43 Stat. 376.

An Act to amend the act of June 30, 1919, relative to per capita cost of Indian schools, February 21, 1925; 43 Stat. 958.

An Act to appropriate certain tribal funds for the benefit of the Indians of the Fort Peck and Blackfeet Reservations, April 19, 1926; 44 Stat. 303.

An Act to provide for the erection at Burns, Oregon, of a school for the use of the Piute Indian children, June 23, 1926; 44 Stat. 761.

An Act to provide for the construction of a hospital at the Fort Bidwell Indian School, California, March 28, 1928; 45 Stat. 375.

An Act authorizing an appropriation for the survey and investigation of the placing of water on the Michaud division and other lands in the Fort Hall Indian Reservation, March 28, 1928; 45 Stat. 378.

An Act to provide for the recording of the Indian sign language through the instrumentality of Major General Hugh L. Scott, retired, and for other purposes, April 8, 1930; 46 Stat. 147.

An Act authorizing the appropriation of Osage funds for attorney's fees and expenses of litigation, January 31, 1931; 46 Stat. 1047.

An Act providing for payment of $25 to each enrolled Chippewa Indian of the Red Lake Band of Minnesota from the timber funds standing to their credit in the Treasury of the United States, June 14, 1932; 47 Stat. 306.

An Act to authorize the Secretary of the Interior to adjust reimbursable debts of Indians and tribes of Indians, July 1, 1932; 47 Stat. 564.

An Act authorizing the Secretary of the Interior to arrange with States or Territories for the education, medical attention, relief of distress, and social welfare of Indians, and for other purposes, April 16, 1934; 48 Stat. 596.

An Act to conserve and develop Indian lands and resources; to extend to Indians the right to form business and other organizations; to establish a credit system for Indians; to grant certain rights of home rule to Indians; to provide for vocational education for Indians; and for other purposes, June 18, 1934; 48 Stat. 984.

An Act to provide funds for acquisition of the property of the Haskell Students Activities Association on behalf of the Indian School known as "Haskell Institute," Lawrence, Kansas, August 13, 1935; 49 Stat. 612.

An Act to establish a Civilian Conservation Corps, and for other purposes, June 28, 1937; 50 Stat. 319.

An Act authorizing the establishment of a revolving loan fund for the Klamath Indians, Oregon, and for other purposes, August 28, 1937; 50 Stat. 872.

An Act to regulate the leasing of certain Indian lands for mining purposes, May 11, 1938; 52 Stat. 347.

An Act to authorize the deposit and investment of Indian funds, June 24, 1938; 52 Stat. 1037.

An Act to confer jurisdiction on the State of North Dakota over offenses committed by or against Indians on the Devil's Lake Indian Reservation, May 31, 1946, 60 Stat. 229.

An Act to provide for the disposition of tribal funds of the Confederated Salish and Koetenai Tribes of Indians of the Flathead Reservation in Montana, June 24, 1946, 60 Stat. 302.

An Act to set aside certain lands in Oklahoma in trust for the Indians of the Kiowa, Comanche, and Apache Indian Reservation, June 24, 1946, 60 Stat. 305.

An Act to amend the act of June 8, 1936, relating to vocational education, so as to provide for the further development of vocational education in the several States and Territories, August 1, 1946, 60 Stat. 775.

An Act to authorize the use of the funds of any tribe of Indians for insurance premiums, August 2, 1946, 60 Stat. 852.

An Act to facilitate and simplify the administration of Indian affairs, August 8, 1946, 60 Stat. 939.

An Act to create an Indian Claims Commission, to provide for the powers, duties and functions thereof, and for other purposes, August 13, 1946, 60 Stat. 1049.

An Act to define the exterior boundary of the Uintah and Ouray Indian Reservation in the State of Utah, and for other purposes, March 11, 1948, 62 Stat. 72.

An Act to give to members of the Crow Tribe the power to manage and assume charge of their restri-ted lands, for their own use or for lease purposes, while such lands remain in trust patents, March 15, 1948, 62 Stat. 80.

An Act to provide for the general welfare and advancement of the Klamath Indians in Oregon, March 29, 1948, 62 Stat. 92.

An Act providing for payment of $50 to each enrolled member of the Mescalero Apache Indian Tribe from funds standing to their credit in the Treasury of the United States, April 30, 1948; 62 Stat. 206.

Joint Resolution to provide for the issuance of a special postage stamp in honor of the Five Civilized Tribes of Indians in Oklahoma, May 4, 1948; 62 Stat. 211.

An Act to authorize loans for Indians, and for other purposes, May 7, 1948; 62 Stat. 211.

An Act to authorize the sale of individual Indian land acquired under the Act of June 18, 1934, and under the Act of June 26, 1936, May 14, 1948; 62 Stat. 236.

An Act to authorize payments to the public school district or districts serving the Fort Peck project, Montana, for the education of dependents of persons engaged on that project, June 3, 1946; 62 Stat. 297.

An Act to amend the act approved May 18, 1938 (45 Stat. 602), as amended, to revise the roll of the Indians of California provided therein, June 30, 1948; 62 Stat. 1166.

An Act to confer jurisdiction on the State of New York with respect to offenses committed on Indian reservations within such state, July 2, 1948; 62 Stat. 1224.

An Act providing for more expeditious determination of certain claims filed by the Indians, July 2, 1948; 62 Stat. 1228.

An Act to provide for the use of the State course of study in schools operated by the Bureau of Indian Affairs on Indian reservations in South Dakota when requested by a majority vote of the parents of the students enrolled therein, September 7, 1949; 63 Stat. 694.

An Act to authorize the Secretary of the Interior to exchange certain Navajo Tribal Indian land for certain Utah State land, September 7, 1949; 63 Stat. 695.

An Act to provide for the construction, extension and improvement of school buildings in Hoopa, California, October 6, 1949; 63 Stat. 722.

An Act to effect an exchange of certain lands in the State of North Carolina between the United States and the Eastern Band of Cherokee Indians, and for other purposes, October 10, 1949; 63 Stat. 726.

An Act to Authorize the Secretary of the Interior to transfer to the Crow Indian Tribe of Montana the title to certain buffalo, October 25, 1949; 63 Stat. 904.

An Act to promote the rehabilitation of the Navajo and Hopi Tribes of Indians and a better utilization of the resources of the Navajo and Hopi Indian Reservations, and for other purposes, April 19, 1950; 64 Stat. 44.

An Act to regulate the collection and disbursement of moneys realized from leases made by the Seneca Nation of Indians of New York, and for other purposes, August 14, 1950; 64 Stat. 443.

An Act to authorize the commutation of the annual appropriation for fulfilling various treaties with the Choctaw Nation of Indians in Oklahoma, and for other purposes, September 1, 1950; 64 Stat. 573.

An Act to provide for medical services to non-Indians in Indian hospitals, and for other purposes, April 9, 1952; 66 Stat. 35.

An Act to authorize the Choctaw, Chickasaw, Cherokee, Creek, or Seminole Tribes of Indians to make contracts with approval of the Secretary of the Interior, or his authorized representative, under such rules and regulations as the Secretary of the Interior may prescribe, July 3, 1952; 66 Stat. 323.

An Act to vest title in the United States to certain lands and interests in lands of the Shoshone and Arapaho Indian Tribes of the Wind River Reservation and to provide compensation therefrom, and for other purposes, July 18, 1952; 66 Stat. 780.

An Act to authorize payment of salaries and expenses of officials of the Klamath Tribe, May 29, 1953; 67 Stat. 41.

An Act to eliminate certain discriminatory legislation against Indians of the United States, August 15, 1953; 67 Stat. 586. (Indian liquor laws)

An Act to terminate certain Federal restrictions upon Indians, August 15, 1953; 67 Stat. 590.

An Act to extend the time for enrollment of the Indians of California, and for other purposes, June 8, 1954; 68 Stat. 240.

An Act to provide for a per capita distribution of Menominee Tribal funds and authorize the withdrawal of the Tribe from Federal supervision, June 18, 1954; 68 Stat. 253.

An Act to provide for the use of tribal funds of the Southern Ute Tribe of the Southern Ute Reservation, to authorize a per-capita payment out of such funds, and for other purposes, June 28, 1954; 68 Stat. 300.

An Act to provide that each grant of exchange assignment on tribal land on the Cheyenne River Sioux Reservation and the Standing Rock Sioux Reservation shall have the same force and effect as a trust patent, and for other purposes, July 14, 1954; 68 Stat. 467.

An Act to aid in the provision and improvement of housing, the elimination and prevention of slums, and the conservation and development of urban communities, August 2, 1954; 68 Stat. 590.

An Act to provide for the termination of Federal supervision over the property of the Klamath Tribe of Indians located in the State of Oregon, and the individual members thereof, and for other purposes, August 13, 1954; 68 Stat. 718.

An Act to provide for the termination of Federal supervision over certain tribes and band of Indians located in western Oregon and the individual members thereof, and for other purposes, August 13, 1954; 68 Stat. 724.

An Act to provide for the termination of Federal supervision over the Alabama and Coushatta Tribes of Indians of Texas and the individual members thereof; and for other purposes, August 23, 1954; 68 Stat. 768.

An Act to provide for the partition and distribution of the assets of the Ute Indian Tribe of the Uintah and Ouray Reservation in Utah between the mixed-blood and full-blood members thereof; and for the termination of Federal supervision over the property of the mixed-blood members of said tribe; to provide a development program for the full-blood members of said tribe, and for other purposes, August 27, 1954; 68 Stat. 868.

An Act to provide for the termination of Federal supervision over the property of certain tribes, bands and colonies of Indians in the State of Utah and the individual members thereof, and for other purposes, September 1, 1954; 68 Stat. 1099.

An Act relative the exploration, location, and entry of mineral lands within the Papago Indian Reservation, May 27, 1955; 69 Stat. 67.

An Act to amend Section 2 of the Act of March 2, 1945, pertaining to the Columbia River at Bonneville, Oregon, June 8, 1955; 69 Stat. 85.

An Act to authorize the leasing of certain lands of the Yakima Tribe to the State of Washington for historical and for park purposes, July 28, 1955; 69 Stat. 391.

An Act to authorize the purchase, sale, and exchange of certain Indian lands on the Yakima Indian Reservation, and for other purposes, July 28, 1955; 69 Stat. 392.

An Act to authorize the leasing of restricted Indian lands for public, religious, educational, residential, business, and other purposes requiring the grant of long-term leases, August 9, 1955; 69 Stat. 540.

An Act to provide for the conveyance to the State of North Dakota, for use as a State historic site, of the lands where Chief Sitting Bull was originally buried, August 9, 1955; 69 Stat. 543.

An Act to authorize the execution of mortgages and deeds of trust on individual Indian trust and restricted land, March 29, 1956; 70 Stat. 62.

An Act to provide for the segregation of certain funds of the Fort Berthold Indians on the basis of a membership roll prepared for such purposes, June 4, 1956; 70 Stat. 228.

An Act relating to the Lumbee Indians of North Carolina, June 7, 1956; 70 Stat. 254.

An Act to authorize the partition or sale of inherited interests in allotted lands in the Tulalip Reservation, Washington, and for other purposes, June 18, 1956; 70 Stat. 290.

An Act to transfer six hundred acres of public domain to the Kanosh Band of Indians, Utah, July 11, 1956; 70 Stat. 528.

Joint Resolution directing the Secretary of the Interior to conduct a study and investigation of Indian education in the United States, July 14, 1956; 70 Stat. 531.

An Act restoring to tribal ownership certain lands upon the Colville Indian Reservation, Washington, and for other purposes, July 24, 1956; 70 Stat. 626.

An Act to encourage and assist the States in the establishment of State committees on education beyond high school, and for other purposes, July 26, 1956; 70 Stat. 676.

An Act to authorize the Secretary of the Interior to charge for special services to purchasers of timber from Indian lands, July 30, 1956; 70 Stat. 721.

An Act to provide for the termination of Federal supervision over the property of the Wyandotte Tribe of Oklahoma and the individual members thereof, and for other purposes, August 1, 1956; 70 Stat. 897.

An Act relative to employment for certain adult Indians on or near Indian reservations, August 3, 1956; 70 Stat. 986.

An Act to amend the Act of August 24, 1912, as amended, with reference to educational leave to employees of the Bureau of Indian Affairs, July 10, 1957; 71 Stat. 282.

An Act to stimulate industrial development near Indian reservations, August 28, 1957; 71 Stat. 468.

An Act to provide means of further securing and protecting the civil rights of persons within the jurisdiction of the United States, September 9, 1957; 71 Stat. 634.

An Act to provide for the restoration to tribal ownership of all vacant and undisposed of ceded lands on certain Indian reservations, and for other purposes, May 19, 1958; 72 Stat. 121.

An Act to determine the rights and interests of the Navajo Tribe, Hopi Tribe, and the individual Indians to the area set aside by Executive order of December 16, 1882, and for other purposes, July 22, 1958; 72 Stat. 403.

An Act to provide for the distribution of the land and assets of certain Indian rancherias and reservations in California, and for other purposes, August 18, 1958; 72 Stat. 622.

An Act to amend the law relating to the execution of contracts with Indian tribes, August 27, 1958; 72 Stat. 927.

An Act to transfer certain property and functions of the Housing and Home Finance Administrator to the Secretary of the Interior, and for other purposes, August 28, 1958; 72 Stat. 974.

An Act to regulate the handling of student funds in Indian schools operated by the Bureau of Indian Affairs, and for other purposes, April 27, 1959; 73 Stat. 20.

An Act to authorize the use of the revolving loan fund for Indians to assist Klamath Indians during the period for terminating Federal supervision, June 11, 1959; 73 Stat. 70.

An Act to make payments to Indians for destruction of fishing rights at Celilo Falls exempt from income tax, July 31, 1959; 73 Stat. 271.

An Act to set aside certain lands in Washington for Indians of the Quinault Tribe, August 25, 1959; 73 Stat. 427.

An Act to declare that the United States holds title to certain land in trust for the White Mountain Apache Tribe, Arizona, March 18, 1860; 74 Stat. 8.

An Act to amend the Act of April 19, 1950 (64 Stat. 44; 25 USC 635), to better promote the rehabilitation of the Navajo and Hopi Tribes of Indians, and for other purposes, June 11, 1960; 74 Stat. 199.

An Act concerning payment of debts out of compensation for trust land on the Standing Rock Sioux Reservation taken by the United States, June 29, 1960; 74 Stat. 254.

An Act to amend Title 18 of the United States Code to make it unlawful to destroy, deface, or remove certain boundary markers on Indian reservations, and to trespass on Indian reservations to hunt, fish, or trap, July 12, 1960; 74 Stat. 469.

An Act to amend the Housing Amendment of 1955 to make Indian tribes eligible for Federal loans to finance public works or facilities, and for other purposes, October 15, 1962; 76 Stat. 920.

An Act to establish a revolving fund from which the Secretary of the Interior may make loans to finance the procurement of expert assistance by Indian tribes in cases before the Indian Claims Commission, November 4, 1963; 77 Stat. 301.

An Act approving a compromise and settlement agreement of the Navajo Tribe of Indians and authorizing the tribe to execute and the Secretary of the Interior to approve any oil and gas leases entered into pursuant to the agreement, November 20, 1963; 77 Stat. 337.

An Act to amend the Act of August 3, 1956 (70 Stat. 986), as amended, relating to adult Indian vocational training, December 23, 1963; 77 Stat. 471.

An Act to amend the Act of June 25, 1910 (36 Stat. 857; 25 U.S. Code 406, 407), with respect to the sale of Indian timber, April 30, 1964; 78 Stat. 186.

An Act to fix the beneficial ownership of the Colorado River Indian Reservation located in the States of Arizona and California, April 30, 1964; 78 Stat. 188.

An Act to enforce the Constitutional right to vote, to confer jurisdiction upon the district courts of the United States to provide injunctive relief against discrimination in public accommodations; to authorize the Attorney General to institute suits to protect Constitutional rights in public facilities and public education, to extend the Commission on Civil Rights, to prevent discrimination in federally-assisted programs, to establish a Commission on Equal Employment Opportunity, and for other purposes, July 2, 1964; 78 Stat. 241.

An Act to mobilize the human and financial resources of the Nation to combat poverty in the United States, August 20, 1964; 78 Stat. 508.

An Act to increase the amounts authorized for Indian adult vocational education, April 20, 1965; 79 Stat. 74.

An Act to authorize the Secretary of the Interior to enter into contracts for scientific and technological research, and for other purposes, October 15, 1966; 80 Stat. 951.

An Act to amend the provisions of Title 18 of the United States Code relating to offenses committed in Indian country, Novermber 2, 1966; 80 Stat. 1100.

An Act to increase the amounts authorized for Indian adult vocational education, February 3, 1968; 82 Stat. 4.

An Act to authorize the consolidation and use of funds arising from judgments in favor of the Apache Tribe of the Mescalero Reservation and of each of its constituent groups, March 12, 1968; 82 Stat. 47.

An Act relating to Federal support of education of Indian students in sectarian institutions of higher education, March 30, 1968; 82 Stat. 71.

An Act relating to the Tiwa Indians of Texas, April 12, 1968; 82 Stat. 93.

An Act to amend the Act of February 14, 1931, relating to the acceptance of gifts for the benefit of Indians , June 8, 1968; 82 Stat. 171.

An Act to provide for sale or exchange of isolated tracts of tribal lands on the Flathead Reservation, Montana, July 18, 1968; 82 Stat. 356.

An Act to assist in the provision of housing for low and moderate income families, and to extend and amend laws relating to housing and urban development, August 1, 1968; 82 Stat. 476.

An Act to compensate the Indians of California for the value of land erroneously used as an offset in a judgment against the United States obtained by said Indians , August 25, 1969; 83 Stat. 105.

An Act to provide for loans to Indian tribes and tribal corporations, and for other purposes, April 11, 1970; 84 Stat. 120.

An Act to further the economic advancement and general welfare of the Hopi Indian Tribe of the State of Arizona, May 22, 1970; 84 Stat. 260.

An Act to further extend the period of restrictions on lands of the Quapaw Indians, Oklahoma, and for other purposes, June 24, 1970; 84 Stat. 325.

An Act to reimburse the Ute Tribe of the Uintah and Ouray Reservation for tribal funds that were used to construct, operate, and maintain the Uintah Indian irrigation project, Utah, and for other purposes, September 18, 1970; 84 Stat. 843.

An Act to authorize each of the Five Civilized Tribes of Oklahoma to popularly select their principal officers, and for other purposes, October 22, 1970; 84 Stat. 1091.

An Act to authorize grants for the Navajo Community College, and for other purposes, December 15, 1971; 85 Stat. 646.

An Act to extend the life of the Indian Claims Commission, and for other purposes, March 30, 1972; 86 Stat. 114.

An Act to amend the Higher Education Act of 1965, the Vocational Education Act of 1963, the General Education Provisions Act (creating a National Foundation for Post-Secondary Education and a National Institute of Education), the Elementary and Secondary Education Act of 1965, Public Law 874, Eighty-First Congress, and related Acts, and for other purposes, June 23, 1972; 86 Stat. 235.

Note: The above listing of Congressional legislation does not include each and every act passed by the Congress. It does not include, for example, the numerous appropriation acts which contain much of the authority for the activities of the Bureau of Indian Affairs. At least one appropriation act for the expenses of the Bureau of Indian Affairs has been enacted each year since 1792. The list does not contain, either, all the acts providing for the distribution of judgment Funds. These were quite numerous in the years 1969 through 1973.

BOOKS

Abel, Annie Heloise. The American Indian Under Reconstruction. Cleveland: The Arthur H. Clark Company, 1925.

Adams, Evelyn C. American Indian Education, Government Schools and Economic Progress. Morningside Heights: King's Crown Press, 1946.

American Indian Historical Society. Textbooks and the American Indian. San Francisco: American Indian Historian Press, Inc., 1970.

Bailey, L. R. The Long Walk, A History of the Navajo Wars, 1846-68. Los Angeles: Westernlore Press, 1964.

Baldwin, Gordon C. Indians of the Southwest. New York: Capricorn Books, 1970.

Billington, Ray Allen. The Far Western Frontier 1830-1860. New York: Harper and Row Publishers, 1956.

Blauch, Lloyd E. Educational Services for Indians. Staff Study No. 18 Prepared for the Advisory Committee on Education. Washington: Government Printing Office, 1939.

Cohen, Felix S. Handbook of Federal Indian Law. Washington: Government Printing Office, 1945.

David, Jay (Ed.). The American Indian: The First Victim. New York: William Morrow and Company, 1972.

Debo, Angie. A History of Indians of the United States. Norman: University of Oklahoma Press, 1970.

Deloria, Vine, Jr. <u>Custer Died for Your Sins</u>. New York: The Macmillan Company, 1969.

_____ (Ed.). <u>Of Utmost Good Faith</u>. San Francisco: Straight Arrow Books, 1971.

Embree, Edwin Rogers. <u>Indians of the Americas</u>. Boston: Houghton Mifflin Company, 1939.

Every, Dale Van. <u>Disinherited: The Lost Birthright of the American Indians</u>. New York: William Morrow and Company, 1966.

Forbes, Jack D. (Ed.). <u>The Indian in America's Past</u>. Englewood Cliffs: Prentice-Hall Inc., 1964.

Foreman, Grant. <u>Indians and Pioneers</u>. New Haven: Yale University Press, 1930.

_____. <u>Indian Removal: The Emigration of the Five Civilized Tribes</u>. Norman: University of Oklahoma Press, 1953.

Goddard, Pliny Earle. <u>Indians of the Southwest</u>. New York: American Museum Press, 1921.

Greymont, Barbara. <u>The Iroquois in the American Revolution</u>. Syracuse: Syracuse University Press, 1972.

Gridley, Marion E. (Ed.). <u>Indians of Today</u>. New York: ICEP , Inc., 1971.

Harmon, George Dewey. <u>Sixty Years of Indian Affairs, Political, Economic and Diplomatic, 1789-1850</u>. Chapel Hill : The University of North Carolina Press, 1941.

Hodge, Fredrick Webb (Ed.). <u>Handbook of American Indians North of Mexico</u>. New York: Pageant Books Inc., 1960.

Hoopes, Alban W. <u>Indian Affairs and Their Administration</u>. Philadelphia: University of Pennsylvania Press, 1932.

Institute of Government Research. <u>The Problem of Indian Administration</u>. Baltimore: The Johns Hopkins Press, 1928.

Josephy, Alvin M., Jr. <u>The Nez Perce Indians and Opening of the Northwest</u>. Abridged edition. New Haven: Yale University Press, 1971.

_____. <u>The Patriot Chief</u>. New York: The Viking Press, 1958.

_____. <u>The Indian Heritage of America</u>. New York: Bantam Books, 1968.

_____. <u>Red Power The American Indians' Fight for Freedom</u>. New York: McGraw-Hill Book Company, 1971.

Kappler, Charles J. <u>Indian Affairs, Laws and Treaties</u>. Washington: Government Printing Office, 1903.

Kluckholn, Clyde and Dorothea Leighton. <u>The Navajo</u>. (Revised Edition). Garden City: Doubleday and Company, Inc., 1962.

LaFarge, Oliver. <u>The Changing Indian</u>. Norman: University of Oklahoma Press, 1942.

Linton, Ralph. <u>Acculturation in Seven American Indian Tribes</u>. New York: D. Appleton-Century Company, 1940.

Martin, Paul S., George I. Quimby and Donald Collier. <u>Indians Before Columbus</u>. Chicago: University of Chicago Press, 1947.

Marriott, Alice and Carol K. Rachlin. <u>American Epic--The Story of the American Indians</u>. New York: New American Library, Inc., 1969.

Mead, Margaret. <u>The Changing Culture of an Indian Tribe</u>. New York: Capricorn Books, 1966.

Merk, Frederick. <u>Manifest Destiny and Mission</u>. New York: Vantage, 1963.

Meyers, William. <u>Native Americans--The New Indian Resistance</u>. New York: International Publishers, 1971.

Meriam Report. (See Institute of Government Research.)

Moorhead, Warren King. *The American Indian in the United States*. Andover: The Andover Press, 1914.

Morgan, Henry Lewis. *The Indian Journals, 1859-62*. Edited by Leslie A. White. Ann Arbor: The University of Michigan Press, 1959.

McNickle, D'Arcy. *Native American Tribalism-Indian Survivals and Renewals*. New York: Oxford University Press, 1973.

Neihardt, John C. *The Twilight of the Sioux*. Lincoln: University of Nebraska Press, 1961.

Oswalt, Wendell H. *This Land Was Theirs*. New York: John Wiley and Sons, Inc., 1966.

Parker, Mack. *The Amazing Red Man*. San Antonio: The Naylor Company, 1960.

Porter, Fayne C. *Our Indian Heritage--Profiles of 12 Great Leaders*. Philadelphia: The Chilton Press, 1964.

Priest, Loring Benson. *Uncle Sam's Stepchildren*. New Brunswick: Rutgers University Press, 1942.

Prucha, F. P. *American Indian Policy in the Formative Years*. Cambridge: Harvard University Press, 1962.

Roessel, Robert A., Jr. *Handbook for American Indian Education*. Los Angeles: Amerincian Publishing Company, n.d.

Schmeckebier, Lawrence F. *The Office of Indian Affairs: Its History, Activities, and Organization*. Baltimore: The Johns Hopkins Press, 1927.

Seymour, Flora W. S. *The Story of the Redman*. New York: Longmans, Green and Company, 1929.

Spicer, Edward S. (Ed.). *Perspectives in American Indian Culture Change*. Chicago: University of Chicago Press, 1961.

_____. *A Short History of the Indian of the United States*. New York: Van Nostrand Reinhold Company, 1969.

Steiner, Stan. *The New Indians*. New York: Harper and Row, 1968.

Steward, Julian A. *Basin Plateau Aboriginal Socio-Political Groups*. Smithsonian Institute Bulleting No. 120. Washington: Government Printing Office, 1938.

Wallace, Anthony F. C. *The Death and Rebirth of the Seneca*. New York: Vintage Books, 1969.

Walker, Deward E., Jr. *The Emergent Native Americans*. Boston: Little, Brown and Company, 1972.

Wissler, Clark. *Indians of the United States: Four Centuries of Their History and Culture*. Garden City: Doubleday, Doran and Company, 1946.

PUBLICATIONS OF BUREAU OF INDIAN AFFAIRS

American Indians and the Federal Government. Washington: Government Printing Office, 1965.

American Indian Calendar. Washington: Government Printing Office, 1965.

Coombs, L. Madison. *Doorway Toward the Light*. Ogden: Defense Printing Service, 1962.

Directory of Gield and General Offices. Lawrence: Haskell Printing Department, Quarterly, 1934-19--.

Education for Action. Chilocco: Chilocco School Printing Department, 1944.

Education for Cultural Change. Chilocco: Chilocco Printing Department, 1953.

Education for Cross-Cultural Enrichment. Chilocco: Chilocco School Printing Department, 1944.

Education Dialogue. Washington: Bureau of Indian Affairs, Monthly, 1971-19--.

Fact Sheet on BIA Programs and the American Indians. Printed on Bureau of Indian Affairs letterhead, n.d.

General Information Bulletin for Intermountain School Employees and Their Families. Brigham City: Intermountain School, Annual, 1950-19--.

Indian Affairs Manual. 9 Vols. Washington: Government Printing Office, dated as released.

Indian Education. Lawrence: Haskell Printing Department, bimonthly.

Indian Record. Washington: Bureau of Indian Affairs, Monthly, 1967-19--.

Indians at Work. Lawrence: Haskell Printing Department, semimonthly, 1933-1937.

Report of the Commissioner of Indian Affairs. Washington: Government Printing Office, annual, 1825-19--.

Report to the Secretary of the Interior by the Task Force on Indian Affairs. Mimeographed pamphlet, July 10, 1961.

You Asked About ... (Informational Bulletins). Washington: momeographed, periodically published.